Christians In Families

An Inquiry into the Nature
and Mission of the Christian Home

Roy W. Fairchild

THE COVENANT LIFE CURRICULUM

PUBLISHED BY
THE CLC PRESS
RICHMOND, VIRGINIA

The Covenant Life Curriculum
the authorized curriculum
of the following denominations

Associate Reformed Presbyterian Church
Cumberland Presbyterian Church
Moravian Church in America
Presbyterian Church in the United States
Reformed Church in America

Unless otherwise noted, Scripture quotations are from the *Revised Standard Version of the Bible*, copyrighted 1946 and 1952 by the Division of Christian Education of the National Council of Churches, and used by permission.

© Marshall C. Dendy 1964
Printed in the United States of America

First Printing 1964
1078(K)37859

Preface

The Home and Family Nurture aspect of the Covenant Life Curriculum is designed to help churches minister to their families. It rests on these convictions: that basic nurture in the Christian faith for people of all ages takes place through home and family relationships; that the primary witness of the church to the community takes place as its families live and work in the community; and that families are under such serious pressures from the world around them that they are unable to bear effectively the burden of nurture or witness without the continual ministry of the church to them.

Like the whole of the Covenant Life Curriculum, this aspect begins with the fact of revelation and seeks to make clear the message of God's redeeming love to man in his predicament. It deals with the Christian family as part of the covenant community which knows itself and all of its members as recipients of God's promise of grace and his demand for righteous living in response to his grace.

This approach to Christian family education, therefore, includes three features:

First, it offers a Christian interpretation of the nature and mission of the family, including the Christian view of sex, marriage, and parenthood. This interpretation is intended to help the family and all of its members to know who they are in the light of the acts of God for their salvation.

Second, it provides resources to assist families in living under the Lordship of Christ. These resources are intended to aid families in coming to a deeper understanding of the faith and in shaping their response to God in worship and in their lives together. They are based on the conviction that if the family is committed to its distinctive Christian nature and mission as a part of the church and society, it will be enabled, in response to the work of God in Christ, to build its own pattern of life and to create its own expression of its faith in the life of the community.

Third, it proposes specific ways by which the larger fellowship of the church may support and assist each family as it faces critical issues and is threatened by the heavy pressures of life.

This approach to Christian family education necessitates a procedure that is in harmony not only with the fact of revelation but also with the nature of the gospel, the needs and types of families, and the nature of the church. This kind of program developed by any particular church should include such elements as the following:

> Devising ways of increasing the sensitivity of the whole church to its own nature and mission and the significance of the family in fulfilling the mission.

> Grouping the membership of the church in particular ways so as to facilitate the development of a strong supporting fellowship of concern.

> Developing channels for ministering to the needs of each family and for equipping all families for their ministry to the community.

The Home and Family Nurture aspect of the Covenant Life Curriculum is a challenge to the whole church to move forward in a teaching ministry that takes seriously the Christian nature and mission of the family. It is offered in the hope that God will bless those who use it and in the prayer that through it families will be nurtured in the faith.

THE FAMILY STAFF COUNCIL

Contents

PART I
The Christian Looks at the World's Family Values

1. **The Point of View** 11
   The Terms 11
     What Constitutes a Family?
     The Modern Family Is Confused
   The Perspective 15
     Where Shall We Look for Guidance?
     A Christocentric Perspective Is Our First Assumption
   The Implications 19
     All of Life Is of One Piece, Unified
     A Christian View of the Family Is Realistic
   The Direction 23

2. **Conflicting Family Ideals in America** 25
   There Is No "Typical American Family" 26
   Social Forces Have Changed the American Family . . 29
     Who Is "the Head-of-the-House"?
     The New Husband-Father Image
     The New Wife-Mother Image
     What Are the Problems of Child Rearing?
   What Marriage Means to Americans 37
     Complete Fulfillment, an Unrealistic Goal
     Love, a Romanticized Ideal
     Divorce, a Convenient Escape Hatch

3. **Looking at Marriage Through the Eyes of Faith** . . 47
   Faith and the Family 48
     Family Influence and Individual Faith
     Christians in Families
     One World, Many Family Patterns

Faith and the Marriage Relationship 54
  Sexuality in Marriage
    The Husband-Wife Relationship Is Central
    Sexuality Can Be Spiritual
    Sexuality Has Two Main Purposes
  Unity in Marriage
    The Mystery of Unity
    Unity Without Uniformity
    The Renewal of Unity
  Failure in Marriage
    The Recognition of Divorce
    Divorce and Realized Forgiveness
    The Idolatry of Marriage
    The Transformation of Love

4. The Sexual Revolution: A New Challenge 73
  The Challenge to Christians 73
  The Breakdown of the Moralistic View of Sex . . . 75
    Prevailing Philosophies of Sexual Expression
      Natural Expression and Romantic Love
      Homosexuality
    The Results of Sexual License
  Guidance for Christians in the Sexual Revolution . . 86
    Responsible Sex Education
    Responsible Parenthood

5. The Vocation of Parenthood 96
  What Parenthood Requires 97
  What Children Can Do for Parents 99
  What Parents Can Do for Children 100
    The Need for a Mature Faith
    The Nurture of the Lord
      Physical Care and Emotional Protection
      A Sense of Identity
      Life and the Grace of God
    The Admonition of the Lord
      The Need for Discipline
      The Development of Conscience
      A System of Values
  What Family Worship Can Be 118

PART II
The Family: The School of Christian Relationships

6. **Family Communication and Authentic Personhood** . 125
   The Individual and Family Communication 127
      The Search for Genuine Intimacy
      The Mystery of the Individual
   Human Sin and Family Communication 131
   Christian Freedom and Family Communication . . . 136
      The Freedom to Understand
      The Freedom to Respond
      The Freedom to Be Real

7. **Family Unity and Personal Differences** 145
   The Need to Recognize Differentness 145
      The Discovery of Differentness
      The Denial of Differentness
   The Need for a Balance of Individuality and Unity . . 150
      A Foundation of Unity
      Differentness Within Unity
   The Need for Parental Teamwork 155

8. **Christians and Creative Conflict** 159
   The Reality of Anger 161
      The Need to Express Anger
      The Need to Resolve Anger
        Separation and Silence
        Speaking the Truth in Love
        Humility and Patience
   The Reality of God's Forgiveness 171
   When Professional Help Is Needed 174

9. **Decision Making and Discipleship** 177
   The Activity of Responsible Decision Making . . . 179
      Choice
      Evaluation
      Total Involvement
   The Freedom and Limitations of Commitment . . . 186
      Time
      Society

  The Guidance of Faith 189
   Fellowship
   Prayer

PART III
Families in the Church and in the World

10. **Christ's Family of Families** 199
  The Family of Faith Biblically Understood 199
  The Family of Faith Gathered 204
   God's Call and Covenant
   Our Response: Confession and Participation
    Baptism; The Lord's Supper
   Our Response: Worship and Study
    The Sermon; Group Study; The Worship Service
   Our Response: Ministering to One Another
  The Family of Faith Scattered 213

11. **Arenas of Family Witness: The Community** . . . 218
  Witnessing Responsibly 219
  Witnessing to Youth 222
  Witnessing to Local Situations 227
   Housing and Schools
   The Racial Crisis
  Witnessing in the Neighborhood 230

12. **Arenas of Family Witness: The Economic Realm** . . 233
  The Relationship of Home and Work 234
  The Relationship of Faith and Work 236
   The Dangers of Modern Business and Industry
   The Biblical Understanding of Vocation
    Responsible Use of Abilities
    Responsible Work Relations
    Responsible Spending

13. **Arenas of Family Witness:**
  National and International Affairs 247
  World Crisis and Tension 247
  Christian Response 248
   In International Affairs
   In Politics

A Problem Index 257

Part I
The Christian Looks at the World's Family Values

1 The Point of View...............................11
2 Conflicting Family Ideals in America...................25
3 Looking at Marriage Through the Eyes of Faith...........47
4 The Sexual Revolution: A New Challenge...............73
5 The Vocation of Parenthood........................96

1
The Point of View

In a good mystery novel suspense is a key ingredient. We may not discover until the last page the clue which ties the whole story together. We see a Perry Mason or a Hercule Poirot walk through its pages—cerebral cortex on twenty-four-hour duty, teasing out evidence from every human conversation, and, finally, the answer to the whole puzzle suddenly drops into place. The motive and theme which makes sense out of the miscellany of events is found; the thread upon which all apparently unrelated items can be strung is disclosed. And the book is finished. Not so this volume; the key will be obvious, and the theme set in the first chapters.

This book will focus upon *Christians* living in *families*. It will speak about that group of people who have a particular outlook on life as they seek to live out its understandings within and through the universal experience of the family. Those who look to the biblical view of life as the main clue to the meaning of the family soon discover that it has great, even revolutionary, implications.

THE TERMS

What Constitutes a Family?

The employer speaks of his office staff as "one big happy family." The theologian, with biblical warrant, refers to the church as the "family of God." What constitutes a family? Is it any group animated by a friendly attitude, an *esprit de corps?* An adolescent or young adult, alienated from his parents—as most are at some time or other—may turn to the other persons or groups with whom he feels he can be himself and say about them, "Here is my *real* family." There is some justification for saying that our family exists where we feel at home, where there are people who affirm us as authentic selves. We are reminded of Jesus' words to his own kinfolk, when, embarrassed by his pronouncements, they sought to bring him home and divert him from his calling. Looking at those he was teaching, he said, "Here are my mother and my brothers! Whoever does the will of God is my brother, and sister, and mother" (Mark 3:34–35). We must remind ourselves that we also belong to a larger family than our family of origin.

For now, a more restricted definition of the family will be used. *"Family" will mean for us, primarily, married parents living together with their children who are related to them by blood or adoption.* If a couple have no children, if their children have left home to be on their own, or if a parental partner is missing, we speak of an "incomplete family." When relatives live with the "nuclear" unit of parents and children, or are in close contact with them, we see this as the larger or "extended" family group. Any combination of persons living together or alone, such as a couple of unmarried men or women, are considered "adult households."

In a period of two or three decades, our family changes a great deal. It expands with the arrival of new members. It contracts when grown youngsters leave home or when death claims loved ones. And as the family unit changes, so do we. When that first baby was brought home from the hospital, we were untried, fearful that the little one would break. In later years, with more experience in our parenting, we become more and more relaxed. As children grow older, they lead us into new experiences that expand our horizon and create new needs within us. Any serious change that affects *any* one member of our family, affects each of *us* because we are bound together. Let an older son leave for college, and all of us who are left at home alter our relationships to each other and to him. The family is a sensitive organism similar to the human body. It keeps its recognizable identity although it is actually changing day by day.

Also like the body, the family is deeply influenced by its surroundings. However hard we try to insulate it, it cannot be a world unto itself. One can, of course, assert that the family is a group separate and different from other groups in our society. It is unique. A close look reveals that the walls of privacy which separate it from the wider world are permeable, tissue-paper thin. Through the newspaper, TV, and the comings and goings of family members there is an active interchange of ideas and values between the family and the other institutions of society. *Living in the "sea of influence" around it, it is the problem and the privilege of the Christian family to both filter and flavor that sea.*

The Modern Family Is Confused

No one with eyes to see can miss the loneliness and boredom which seem to haunt our time. These malignant moods frequently invade even the most cohesive families. At times of uneasiness they ask how they can find a sense of steady purpose in the midst of the pilgrimage from birth to death. Countless people reflect a desperate attempt to dispel the meaninglessness of life by their restless urge to move, to change their jobs, and to take exciting risks. They act as if life were "full of sound and fury, signifying nothing," as Shakespeare noted (*Macbeth,* Act V). They are caught in limbo between the goals for life absorbed from their parents and the values which they attempt, in trial and error fashion, to carve out of their confused experience. They find it hard to be committed to either past or future. And in the present they are rudderless, unable to design and organize a style of life to fit their families or themselves as individuals.

Is it possible that the view of life, marriage, and family found within the Christian faith can furnish them with a solid identity, with a conviction that God has placed their own family within a stream of history-making in which he is the author? Can they, within the covenant community of faith, find that degree of certitude about life's meaning which would enable them to hold a plumb line to vacillating moods and mores of the day? Is there, in that fellowship in which we are "members of one another," the dynamic by which to find creative solutions to the pressures faced by all families in our society? These are a few of the questions this book seeks to answer.

Such possibilities for family living do not mean that the homes of Christians are free from confusion and anxiety. Not at

14 CHRISTIANS IN FAMILIES

all. A few examples of what families in the church do face will relieve us of such an illusion.

ITEM: The titles of articles in newspapers and magazines tell of the changing roles of mothers and fathers and of the disturbance about the change:
"Are the Two Sexes Merging?"
"Fathers Shouldn't Be Mothers!"
"Trousered Moms and Dishwashing Dads"

ITEM: Many church parents are at a loss to know when to give in to the pleadings of their children when they say, "But all the kids are doing it." They wonder if they should say no and run the risk of having their children disliked.

ITEM: "The church's magazines keep talking about family worship, but we've never been able to pull it off without becoming more tense than when we started. I guess we just don't have a Christian family," said one mother despairingly.

ITEM: "Sometimes I wish we could recapture the warmth and excitement of our early years together," mused John to himself on their tenth anniversary. "Somehow we've just drifted apart as the family has grown and work has claimed more of my time. Can we find our way back to each other?"

ITEM: Jimmy's mother and father were divorced a year ago when he was six years old. Since that time he has returned to baby ways, has grown hostile with other children, and has not learned to read. What can the parent without a partner do to help her boy find the masculine companionship he seems to need?

ITEM: Parents no longer have confidence that they know what is the "good child" or the "good parent" or the "good mate." Why else, one expert asks, would so many Americans anxiously check Dr. Spock for baby care, Dr. Gesell for child growth, and Dr. Kinsey for the record of success and failure in sexual life?

This is but a sampling of the everyday concerns of Christians in families. Some people maintain that "the family in America is disintegrating" and use these and other more serious examples of confusion and conflict to support their contention. We have a right to distrust such blanket indictments of the families of the American scene. They may indeed be mixed up, often not knowing which way to go for guidance. Yet the family can be a wonderfully warm configuration of human beings bound together by a purpose that is larger than their tension and deeper than their uncertainty about how to manage their homes.

THE PERSPECTIVE

Where Shall We Look for Guidance?

Some readers will question this attempt to seek a biblical understanding of family experiences. Holding that "scientific facts" about families are a better source of guidance, they wonder about the usefulness of the effort to see everything through a screen of Christian values. On the other hand, some readers will approach the subject convinced that a complete and detailed blueprint for family life is to be discovered in the Bible. They will ask why we should concern ourselves with the discoveries of modern social science about how people behave in families.

This book adopts neither of these viewpoints. It is interested in meanings as well as facts. No factual description of family life is enough to *understand* a family; its experiences must be understood in light of the family's goals, its way of seeing itself, and its purposes. Families do not differ so much in the experiences they have; often they are monotonously similar. Families are different because of their *interpretation* of those experiences, the *meaning* they give to what they do as families.

Where does the modern person find meaning in the family existence he shares? A great many turn to "science" in its popular expressions. They ask, "Doesn't faith, with its legendary stories, occupy the short end of the seesaw when compared with the exact descriptions of science about the origins and workable patterns of family life? Why not trust the carefully gathered evidence of the cultural and biological sciences instead of the speculations of theology?"

Such questions offer a false contrast. I can ask the psychologist about the patterns of mothering and their effect on children's personalities and receive some very useful information. I can ask the cultural anthropologist, who studies the socially inherited behavior patterns in different societies, about the first forms of family life and I will receive a detailed description of the evidence and the hypotheses. I can, for example, with the aid of the Carbon 14 technique, date material and artifacts of the past with almost absolute confidence.

When we ask *what is the purpose of man and his ultimate origin, nature, and destiny,* we do not look to science for an answer. It is the Bible's purpose to reveal the Source of all life and its meaning and purpose in history. It is not concerned primarily with the details of what happened in nature; it does not ask through what various forms man and his institutions have evolved. The narrators of Genesis, for example, were quite content to use the ancient scientific and historical understandings available to them as a vehicle for dealing with the central questions of the meaning and destiny of human beings and of the family itself. Once this is clearly understood, we find that we need not contrast science and faith to the detriment of one or the other. Questions about the *development* of man and about the *purpose* of man do not necessarily contradict one another because their affirmations lie on different levels. Science is to be asked about the "what," "when," and "how" of these human patterns. Faith, as viewed by the Bible, should be asked about the meaning and the purpose of it all, what stands in the way of our realizing this purpose, and where human beatitude might be found. This, after all, is the point of every book of the Bible.

This book faces both ways—toward the biblical faith and toward scientific discovery—in the attempt to understand the human family. In the chapters that follow, the reader will be scanning the domestic terrain through a prism which refracts three words which, like colored rays of a spectrum, cast their hue upon the text as a whole. These words are affirmations of the author and keys to the interpretation of the domestic map which will be unrolled: *Christocentric, unified,* and *realistic.*

A Christocentric Perspective Is Our First Assumption

Here the question might be raised, "How can we turn to Jesus for any guidance as to the meaning of our family life today? Indeed, how can we turn to any of the biblical figures whose circumstances were so different from our own?" But is not the chief problem of church people our tendency to affirm that Jesus Christ is decisive for us without knowing or being willing to see what this means for our concrete existence?

No one can live without commitment to *some* values, to some basic notion of what is "good" and "evil" in the world. This is a built-in necessity for human personality. We order our lives, sometimes unconsciously, according to one or another of the rival gods available in our society. It may be our nation, or social approval, or democracy or science. The biblical prophets were profoundly right in declaring that man is *homo religiosus* (a religious animal). We are never without some god; we cannot choose to be religious or irreligious. The important question to be asked of each one of us is, "What (or who) is your god?" Or, as Martin Luther put the issue, "Whatever, then, thy heart clings to . . . and relies upon, that is properly thy God."[1]

When we speak of a "Christocentric" perspective in family living, we are not advocating an attempt to imitate the specific pattern of Jesus' life—remaining unmarried, "living on the land" with friends, and so on. The Christian life is not a slavish copying of Jesus' life, but our intention, in spite of repeated failure, is to fulfill God's purpose for our unique existence as Christ did for his.

Thus we are called to see life and our own decisions under the impact of what Christ said, what he did, and in the light of his presence in the fellowship of faith today. We cannot ignore his relatively few words about marriage and family life; we must go far beyond them. Thus even when we come across pictures of

---

1. Martin Luther, "The Greater Catechism," *Luther's Primary Works* (London: Hodder and Stoughton, Ltd., 1896), p. 34.

family life and sexual behavior in the Old Testament, we are not to assume that they represent a Christian view of the matter. The heartrending story of Jacob who labored seven years for Rachel only to be deceived by his father-in-law who gave him her sister instead (Genesis 29) is not to be considered an ideal pattern. Nor are we to regard Solomon and his 700 wives and 300 concubines (1 Kings 11:3) as the will of God for the family. Who can forget the pathetic story of Abraham and Sarah (Genesis 16) who were desperate to have a child because they shared the Hebrew belief in social immortality through male children? They were not successful and, as in the Near East today, assumed that it was the *woman* who was obviously sterile. Sarah, the concerned but childless wife, suggests a solution to her husband in words which would shock the average wife even in this day of artificial insemination: " 'Go in to my maid; it may be that I shall obtain children by her.' And Abram hearkened to the voice of Sarah . . . And he went in to Hagar, and she conceived" (Genesis 16:2, 4).

The biblical characters move in the context of their own society and are to be understood in the light of God's will. We must recognize that even Israel imperfectly understood what God was trying to make clear to them until at last the world was confronted by the "stature of the fulness of Christ" (Ephesians 4:13).

A Christocentric perspective sees God *continuing* his presence in the fellowship of his faithful people. *It is in this covenant community that he chooses to guide us in the concrete decisions of an ever-changing family life.* Unlike the Muslims for whom the Koran attempts to fix behavior for all time, Christians can stand in awe of the fact that God waits for his Spirit to be heard in the church. For "where two or three are gathered in my name, there I am in the midst of them" (Matthew 18:20). And as Paul put it, "a new covenant, not in a written code but in the Spirit; for the written code kills, but the Spirit gives life" (2 Corinthians 3:6).

Our first assumption is that, in Jesus Christ, God has entered human life and has broken it open in such a way that its deepest issues are revealed and its depths and dilemmas are laid bare. We assert that in him is seen the profoundest answer to the questions that every person asks about himself and his existence. The church has contended that here, in this one Life, God did something and said something that changed our relationship to him, to our fellow human beings (even those we live with), and to ourselves.

THE IMPLICATIONS

All of Life Is of One Piece, Unified

Jesus saw life as a unity under the sovereignty of God. A neat division of life into the sacred and profane, the "spiritual" and the "material," is precisely what he came to eradicate. His insistence that all of life is of a piece, to be lived under the sovereignty of God, runs afoul of the deep-rooted tendency in the human spirit—to hide from God, and carve its life into two insulated compartments. Our temptation is to keep the "religious" realm and the "earthly" concerns of life from getting mixed, homogenized. In such a split-level existence, Christianity is thought to be relevant to our praying, Bible-reading, church-going, hymn-singing life. But we cannot believe that it could speak to the decisions about our bill-paying, car-buying, love-making, nose-wiping, and dish-drying existence in the family realm, not to mention our citizenship in town or in our life at work. Yet, unless our Christian faith has the promise of enlightening these events of our life and will teach us to live as disciples within them, has it really anything to say?

Everyday experiences are important to God who entered our life as "Emmanuel" (God with us), and the Bible affirms that he will finally "reconcile to himself *all things* . . . making peace by the blood of his cross" (Colossians 1:20; author's italics). Jesus Christ talked very little about religion but he was always disclosing the relationship of God to the ordinary events of life as well as to the life and death issues confronting people. Can anyone even scan the four Gospels and not sense the close touch which Jesus had with the common life about him? One looks almost in vain for "religious" talk or "sacred" vocabulary. In contrast, his words and stories tell of salt, a lamp and a bushel basket, the farmer sowing a crop, wild birds, wild flowers, grapes and thorns, the foundation of a house, sick people and a doctor, children playing at a street corner, weeds, mustard, yeast, three loaves of bread, buried money, puppies eating under a table, a hen and her chicks, bridesmaids, a bridegroom, a lost coin, a coat left in a house, a dishonest manager, to list but a few of his images. In his incarnation in Jesus Christ, God was deeply identified with the world. And if God relates himself to all of life inside and outside the family and not solely or even chiefly to what men have called religion, this fact has some startling implications.

Religion can be but an external form, a series of practices, a superficial avoidance of the obvious immoralities such as murder, adultery, robbery. It is sometimes a desperate effort to prove one's virtue. God is not content with niceness on the outside of life, but only with "truth in the inward being" (Psalm 51:6). Jesus bitingly criticizes the "phonies" of his day, those hypocrites who refused to look at themselves squarely, pretending to be something other than they were. What a devastating attack on the sacred-secular division of life he makes! When Jesus unfavorably compares the religious leaders of his day with the traitorous tax collectors, prostitutes, murderers, adulterers, and thieves (because they, at least, had given up pretense) he says in no uncertain terms that "religion," as commonly understood, *can be* an enemy of God!

True spirituality is not confined to religious practices, religious places, or religious persons. It has as much to do with the physical life as with the mental or spiritual. Indeed, both the Bible and modern psychology would challenge this kind of division of the person. In his Letter to the Romans, Paul writes, "I appeal to you therefore, brethren, by the mercies of God, to present your *bodies* as a living sacrifice, holy and acceptable to God, which is your *spiritual* worship" (Romans 12:1; author's italics). The key to understanding this verse lies in the word "therefore." Paul has already written about God taking the initiative in Christ to meet and overcome our sin and despair and discouragement; he has indicated how this redeeming activity of God will affect all of human history and destiny. Our response in the light of this, therefore, is to render a spiritual service by presenting our bodies, *the full physical and material side of our life*, that it might be used for the overarching purpose God has in store for his people—that they might be reconciled to him, to each other, and to themselves. All of life, indeed *every facet of family living, can become a form of "spiritual service":* disciplining the children, earning the "bread and butter," entering into sexual oneness with one's mate. The ordinary always has a spiritual dimension. For example, family devotions, so often considered the hallmark of the Christian family, may not be more sacred nor more important to God than recreation at a crucial time in a family's life. Fun might be needed just then to bring laughter and to build a common world among those who have grown tense in their togetherness.

Of course, there *is* a place for legitimate worship, as *the church in the home*, but that worship must be conducted in spirit and in truth. Worship without truth in relationships is but an empty form, as Jesus implies when he says, "So if you are offering your gift at the altar, and there remember that your brother has something against you, leave your gift there before the altar and go; first be reconciled to your brother, and then come and offer your gift" (Matthew 5:23-24). Contrast this word of our Lord with the unbiblical "inspirational" view of worship suggested by David Head in *He Sent Leanness*, a book of "prayers for the natural man":

> Lord, give us all a nice feeling this morning. . . . We pray that we may enjoy the preliminaries, and that the sermon may give us all a glow. I know I have offended at least two people this week with my quick temper, but please do not let the thought of that intrude upon this spiritual feast. Praise God. Amen.[2]

A Christian View of the Family Is Realistic

Christian people must not succumb to the temptation of living in a little cardboard world of family ideals. A perfect family does not exist. God knows this and accepts us in spite of our sin

---
2. David Head, *He Sent Leanness* (New York: The Macmillan Company, 1959), p. 27. Used by permission of The Macmillan Company.

and our mistakes. Christians must learn to look at the realities of family life and not merely emphasize what families ought to be. We can ill afford to turn our eyes away even from such unpleasant realities as family conflict, divorce, and the sexual excesses of our time. The day has come when repeating sentimental truisms about what *ought* to be will not do. Such an attitude denies both the complexities of the world which God loves and his own power to deal with the rawest of family realities. We must look squarely at all kinds of homes, homes in which children are grimy and sticky and father remains unshaven on the weekend; homes in which mothers get pushed beyond endurance and shout at their small fry to get out of the house and stay out; homes in which fathers resort to "shut up" or "because I said so" when confronted by their children's annoying behavior; homes in which offsprings do not docilely obey their parents but mutter under their breaths, "Go climb a tree." The families this book will speak to have homes in which illness and death and tragedy are not strangers; in which disappointment is not unknown. In homes of Christians, men do lose their jobs or fail to win promotions; a few may be unfaithful to their wives. This book is not speaking merely to families that seem to live with mild unending joy, but to those in which a woman may become depressed at menopause and children may turn out lazy or irresponsible.

Because he is there as he is present elsewhere, God enables us to look at the family sector of our life with our eyes wide open. It is the Christian faith that whatever help we have is not in turning our backs upon the unpleasant features of family life but in confronting the terror of our condition. Otherwise we deceive ourselves and fail to realize that *the gospel is good news for our actual existence in the family.* The Bible does not approach the family as a place where the Kingdom of God can be more easily realized than anywhere else. For here the deepest hurts as well as the deepest healing can come; here we both enjoy and are damned by our relationships. No, the family has no special grace at its disposal that Christ's men or women, single or married, cannot have.

Biblical realism about the family calls for another insight on our part, one that might not set well with religious activists and

American self-made men and women. *You cannot make your family Christian!* Many people think that if they do this or that or believe this or that, their effort will *create* a Christian home. The simplest misunderstanding of the matter is the belief that if two people are married by a clergyman, if they say the vows in church, the result is a "Christian marriage." It does not take very much thought to realize that having a church wedding does not necessarily mean one has the intention of living out married life under the sovereignty of Almighty God.

There are those who would identify a Christian family with that collection of people who engage in certain practices, such as going to church and carrying out family devotions, and who are nice to each other (at least in public). But these families miss the mark if they do not see that they can go through all these motions and not really understand what the story is all about. If these practices are the *result* of living with an understanding of God's word they can have meaning. But they never *earn* for us the label "Christian." That description is given to us by him whose love we can only accept and make our own. In contrast, many engage in Christian practices not as a response to God's love, but to demonstrate a proof of their goodness to themselves and others. "They have their reward," said Jesus (Matthew 6:16).

THE DIRECTION

The purpose of this book is to provide a means by which Christians in families can come to understand better that part of life in which they spend most of their time and energy. Of the 900 months, more or less, loaned to us at birth, perhaps one-third to one-half of them will find us in close relationships with family members. Does Christian faith add meaning to our life together? Does it also contribute to a new conception of our families as effective agents of God's reconciliation to the world in which we live?

The next two chapters of Part I will take a close look at the unique understanding that Christian faith contributes to marriage. Then the reader will look out upon the broad American scene and view the conflict of family ideals that contributes to our uncertainty. The sexual revolution which threatens to change our way of life drastically will be examined from the perspective of faith. Having examined a picture of the world in which our families will be brought up, we close with a consideration of the responsibilities of Christian parents to their children in the light of these pressures.

Part II will lead the reader into the Christian dimensions of life within the home: what resources are available for learning better to communicate with each other and resolve our tensions; how it is possible for family members to keep their own individuality and not disrupt family unity; how Christians in families can develop strategies of creative conflict. These will be our concerns.

Part III takes the family beyond the four walls of the home into Christ's family of families and then into the broader world: Quick strokes on a broad canvas will provide a sketch of the Christian family's life both in the fellowship of faith and in the rough-and-tumble world. How the family unit can prepare to be the church, the front-line fighters for the Kingdom of God in the arenas of community, of work, and of the national and international scene. Here is a portrait of the Christian family in action.

2
Conflicting Family Ideals in America

"Many of our misunderstandings are just quick little passes that are made about problems when children or parents are on their way out," says one father. "It's a geared society—the children have plans—a very social society. My wife and I are getting worn out just trying to regulate our schedule. The whole thing to me is just a rat race, and it is hard to keep it on the level of a smooth-running family unit. Yet, you wouldn't want your children to operate any other way."[1]

These words of a typical American father express many of the ideals and the dilemmas of the modern home:

- family freedom vs. a tightly organized schedule
- family cohesiveness vs. loyalty to community or school
- the need for understanding vs. no time to communicate
- parents' desire for children's social success vs. their own self-fulfillment.

As we look at the contemporary family, one thing is certain: it is uncertain. It is caught in a tug-of-war between the conflicting ideals and goals for life. Can all of these be achieved, or is it possible that we want contradictory things?

Most families aspiring to discover and live out a Christian "style of life" in the home will feel the same pulls that their neighbors do. For this reason, we must look at some of the goals for marriage and family which subtly influence us all even as we try to judge our society from the perspective of Christian faith. We begin absorbing the values of our culture long before we learn them in our formal schooling. These acquired customs and meanings seem right to us because we were indoctrinated before

---

1. Roy W. Fairchild and John Charles Wynn, *Families in the Church: A Protestant Survey* (New York: Association Press, 1961), p. 133.

we had any critical judgment to bear upon the matter—not a biblical standard of judgment, at any rate. In this chapter we will take off the cultural eyeglasses which have become so natural that we forget we have them on, and look *at* these lenses, rather than *through* them, in order to ask ourselves what it is we really want.

THERE IS NO "TYPICAL AMERICAN FAMILY"

A part of our uncertainty comes from the fact that we live in a "pluralistic" society, a society which embodies many ways of life within it. Furthermore, there is no one "American Family." A quick look at the variety of families which have existed and do now reside in the United States will reveal that they have lived according to many different family ideals.

When we think of "the American Family," our mind's eye pictures young parents with two or three well-dressed children driving to church together in a station wagon. There are, to be sure, forces in American society which urge *all* of its families toward this common mold. We who think our particular family type is natural should be aware that many patterns have existed in American history.

There have been at least two experiments in nonmonogamous marriage in our history. Both of them were prompted by religious motivations which fall considerably short of the New Testament position.

The Mormons practiced polygamy as early as the 1830's, although the doctrine of plural wives for one husband ("The Principle") was not officially promulgated until 1852. Never a practice among the majority of Mormons, polygamy continued for a few years after our entrance into the twentieth century. Protestants should note that plural marriage was closely related to the Mormon belief that there are two kinds of marriage, one for earthly life only and one for eternity.

The group marriage custom of the Oneida Community, which had its origin in Vermont, is almost unknown to us. John Humphrey Noyes, its founder, believed that the Kingdom of God had already come on earth in its fullness and that complete liberation from sin was an accomplished fact, an affirmation which Protestants would contest. He was convinced that in the now-realized Kingdom, all beings, male or female, were to love each other equally. The result was a sexual communalism in which every adult male had sexual privileges with every adult female and vice versa. The community flourished for several decades after 1848 when it reassembled in central New York state following court trials and persecution. Poverty, crime, alcoholism, divorce, desertion, and children (surprisingly) were virtually lacking in the community. Adults exercised "birth control" because proper child care and education were impossible for the persecuted group.

Today in the American culture we are not given to such experimentation with marriage forms. The changes in the relations between men and women, while increasingly experimental, are generally taking place *within* monogamous marriage as we know it.

At least five different types of families can be identified in today's American society.

We still see, principally in the Midwest, the *rural family* which regards the farm as a family enterprise in which each member has a part until the children grow up, disperse, and get married. The movement to the cities and the invasion of television and technology, however, seem to be slowly erasing a unique rural way of life for the families of America.

A second type is the *"old family"* unit, located principally in New England and the South. Here wealth, pride of social position and ancestry, and the desire to stay geographically where the family has been since this country's birth are important family values. Such a family wants to keep its family history and rituals alive, often against great odds.

A third type of family is represented by those parents who, one or two generations ago, have moved from the *"old country."* In spite of opposition from their "Americanized" children, they want to hold on to their traditions in the face of a strange and fast-changing American environment. Irish, Italian, Jewish, Polish, Greek, Chinese and Japanese-originated families have formed enclaves in the American society, holding what they can of their heritage in the face of a break between the generations. Some adapt rather quickly to the new ways, some compromise; others express an urgency in their tenacious attempt to preserve the old patterns of life. Almost always, however, the children of such families have the painful struggle of choosing between two ways of life in a stormy adolescence.

A fourth distinct group is the *Negro family* which is in the process of rapid change at the present time. Shaped by its origin in slavery, the *lower*-class Negro family is, according to reputable sociologists, still the most loosely organized and easily broken in the United States. The slave family found its center in the mother rather than the father, since she was usually the stable household servant of Southern families. The father, who was often sold separately, was a casual member of the family. A stronger family system is developing among middle-class and upper-middle class Negroes, with the father playing a much more decisive role. In these families divorce and desertion is average compared with the nation as a whole, and sexual morals are often even more stringently observed than in Caucasian middle-class groups.

It is the fifth group, the large *American middle class,* that most readers will recognize as their own. Whether living in small town, big city, or suburbia, this mobile, equalitarian, mother-organized, child-centered family has become the "ideal" for all classes and groups in the American culture. The paradox is this: It has become the preferred family image on TV and in the magazines even while it is still struggling to find its own bearings. It is anxious about its goals, the place of father and mother in the home, and its child rearing. It is frequently torn between contradictory values; it may cling simultaneously to the values of romantic love *and* of competitive achievement, of togetherness *and* extreme individualism, of inward peace *and* a nervous scramble for status. It often holds in tension the values of lifelong marital commitment *and* the values of the supremacy of the individual's happiness. Yet there are resources in this family which we cannot underestimate. It is an adaptable unit with a genius for innovation. American husbands and wives believe that sexual love cements their relationship. Further, they are eager to try the democratic experiment in the family. And they want to make a go of marriage and parenthood.

SOCIAL FORCES HAVE CHANGED THE AMERICAN FAMILY

The problems of this mainstream American home and its conflicts are intimately connected with the vast panorama of social changes occurring in the past few decades. What are the gigantic social forces which have changed the American family in the last decades? The most influential are:

- The industrialization of the country with the resulting enormous migration into the great urban centers.
- The "emancipation" of women with consequent legal, political, educational, and economic gains for them.

These massive changes have left us with a family which frequently moves. One family in five moves its residence across county lines each year. It is often isolated from grandparents and other relatives which were so much a part of the earlier rural scene. In this home, the traditional subordination of wife to husband and of children to parents has been whittled away by the absence of the father at work and by the increasing competence of wife and children to take over.

"Mobile," "lonely," and "democratic," these are the words which describe the new middle-class family of America. Hungrily the American family reaches out to the suburbs which promise to provide the stability, roots, and friendship so often lacking. No longer guided by a rigid structure of authority, this new family sinks or swims, depending on whether or not its members can find the spirit and devise the means by which it might become a meaningful cooperative venture instead of sheer anarchy on the one hand or despotism on the other.

Who Is "the Head-of-the-House"?

Suppose a hypothetical Martian stepped out of his spaceship to ring the doorbell at your home. Suppose one of your children opened the door and the visitor from outer space said, "Take me to your leader." To whom would the children go? To mother? To father? To both? Or would he say, reflecting the situation in many a modern American home, "I am the leader."

Who *does* take the lead in the modern American home? This question must be countered by another question, "The lead in what?" Every family that operates as a family at all must find a way to operate harmoniously as a small group that has certain important functions to accomplish. Someone must provide the income, keep track of it, disperse it. Someone must manage the household with all that such implies. Someone must care for and nurture the children. Asking who decides what and who does what among the dozens of family tasks that must be accomplished is another way of asking, "Who is the head of the family in this sphere of its life?"

When compared with European families, the American family is remarkably equalitarian in decision making. Usually neither parent is in a position of recognized final authority. German students visiting the United States have reacted with dismay at the way in which the American male seems to be stripped of his power and authority and at what they regard as the excessive and uncontrolled freedom of American children. But they also seem to envy the easy give-and-take between the sexes and between parents and their children. Can we have both?

Because of the biblical picture of clear male dominance in the family, one might expect devout religious people to be less equalitarian in the home. *On the contrary,* some research studies indicate that the more devout the family, whether Roman Catholic or Protestant, the more young people report a fifty-fifty pattern of dominance in their homes. Youth who are indifferent to religion, however, are much more likely to have a father- or mother-dominated home. Apparently, Christian faith as understood today fosters an attitude in husband and wife toward each other which reflects more closely the words, "there is neither male or female . . . in Christ" (Galatians 3:28) and "Be subject to *one another*" (Ephesians 5:21; author's italics), than the admonition, "Wives, be subject to your husbands . . ." (Ephesians 5:22).

A family's organization and leadership can best be understood if we view its process of decision making and the divisions of labor by which it gets needed tasks done. Who provides for the economic needs, disciplines the children, hosts the guests, keeps the books, cleans the house, cooks the meals, organizes the recreation, fosters religious nurture? Each family undoubtedly works out its own division of labor, sometimes by trial and error, sometimes by deliberate design, occasionally by default; but assign tasks it must. The particular assignment of roles to be taken by husband and wife depends upon many factors: *the age of the children, the aptitude of the individual for certain work, and the organization of the spouse's own childhood home, as well as where father works and whether mother holds a paying job outside the home.* It is not enough for the Christian family to hearken back to a clearly male-centered, rural society and say that *its* pattern is the will of God for today. All of the factors mentioned above have a bearing on the problem. God's history is real; life moves on. And he nowhere promises to keep this a simple, rural world.

The New Husband-Father Image. In many marriages, especially during the first year or two of life together, couples *share* many jobs. They may find keeping house together is fun. But as the years go on, there is a steady growth of specialization in family tasks, and partners fall into well-worn ruts. In happy marriages, however, some tasks continue to be shared. Christopher Morley has penned these lines:

> The man who never in his life
> Has washed the dishes with his wife
> Or polished up the silver plate—
> He still is largely celibate.[2]

According to research on family life, husbands who *never* share any household jobs with their wives seem to have the least satisfactory marriages in the United States, even though they may work effectively at their own occupations.

Alarmists have warned that the reversal of the traditional roles—wherein the male exercised authority and was economic

---

2. From *Poems* by Christopher Morley. Copyright 1917, 1945 by Christopher Morley. Published by J. B. Lippincott Company.

provider while his wife was his helper and was almost completely confined to the household—is fraught with danger. They visualize a "feminizing of the male." They see the seeds of confusion being scattered among the children concerning their sexual roles.

There is no doubt that the father's role in the new American family has been transformed since his great-grandfather's day. No longer sternly in command, nor apparently wanting to be, he sees himself as the "head" of the family chiefly in his providing task and as an assistant to his wife in practically everything else. His responsibility seems to have increased while his authority has decreased. Someone has pointed out that the "head of household" is a term now used chiefly in federal income tax instructions and there only to denote one who is married to an alien or not married at all! Busy at the job—which often demands massive amounts of time for specialization—the father has delegated other family tasks or has abdicated them.

The New Wife-Mother Image. Whatever the reason for the father's rejection of traditional authority and responsibilities, the result is generally the same: The American mother has more responsibility than ever before for the family's well-being inside and outside the home. This change in family leadership and organization is not due solely to the father's preoccupation with work which takes so much time and energy. The shift may simply be evidence of the influence of the idea of democracy which distributes more evenly our rights and responsibilities in American society. But it may also reflect the growing *competence* of wives and mothers to do the kinds of things which were the male prerogative in the earlier days of our history.

- Women are now less economically dependent; many more of them are working for wages before and during marriage. (Almost one-third of all mothers with children under eighteen are in the labor force full or part-time.)
- Modern women are better educated and have developed specialized skills, including the ability to handle expenditures and carry responsibility in the community.

These are but two of the influences which bear upon the wifely role in the family today.

The increased competence of the modern wife makes it possible and often desirable for her to take a more responsible role in home and community. But this greater ability has not made life easier for her in the average American home. Rather, the average wife and mother is bedeviled by too many functions. She is expected to be a home manager, hostess, nurse, shopper, glamour girl, supervisor of children's informal education, clubwoman, and often worker or careerist. *How can she find her identity as a woman in the midst of her fragmented life?* While she increases her general competence and uses her newfound rights, she suffers from self-doubt. The sexual revolution, the job revolution, and the kitchen revolution have fantastically extended the possibilities open to her and have brought keen satisfaction. Yet often intermingled with this satisfaction are anxiety, guilt, boredom, and resentment as she attempts to find herself in this new world. There is a persisting uncertainty about how to encompass the roles of wife, mother, and self, and how to find room for all three.

The American woman has three models of the "good wife" to draw upon in our society.[3] The first is the *mother-wife* role, the traditional role of the married woman. This image is of a woman who is totally devoted to her home and husband. She sees as her obligations bearing and rearing children, caring for the home, and subordinating herself to the economic or professional interests of her husband.

While the majority of women think they would prefer this role, they also say it has its disadvantages. Boredom with and resentment of children and housework may set in as they see other women doing what looks exciting and significant. Their husbands may outgrow them intellectually because they lack stimulation. (Adult education possibilities can change that.) The security of the role may lose its luster when the reward for this steady loyalty is not paid in gratitude. Furthermore, these women

---

3. Clifford Kirkpatrick, *The Family* (New York: The Ronald Press Co., 1955), pp. 163–164.

may feel lost when their last child leaves home and they are still in their early fifties. They may have to *learn* to be wives again for the remaining one-third of their married lives.

The other two images of the "good wife" are peculiar to the modern era and are gaining increased popularity. It is too early to say what their effect on the home will be.

The second is the *companion-wife*, a product of college education and ample leisure. She attempts to share her husband's life fully, especially in recreational and social spheres, which, the couple reasons, may aid his business success. She swims, golfs, and boats with her husband. She is his intellectual companion and attempts to keep up with his interests, hoping in this way to exorcise the demon of boredom which overtakes many a marriage. She is family-centered without being homebound. Theaters, nightclubs, and elaborate vacations all demand a husband who has the earning power to afford such luxuries as well as some household help. For her part, the companion-wife is expected to stay alert, young, sexy, and entertaining. Her main function, as she sees it, is to provide constant ego satisfaction to her husband in the sexual-social arena. Children in this kind of family are trained to be well-adjusted "colleagues," primed for the team life of the "organization man." The companion-wife feels her insecurity in the constant struggle to keep up the hectic pace of community activity and in the fear of growing old and uninteresting.

The third model is the *partner-wife*. Because of her full-time job, she is entitled to equality in authority and decision-making in all family matters. She expects a strong voice in family finances and freedom in her personal life. She may find fulfillment and stimulating contacts in the professional or business life beyond her home, but for this she, too, must pay. Much of her marital life will run parallel to her husband's, even to the point of keeping separate bank accounts. Household management is necessarily divided, although two incomes often make it possible to hire outside help. The risks which the partner-wife must assume come both from her desire and ability to be fairly independent and from the economic competition which might develop with her husband. A woman fulfilling this American model can get tired of the double job she has to carry as careerist and wife. And in the rare moments when she has time to reflect, she may sometimes yearn for children or for more time with those she has. If she is Christian she may have a constant inward struggle about whether or not to "bury her talents," which may be outstanding, in order to fulfill the roles society seems to desire and expect. Can she find room for both?

Christians in families living in an industrial age, an age which has witnessed the emancipation of women on every front, cannot simply return to the past when asking which road to take. Any answer must be worked out for a particular, unique, one-flesh relationship which has never been before and will never be again. And in their search, such inquirers are blessed if they find the community of faith willing to be a forum for their clarification of roles in the modern home.

What Are the Problems of Child Rearing?

When Jesus said, ". . . henceforth in one house there will be five divided . . ." (Luke 12:52), he was referring to the higher loyalties that might separate kin from each other when he came into the picture. In our day, we are cursed with another kind of division. We can't agree on how children should be reared: What kind of child do we want to have? What is the good child? Do we want a child who will think for himself or one who will obey? Do we want a child who is "popular" in high school, a "leader" in college, a "success" at his job, even if these attributes make him indifferent to a sense of wonder, or honor, or a dedication to what will not pay off? Do we want a social extravert or a creative introvert? Or have we a choice?

We are confused about our child-rearing goals and the "authorities" in child-rearing have added to our already abundant parental anxieties. In the 1920's John B. Watson's behavioristic psychology made parents feel that the child's parental environment was totally responsible for what he turned out to be. A decade later the Freudians added to parental anxiety by claiming that the child's destiny is fashioned in the nursery. Everything crucial was alleged to happen in the first five years of life.

Even with these extreme views now modified greatly by students of child development, we can understand the confusion of parents. The hopes of parents in the last two or three generations have shifted from goals of economic and material well-being to include psychic health as well. Goals for children are now an interesting blend of mental hygiene principles and the marks of success derived from the business world. "Spiritual values" are assumed to be somehow identical with these American desires. Almost no value is placed upon growth through suffering. The child is not likely to learn from his everyday world that it is by a series of small deaths that men find fulfillment in life. Child-rearing patterns are the way a society perpetuates itself. Therefore, its goals, and the techniques of discipline by which it channels the energies of youth, are important to understand. *Both American parents and children are perplexed and confused because they have not thought through and sorted out their values in this busy world.*

There is another major influence which makes child rearing a problem and divides the household. Children are now very much involved in a society of their own which is often at odds with family standards. As the quotation beginning this chapter implies, parents want their children to be well-socialized and independent. Fearing that their children will be "oddballs" and left to themselves, parents want them to be a part of everything. They often mistake the aloneness which is necessary for creativity for loneliness. In any event, parents are in a dilemma; while wanting their offspring to be "in" solidly with their age-mates, they testify that those groups to which their children belong make parental decision making and discipline more difficult, if not impossible.

Teen-agers, especially, seem to have developed their own small society within society which holds up its own standards, special symbols, and distinct language. High school is the center of "teen-age culture" which is, for the average adolescent, a stronger force than his parents. This should be no great surprise, since teen-agers spend between seven and twelve hours a day with high school associates.

This teen-age society is one of prosperity and power. Seventeen million teen-age buyers had an income of ten billion dollars in 1959 and their buying power is expected to double by 1970! As a result of this huge market, a coalition of advertisers and teen-agers has formed. Unlike the parents and teachers who must often discipline and restrict youth, the advertiser is on the side of teen-agers and flatters and cajoles them into buying. And buy they do. It is estimated that fifty-four million dollars are spent annually on cosmetics alone.

The automobile is another basic material value of the teen-age society. "Without wheels," said one high school young person to the author, "life would not be worth living." In 1960, about six million teen-agers operated cars. They were among the best customers of the used car industry. Records of popular songs, depicting the rocky road of romance, bring seventy-five million dollars from young people annually.

The nonmaterial aspects of this youth culture in America include a special language, numerous periodicals beamed at the pursuit of fun and popularity, and a rating of student activities according to current standards of prestige. Schools and communities differ markedly, but there is great uniformity in one aspect of high school life: athletic ability for boys and glamour for girls are far more rewarded and prized by their peers than intellectual ability.

Here, then, is the teen-age society. More than almost any other influence, it, and its counterparts for younger children, complicates the child-rearing efforts of American parents. *"Youth culture" becomes the measure of all things, and the parents and children seem to have few defenses which the group cannot batter down.* Bewildered as they are, it is little wonder that many parents expect the church to help them in the area of parent-child relations.

WHAT MARRIAGE MEANS TO AMERICANS

If American people believe in anything devoutly, they believe in marriage. Married life is seen as a major goal, a preferred way of life for the vast majority of our people. The specter of divorce, unhappy marital relations, or unruly children, dampens the ardor not one bit. As a matter of fact, census figures over the past two decades show that more than 90 percent of both sexes in America will eventually marry, and many will marry more than one time. It is the "natural thing to do." Unfortunately, the stigma attached to the never-married has not disappeared from our cultural judgments. In this attitude, we are more at home in the Old Testament than in the New Testament, which speaks also of the vocation of singleness. Marriage is lifted up in our society as the *summum bonum*, the highest good of existence.

In a myriad of ways, both open and hidden, we teach our children the supreme value of *ideal* marriage. Most young girls embrace this goal without hesitation; boys do so a bit more reluctantly. Yet even the girl half-seriously thinks about and prepares for a career as insurance against the grim possibility that she will not be married. With the help of the business world which sees the American wedding as the biggest and costliest event in marriage history, the female of the species prepares early for the big step. The average age at which the American girl begins to collect items for her hope chest is fifteen. Of course she has the constant urging and advice of commercial interests in these preparations. Most Americans sense something of a ritualistic, if not religious, meaning to marriage since eight out of every ten weddings are presided over by a member of the clergy.

Americans believe in marriage; there is no doubt about this. Our doubt enters when we ask pointed questions about the *image* of marriage in America. What do Americans expect of their family life? For what ideal do they strive in marriage?

A third-grade girl was asked by her teacher to give the name of the form of marriage in which one man remained married to one woman. Her prompt reply was, "Monotony." An ever increasing number of the populace seem to think so too, if we can judge by the steadily increasing separation, divorce, and desertion figures. We all know that the grounds for divorce are symptoms of already sick marriages for which legal concoctions are prescribed.

To most Americans, the sign of a successful marriage is the

personal happiness of the husband and wife. Happiness is the principal matrimonial goal. When one attempts to break open this elusive concept as it relates to marriage, he is hard put to come up with anything concrete. The cynic might accuse American marriage of being a mutual pact between two individuals who simply want all their desires met—the "I'll scratch your back, you scratch mine" philosophy. That would undoubtedly be an accurate picture of many marriages. For most Americans, however, happiness is an amalgam of romantic love, physical attractiveness, sexual compatibility, partnership with one with whom one can achieve self-expression and financial competence and have children in whom to take pride. The pursuit of happiness in our culture is centered in this intense emotional attachment between husband and wife.

It is no longer enough to think of marriage as useful and necessary for life. In traditional rural America, an enduring marriage was virtually indispensable for the carrying on of economic production and the begetting, education, doctoring, and protecting of the young. Today some of these functions have been taken over by or given to experts and community organizations. The modern home is left with a nucleus of sex and parenthood, companionship, and housekeeping, and less involvement in the duties and responsibilities that our grandparents and their parents had to assume. Marriage now becomes a relationship in which closeness and intimacy are our major concerns.

Complete Fulfillment, an Unrealistic Goal

One would think that American marriage, freed from so many of its utilitarian responsibilities, might have an easier go of it. On the contrary, there is less to hold it together and make it meaningful. All of the eggs are placed in the one basket of "love." Love and affection have come to mean the personal fulfillment of needs.

Entering marriage with romantic expectations, a couple expects to find in marriage *complete* fulfillment, a hope the Christian will regard as idolatrous. Modern Americans expect too much of marriage. They make greater demands of it than any other people; they want greater rewards from it psychically and physically. In our depersonalized, lonely society where it is the rare human being who dares to be more than a "part person" in the competitive swirl of activity, *we try to get everything out of this one relationship.* Satisfactions which, in other cultures, are found in wider family contacts, in work, in religion, and in the community are now expected from husband, wife, and children alone. Thus we make demands upon marriage, but not necessarily the right demands. We have high expectations, but not necessarily reasonable expectations. Consequently, *disillusionment and disappointment are almost inevitable and they follow in the wake of idealized romantic love.* The shock of reality gives birth to a bitter folklore depicting bored, henpecked husbands; dominating, spendthrift wives; and sarcastic talk about the "ball and chain" and "the better half." A comment was made recently by a radio comedian: "Marriage is like a steaming bath. Once you get used to it, it's not so hot."

Unrealistic expectations and hopes are a part of the trouble in American marriage; their root is *idolatry,* the worship of the false gods of marital bliss as the answer to all of life's questions. They will let us down. St. Augustine reminded us, "We are restless until we find our rest in Thee."

Love, a Romanticized Ideal

Marriage in America is a youthful proposition. Half of all American men are married by the time they are twenty-three years of age and half of all women by the age of twenty. It is estimated that 97 percent of today's teen-agers will eventually be married. What is the process by which they select a mate?

UNIVAC'S CALCULATIONS
LEAD COUPLE TO ALTAR

Hollywood, Oct. 16 (UPI) A man and woman who were matched by an electronic computer-analyzer will be married Saturday in the Hollywood First Presbyterian Church. . . .

Most Americans will not be married to each other as a result of the rational mate selection process depicted in this newspaper story. Nor will most of them meet their mates through the assorted formalized introduction services, lonely hearts clubs, and such available in our society. The average boy and girl simply let nature take its course as they meet in the many forums of American life. They meet through a dating system which is a unique American invention; nothing like it is found elsewhere in the world. Yet the American young person takes it for granted that this is the "natural" way by which popularity and sexual attraction are judged, and, ultimately, mates procured. He assumes that out of his many encounters in dating, he will one day be smitten and "fall in love," a feeling he sees as both necessary and sufficient for marriage.

Dating is a product of an open-class society where people move from place to place in their pursuit of happiness and economic security. In early America, the accepted rural pattern was a formal association with a few individuals of the opposite sex. Datable young persons were well-known by one's parents. Today young people meet on their own, often without parental knowledge. Seldom do parents know much of the background of the person encountered by their child if they know him at all. A girl's parents cannot say, as they might have a few decades ago in small-town America, "I've known his pa and ma since he was just a kid, and they've always been hard-working, honest folks." Now it is usually a superficial contact that must suffice to form the parental judgment. And, too often, it is the basis of the young person's decision as well.

The standards for mate selection held by young people, especially those of high school age, are not always conducive to marital success. Physical attractiveness, social charm, dress, and a car are the points of attraction and the magnetism which pulls the sexes to each other as they intermingle in the great metropolitan centers. In such contacts, as in adult social life, dating involves a kind of social maneuvering, which does not often touch upon or reveal those qualities which matter so much if the couple is to live happily together for the next forty years or more. One might even say that in current dating habits there seems to be a conspiracy against deep relationships and the unglamorous events which could be a testing ground for realistic marriage. When one thinks in terms of a lifelong union, being a good mixer and having a presentable pair of legs are somewhat less important than what one thinks about God, money, and a crying baby.

We ought to be encouraged that many young people desire to break through the superficialities and discover what makes for satisfying marriage. With proper education by school and church and home, love can come to mean something more solid than "an itchy feeling around the heart that you can't scratch," an infatuation based on sex appeal.

Dating has real value for American youth. Through the dating experience, a young person attempts to find out *who* he is (male, female, individual) and *whose* he is (where does he belong, who cares for him, and to whom should he be loyal). It is one of the important ways—vocation being the other main avenue—by which he seeks for a *sense of identity*. It is often a painful process, a heartbreaking struggle. Notice that these questions which dating is expected to answer are basically religious questions; they are addressed directly by Christian faith. Does the American dating pattern mask a deeper, unrecognized religious hunger? Is the process of "falling in love," a love which is "bigger than both of us," a search for that which God alone can give? The lonely American wants to be part of something greater than himself, and this desire is accentuated in the teen-ager.

Although he may lose himself for a while in the experience of romantic love, the average American youth sees mate selection as an act of his own free will, accomplished without his parents' having much to say about it. It is inconceivable to him that any marriage which was not inaugurated by extensive dating, courtship, and romantic love could work. This may be one of our cultural blind spots.

Dr. and Mrs. David Mace in their informative book, *Marriage: East and West,* report their discussion with some teen-agers of India who had not yet left the old system of family control over mate selection:

"Wouldn't you like to be free to choose your own marriage partners, like the young people do in the West?"
"Oh no!" several voices replied in chorus.
Taken aback, we searched their faces.
"Why not?"
"For one thing," said one of them, "doesn't it put the girl in a very humiliating position?"
"Humiliating? In what way?"
"Well, doesn't it mean that she has to try to look pretty, and call attention to herself, and attract a boy, to be sure she'll get married?"
"Well, perhaps so."
"And if she doesn't want to do that, or if she feels it's undignified, wouldn't that mean she mightn't get a husband?"
"Yes, that's possible."
"So a girl who is shy and doesn't push herself forward might not be able to get married. Does that happen?"
"Sometimes it does."
"Well, surely that's humiliating. It makes getting married a sort of competition in which the girls are fighting each other for the boys. And it encourages a girl to pretend she's better than she really is. She can't relax and be herself. She has to make a good impression to get a boy, and then she has to go on making a good impression to get him to marry her."
Before we could think of an answer to this unexpected line of argument, another girl broke in.
"In our system, you see," she explained, "we girls don't have to worry at all. We *know* we'll get married. When we are old enough, our parents will find a suitable boy, and everything will be arranged. We don't have to go into competition with each other."[4]

---

4. From *Marriage: East and West* by David and Vera Mace. Copyright © 1959, 1960 by David and Vera Mace. Reprinted by permission of Doubleday & Company, Inc., pp. 130-131.

But even in America, freedom of marriage choice is a myth for the majority who marry. Only the very attractive have a wide range of selection. The limits imposed upon one's choice include considerations of social class, income range, accidents of geography, national background, race, and religion. American youth, in other words, do not have an unlimited number of eligible persons of the opposite sex to choose from. There are strong expectations about whom he should marry although his range of selection is broader than in most societies.

It may surprise American youth to know that, even today, parents are not to be ruled out as playing a significant role in mate choice. Middle-class fathers and mothers quietly or not so quietly influence their young people by providing parties, vacations, and other recreation for the children and their friends. They move to neighborhoods and communities where they think the "right kind" of future mates might be found. They send the youngsters to schools where the "better prospects" are likely to converge. Furthermore, most parents of any social class express their opinions about the dates their children have. They sometimes try persuasion and appeals to loyalty and, occasionally, threats or bribery. Arguments are not uncommon in their homes. The evidence indicates that parental judgment is more likely to be beneficial than harmful. Parental approval is highly associated with good marriage adjustment; disapproval with marital trouble. Of course there are exceptions. Some parents are wrong! In our dating system in the United States, frequent parent-child disagreement is one of the prices to be paid for "freedom."

There is another sense in which marriage choice in America is not free. Romantic love notwithstanding, people are likely to seek out or respond to partners not so much according to conscious likes and dislikes and mutual interests (although this is what they tell themselves) but because of the stronger *unconscious* currents in his life which stem from personal history. When the hidden needs of the psychic life dovetail and supplement those of the partner, a successful marriage is likely to ensue. Thus a woman who is somewhat dependent and agreeable may appeal deeply to a man who needs to be dominant and decisive in his marriage. Our deeper psychic hungers may be more commanding than we think when we "fall in love" and select our mates.

Divorce, a Convenient Escape Hatch

A corollary of American marriage as a pursuit of personal happiness is a relatively easy system of divorce. Only Egypt, where the woman's role in life is changing drastically, has a higher divorce rate than our own. Proportionately, we have three times as many divorces each year as England, France, Australia, and Finland; four to six times as many as Canada, Belgium, Norway, and The Netherlands; and perhaps ten times as many as Soviet Russia. Los Angeles County in California alone often has a greater number of divorces granted in a single year than in all of the British Isles! If marriage is built upon personal happiness, it is assumed that those who marry to find it and find it not should be able to try again.

Surprisingly, the American divorced person does not seem disillusioned with marriage itself, only with his ex-mate. He wants to find what he has been led to feel true marriage promises. And he is too lonely to discard marriage as a goal, no matter how many partners he must try! Some people remarried after divorce do better the second time. Is it possible that they will settle for less in the second marriage? Why did they not learn to do this earlier? Margaret Mead is right when she says that *the most serious thing that is happening in the United States is that people enter marriage with the idea it is terminable.*[5]

The average American today thinks of divorce as the possible escape hatch, even while committing himself to lifelong marriage. Consciously or unconsciously, early or late, the wedding vow is often changed from "as long as we both shall live" to "as long as we both shall love"; from "till death us do part" to "till we get bored with each other"; from "forsaking all others" to "until someone who will make me really happy comes along." This transmutation of vows ordinarily follows disillusionment and frustration in marriage, but it is evident that many couples, just entering marriage, *anticipate* escaping it. A pastor reports that

---

5. From a lecture, Columbia University, 1955.

one couple, after convincing him of their fitness for marriage, went on to agree, "But just in case things don't work out, we're putting money in the bank for the cost of a divorce." Certainly few people plan for divorce before marriage, but the thought may be present nonetheless. A crucial mistake reflected in this couple's words is the assumption that in marriage "things will work out" or "things will not work out." If marriage is anything, it is a costly *achievement,* a persisting *effort,* an artful *creation* within a relationship of mature affection. The raw materials of marriage are ours—that's all. To them we must add our mature faith.

In the face of these staggering changes in marriage and family ideals in America, Christian parents and young people are justifiably perplexed. They cannot turn the clock back and attempt a formula for relationships which comes from a pre-industrial age. Nor can they, if they are serious at all about the Christian faith, simply drift with the tide and conform to this world. It may be that the renewing of their minds can come from honestly facing these dilemmas with each other in the forum provided by a Fellowship which is in the world yet not of it. Christians in families are in the same boat as countless others; they are confused by changing rules and goals. But wherever two or three are gathered together in his Spirit, he has promised to be with them. Can we trust his word?

3
Looking at Marriage Through the Eyes of Faith

"Listen to this, John." Joan Adam had been paging through a church magazine and a particular line caught her eye. She began to read aloud as her husband peered curiously at her over the top of his evening paper, " 'True men and women make great parents and lovers, not because they work hard at being parents and lovers, but because they are committed to the life of faith first.' " They had just gotten the children off to bed and were experiencing that momentary relief of parents who sometimes wonder if it paid to get up that particular morning. "Maybe that's been our trouble," she continued, thinking of the tension at the dinner table. "We've been working so hard at being good parents that we are on edge all the time. Something's wrong, but what?" Seeing that his wife was serious and deeply puzzled, John laid aside the paper and looked at her. Something had come over both of them, he mused to himself. Something that sagged their spirits and created a "fallout" of dissatisfaction in recent weeks. "It's funny," he remarked, "when we were first married we had such a clear sense of where we were going, that God was in this with us. Somehow we've lost that. Maybe we need to look at where we went off the track."

Almost nothing can rob a family of high morale as can a loss of its sense of direction. In our affluent society it is depressingly easy to give so much attention to the means of increasing our happiness and comfort that we soon lose sight of the basic reason for being a family unit. A whole society can be cursed with an apathy that comes from giving over attention to the means and neglecting the purpose for all this effort.

FAITH AND THE FAMILY

Christians hold that the Bible, as the true and lively word, has the ability to reactivate our sense of direction. In a very basic sense the Scripture is the script for the drama of marriage and the family. Before we know how to play our parts, we must read the script to find out what this play is all about. What would our family life be like if played as its Author had intended? Are family members reading the same script?

Maybe a family thinks that their ad-libbing from day to day is all there is to it. Or, if they are serious about a Christian life, people begin to feel that they can create "Christian" families by memorizing the lines of the script and by practicing the rules of expression. But one can learn those lines and rules perfectly and still not grasp what the story is all about! The important thing about Christians in families is the way in which we expose ourselves to the meaning of the script, and let that meaning permeate the whole fabric of our lives together—from floor-mopping to car buying to lovemaking. When we hear that story and know that it is *our* story, God acting for us in Jesus Christ, then something can happen in the most intimate relationships. In this way that highly prized inner security we seek may come, not as an achievement, but as a gift.

Family Influence and Individual Faith

Faith cannot be given to our loved ones intravenously. Hearing and responding is an individual matter. It cannot be presented to our children or handed to our spouse. Simply because we do not live inside another's skin and share his person, we cannot hear or decide for him. Theodore Reik once said, "You cannot tell another being how to live, not even your own child. Perhaps, especially your own child."[1] We must each do our own living, our own deciding, our own dying. Sometimes the very closeness of the family makes us forget this. We may take vows on our child's behalf at his baptism in infancy, but he must be the one to confirm them later. We cannot become a Christian *for*

---
1. From a lecture, Chicago, Illinois, 1947.

another. He must respond to Jesus Christ on his own; faith is highly personal, just as love is.

This does not deny that we have a tremendous influence upon one another, positively and negatively. Each day of our lives we express our values and declare in countless actions what means most to us. Not a day passes that we are not thrust into decisions that reveal what counts with us. Each day that we love, are angry, and find our way back to each other, *we influence each other greatly in matters of faith.* We are bound together. This is the truth behind the biblical story of the Philippian jailer, whose entire family was baptized after the conversion of the father.

But Timothy can be recalled as a signal for another day, for he seems to have come from a religiously split Greek family in which father and grandfather are never mentioned as members of the church. Can a family in which just one person is committed to Christ be Christian? In advising Christian mates not to divorce their non-Christian spouses, the Apostle Paul acknowledges the tremendous influence one person has over another in the family: "For the unbelieving husband is, in a sense, consecrated by being joined to the person of his wife; the unbelieving wife is similarly 'consecrated' by the Christian brother she has married" (1 Corinthians 7:14; Phillips translation[2]).

The First Letter of Peter was also written in a time like ours, when many homes were religiously split. The author gives this advice to the person upon whom a Christian household may depend: "In the same spirit [the willingness to endure suffering] you married women should adapt yourselves to your husbands, so that even if they do not obey the Word of God they may be won to God without any word being spoken, simply by seeing the pure and reverent behavior of you, their wives" (1 Peter 3:1; Phillips translation). When a Christian mate must face the great spiritual loneliness which is present and even confront the antagonism or derision of the rest of the family, it is hard for him not to indulge in self-pity, self-righteousness, moralizing, and scolding. Only when we are secure in God's love and in God's people, can the

---

2. All quotations from *The New Testament in Modern English* © J. B. Phillips, 1958. Used by permission of The Macmillan Company.

influence of Christian grace sweeten the atmosphere of those lives we share.

Christians in Families

Perhaps we have used the clichés "Christian family" and "Christian home" too easily and thoughtlessly. Can we attach the adjective "Christian" to *any* group or institution? For example, can we say that we have a "Christian" nation just because it allows freedom of worship, professes high ideals through the Constitution, and has its coins imprinted with "In God We Trust"?

Only *persons* can be Christian, and these persons can marry and establish families. Is it not better to speak of "Christians *in* families" just as we speak of Christians in business, or Christians at school? Christians witness to their faith in the many arenas of their lives, and the home is one of them. It only confuses the issue to speak of the church and its relationship to the home as if they were two completely separate entities. They are indeed separate if we are thinking of the church as a building and the home as a house. But the same people may be involved in each. When the whole family, or even one member of a family, is *in* the church—that fellowship which proclaims the Good News, which serves the neighbor in need, and which provides a mutual ministry of believers to one another—then we have a new situation.

The gospel ordinarily enters the family by way of the parents who teach their children. In John Calvin's thought the inclusion of children in the covenant is ordinarily by way of the family. Ideally it is through parents that the child derives his understanding of the faith and receives through baptism his "engrafting into the body of Christ." When a parent is Christian, *the church lives in the home* and that family is a part of the larger church. The Bible never speaks of the "Christian family"; rather it speaks of the "church in your house" when a household comes under the sway of the Good News of Jesus Christ and intends to live for him. The relationship of church and home, then, is not the relationship of two separate things to each other. *The church is in the home and the family is in the church when Christian* nurture occurs in families and the families are fulfilling their mission in society.

One World, Many Family Patterns

At the beginning of our inquiry about the Christian meaning of marriage and family, we must face one fact: Family life had been in existence long before there was any Christian understanding of it. The family is a natural group and as such has persisted over thousands of years of recorded history, much longer than any nation or any religious or ethnic group has been able to maintain its identity. It stood as part of God's creation long before man became aware through Scripture of God's intention for this natural group.

We can affirm that God made everything that is, and at the same time realize that not everything we see in the history of marriage and the family has reflected his will. The doctrine of the Fall asserts that man has attempted to become God and to create his own design for what he considers the good life. Thus throughout history marriage has passed through many forms, each of them an attempt to satisfy man's need for companionship, a need implanted within him by his Creator.

Man has tried all the forms of marriage his imagination can conceive. He has even tried to conceive of life without marriage as we know it. He has lived in polygamy, the marriage of one mate to several persons of the opposite sex. And at different periods of history, he has tried group marriage, the relationship of several women to several men. The overwhelming majority of marriages in the world can be classified as monogamous, or pair-marriage, if the definition does not include any idea of the permanency of the particular union.

Monogamy is the only form of marriage found in *all* societies, although many approve of polygamy as well. There is every reason to believe that as societies develop and become more complex, they will become more exclusively monogamous. The near-equal ratio of men to women in most societies is a prime consideration. If one man has two wives, another is consigned to bachelorhood. There is the practical matter of the expense of supporting more than one spouse. Add to these disadvantages the housing problems, the child-rearing issues, sexual rivalry, and conflicts over property, and it is not difficult to see why legal polygamy is becoming obsolete in the world. Paradoxically, as societies develop toward monogamy, we can expect in them an increase in prostitution and other extramarital sexual liaisons.

Even though the United States is considered a monogamous country, we find evidence that many have accepted the notion that monogamy means simply "one mate at a time." One marriage in every eight consummated this year in the U.S.A. will be a second or third marriage. Some who remarry are, of course, deeply concerned to learn from past mistakes and to succeed where once they had failed, but it would not be facetious to apply the terms "sequential monogamy" or "installment plan polygamy" to the marriages of many in our country.

Christians find the rationale for monogamy in revelation; the "one-flesh" relationship is exalted as normative in the Bible. Indeed, *the order of creation itself is established in a way that gives the practical advantage to the monogamous form of marriage.*

What happens when Christianity confronts a polygamous culture? Christians are more concerned with the "spirit" than with the "law" of marriage. Even in our country legal monogamy can be a mask for a polygamy expressed in the faithless desire for variety in mates and sexual experience. In societies where polygamous marriage prevails, it is not sufficient to change the marriage form alone. In fact, to alter such a practice abruptly, not realizing that it is tied in with the life and values of a society, could bring only hardship. It is too easy for a Christian missionary to say bluntly, "To be a Christian you must get rid of all but one of your wives." Is this a condition of *becoming* a Christian? Are we saved by monogamy or by grace? We must consider the consequences of such rigid, abrupt changes: Often the wives turned out upon such missionary orders have been forced into prostitution as a means of making a living, and their children are left destitute. No wonder many Africans regard the missionary as a home wrecker. Christians must be more concerned with demonstrating the Good News in relationships, both marital and racial, than with setting up new legalisms that can throw an entire culture out of joint if imposed without understanding patience.

Each culture develops its practices as a result of a particular history, particular beliefs and values, its physical surroundings, and its attempt to survive. The human beings who live in these strikingly different societies are still fundamentally the same as human beings were in Bible times. Once we conclude, as a Christocentric perspective would lead us to do, that people all over the world are *human* just as we are, having anxieties and fears, reacting in self-protective ways, desiring companionship, striving to be individual persons, struggling to find physical well-being through food, shelter, and sexual experience, we are not surprised to find that family living takes many forms.

In his desire to find God's intention for his family, the Christian might ponder the differences now existing in the world's families. He will know that the American family is just another way man has learned, in his own peculiar circumstances, to satisfy the longings of his heart. And he will not be misled by thinking that it is the last word.

As we view the shifting social scene and contrasting family shapes, we discover that marriage and family seem to satisfy certain universal human needs. One wedding service puts it this way, "Let us therefore reverently remember that God has established and sanctified marriage, for the welfare and happiness of mankind."[3] He has given families a tall order:

- fulfill the need of companionship and belonging;
- provide sexual expression for the mates;
- contribute to the continuance of human life through children;
- bring up offspring so that they might (1) transmit the beliefs of the culture, (2) learn what it is to be a man or a woman, (3) develop a sense of "right"

---

3. *The Book of Common Worship* (Richmond: John Knox Press, 1946), p. 183.

and "wrong" in a particular society, (4) learn how to cope with the inanimate environment, and (5) do the work of the world;

- cooperate in keeping the family group intact by a division of labor and privilege between men and women, parents and children.

This is what every family, in every society, must do to some extent. And this is a "tall order" because no family can, on its own, do all these things adequately. Human weakness, self-centeredness, and the desire for security at the expense of other life prevent this natural group from realizing its full potential.

Christianity contains within itself *the promise of transforming that group into a caring, meaningful community.*

FAITH AND THE MARRIAGE RELATIONSHIP

Sexuality in Marriage

In a real sense sexuality is the most basic fact of our lives. We are not speaking narrowly of sexual love but of the division of human life into male and female. The Magna Charta of humanity is found in the Genesis stories which tell how God completed the creation of man by giving him woman as a companion (Genesis 2:18–25 and Genesis 1:26–29). There are differences in the two stories. In Genesis, chapter 1, which was written *later* than chapter 2, we find that, after making the material and subhuman world, God made man and woman at the same time and with equality of status. "Then God said, 'Let us make man in our image, after our likeness . . .' So God created man in his own image . . . male and female he created them." The original form of Man is a duality, male and female. In Genesis 5:2 we find that Adam is not an individual at all, but a pair: "Male and female he created them, and he blessed them and named *them* Man [Adam] when they were created." Thus Man is not a biped but a quadruped!

God created Man in two types, male and female, for each to fulfill and to complement the other. They have something in common, yet they differ. Without the counterplay of male and female in God's world, we are not fully human. Sex, then, is at the center of God's creation and at the center of our humanity. The sexual difference is the basic difference in life; all other distinctions are less essential or nonessential.

Genesis, chapter 2, contains the "rib" story. Why did God create this partner for man? Because "it is not good that man should be alone." Man cannot live in isolation, nor can he live in communion with only the natural world. Man must have someone who is, as he says, "bone of my bone, and flesh of my flesh" in order to end his loneliness. St. Augustine comments that "Eve was not taken from Adam's feet to be his slave, nor from his head to be his ruler, but from his side to be his beloved partner."[4] This story also answers a quite definite question. Why do the sexes experience such a strong drive for each other? The answer given here is that God took woman from man, that they were originally *one* flesh. Therefore they must come together again and again; they belong to each other.

The Husband-Wife Relationship Is Central. We must consider two points made in both stories. Notice first that these stories deal not with the origin of parenthood, but with the establishment of *marriage*, the relationship of husband and wife. *This* is primary. It is true that the rest of the Old Testament concentrates heavily upon the family—the relationship of parents to children—often viewing children and child rearing as most important. Indeed, the Roman Catholic Church in later centuries followed this same idea, when it called marriage by the Latin word, "matrimony" (the office of motherhood). But in the New Testament Jesus returns the emphasis from the parents-children preoccupation of most of the Old Testament to the husband and wife relationship. "A man shall leave his father and mother and be joined to his wife, and the two shall become one" (Mark 10:7–8). Modern students of the family are discovering that if the husband-wife relation is pushed to the circumference of family concerns and parenthood

---

4. As quoted in *Responsible Marriage and Parenthood* (Philadelphia: Office of The General Assembly, The United Presbyterian Church in the U.S.A., 1962), p. 18.

or relations with the larger family are placed at the center, all of these encounters become distorted.

This insight of faith has great implications for us. We in America give massive amounts of time, attention, and effort on behalf of our children. Perhaps no other people has been as anxious about the behavior and feelings of their offspring. As a result, father and mother put most of their energies into chauffeuring, sponsoring children's clubs, and trying to make them happy and popular. Such parents may be left with little time to be husband and wife to each other. It is possible to get so busy being parents that we forget how to be husband and wife or just persons to each other. To be sure, when new life is first brought into a home, it requires time and effort to give attention to the nurture of our children. This, and nothing more sinister, can disturb the couple and make them feel less close to one another.

In the face of this American emphasis upon children and their worried parents, we may be surprised to find that the Christian view of life stresses the husband-wife relation. "For this reason a man shall leave his father and mother and be joined to his wife." The general order of priority in relationships is seen as: one's mate, children, parents, brothers and sisters, and then other relatives. How much of the difficulty in family life could be avoided if this were realized when conflicting claims are made upon us! Of course, this order can be changed to meet important needs, but the biblical insight is profound, and a biblical view of life can indeed be revolutionary. For example, we know of parents who are starved for affection and who seek emotional gratification in their children. One college girl said, in tears, "I've had to be both daughter and husband to my mother—and I just can't take it any longer." Here the biblical insight and a discovery of the psychology of family relations converge as they speak of the importance of marital relationships to the well-being of the whole family.

Sexuality Can Be Spiritual. A second insight to be gained from these basic biblical stories is that sexuality is God's idea and, as such, is *good*. Puritanical people are often inclined to think of sex as the devil's creation or to at least entertain the notion that God somehow made a mistake. They regard sex with a sort of fascinated horror. In contrast to this attitude, when God finished his work, he "saw everything he had made, and behold, it was very good" (Genesis 1:31).

Male and female are meant to complement each other in all aspects of life. In marriage, a part of that personal community is the sexual union. Marriage is a covenant to be faithful to one another in the "one-flesh" relationship. Both the sexual desire and the relationship of fidelity in which it can be expressed are to be considered gifts of God. To be sure, there are many fruitful relationships between male and female which are not primarily sexual. The relationship between fathers and daughters, mothers and sons, brothers and sisters, co-workers and friends, all need what each sex can bring to the other to find complete humanity. Yet the encounter between the sexes is fully realized only where there is the free and lifetime commitment of one man loving this woman and one woman loving this man in which the sexual relation is an important way in which they become "one." If we read the Bible aright, we cannot conclude that sex itself is evil. The *use* of sex for selfish motives, outside or inside of marriage, can become a very great evil, but the distinction ought to be kept clear.

Why do we so often conclude that the gift of sex is evil? Many Christians have fallen into the trap of regarding the "spiritual" and "physical" as opposites. In so doing, they are not following biblical faith at all, but have become unknowing adherents of the ancient Greek and Persian dualism which divided life into two separate compartments. This movement, which infiltrated the church in the early centuries, gave rise to asceticism, and the emphasis upon celibacy. It sees the body and physical life as a tomb from which an immortal soul must be released. The spiritual life is to soar above the sordid demands of the evil body. But spirit and body are not opposed to each other in biblical thought. In Romans 8: 1–11, for example, Paul is not describing a war between body and spirit but between the "fleshly" or "worldly" motives, which are basically concerned with self, and the "spiritual mind," which is concerned about the Kingdom and the proper use of the body within it. According to biblical faith, a philosophy which tries to drive a wedge between the body and the spirit, calling the one evil and the other good, is anti-Christian. God came to us incarnate, "enfleshed" in Jesus Christ, and because of this, Christianity is joyfully positive in its acceptance of the material world as a gift of God.

Sexuality Has Two Main Purposes. To sum up briefly the positive teachings of Scripture, sex has two equally important functions in life and marriage: *the re-creation of the relationship* of husband and wife—"and the two shall become one" (see Genesis 2:24 and Mark 10:7); and *the procreation of children*—"be fruitful and multiply" (Genesis 1:28). Both of these purposes are encompassed within the compelling desire of human beings for companionship. "It is not good that the man should be alone" (Genesis 2:18). Within this framework, the sexual relationship is characterized by fidelity, loving faithfulness—"A man shall leave his father and mother and be joined to his wife."

Here is where morality comes in and it is morality with a reason. Our faithfulness to each other, our trust in each other, our taking unlimited responsibility for each other allows sex to become more than merely a way of passing on life. *Sex becomes a vehicle that symbolizes the mutuality which a husband and wife have in a language which is precious to both and too deep for words.* A trust of one another in God's covenant furnishes the condition under which the depth, the full intensity of the sexual relation, can be discovered. In faithfulness, we discover the meaning of "one flesh."

To have sexual intercourse before marriage means that a couple will enter into this "holy estate" with no really significant act to mark the importance and the new experience of becoming "one flesh." Is it too much to believe that young people will want to save that precious new gift for the one to whom they will someday commit themselves before the Lord, or that suspense and surprise can still have value for them as they look forward to marriage? In God's intention for us, *our sexuality, when fully expressed, belongs to that one whose life is to be bound with ours in the full communion of life.*

Premarital and extramarital relationships, so often clandestine and frequently accompanied by exploitation, fear, guilt, and resentment, cannot symbolize "oneness." They usually amount to only one thing, tension release. Sex, when it fulfills God's basic purposes, is *not merely the union of two bodies but the union of two persons.* The former is easy; the latter is a great achievement. If sex represents the union of two *persons,* sex technique or the efficient performance of an act, is *not* the all-important thing, in spite of the rationalizations about testing compatibility before marriage. Rather, it is the struggle of growing together in sex, as well as in the other areas of marriage, that welds a couple together and allows them to learn tenderness, humor, and forgiveness in their initial awkwardness. It may take years to find such oneness, but this gift, when it comes, is another reminder of God's presence in our common life.

In Christian faith the sexual relation is seen as involving a kind of knowledge of our mate and ourselves which can be communicated in no other way. When the Bible speaks of the sexual act as "knowing" a woman or a man, it means a deep level of acquaintance. In a relationship of fidelity, you may discover through sex what it means to become a whole person, as you give yourself with abandon and receive the wholehearted love of a trusted husband or wife. You learn what it means to be a man or a woman. And the first occasion of such learning should be when wholeheartedness, unlimited responsibility, security, and comfort exist in a relationship. This is marriage.

Unity in Marriage

There are other ways of communicating deeply with persons which do not require sex—words, art, gestures, music, silence, and the giving and receiving of the work of hand, heart, or head. The unmarried can also develop these fully. Even in marriage, when sexual relations are impossible because of separation or illness or fatigue, other modes of communion can and do express the union of a husband and wife.

The Mystery of Unity. How two persons, male and female, can find a genuine union of spirit and body when they come to marriage with millions of different experiences, a variety of relatives, and quite separate personalities is a deep mystery. Yet they become "one" in God's eyes, if not always in their own feelings. Jesus' sharpest teaching about this biblical arithmetic was evoked when he was challenged by the Pharisees of his day:

> And Pharisees came up and in order to test him asked, "Is it lawful for a man to divorce his wife?" He answered them, "What did Moses command you?" They said, "Moses allowed a man to write a certificate of divorce, and to put her away." But Jesus said to them, "For your hardness of heart he wrote you this commandment. But from the beginning of creation, 'God made them male and female.' For this reason a man shall leave his father and mother and be joined to his wife, and the two shall become one. So they are no longer two but one. What therefore God has joined together, let not man put asunder" (Mark 10:2–9).

American culture fairly shouts at us, "Marriage is a unity created by romantic love and common interests." In the face of this modern practice and thought, the New Testament affirms that "Marriage is a unity created by God." We find the foundation of monogamy in Christ's relationship with the church, for just as Christ makes the church his one bride (Ephesians 5), so man makes one woman his wife.

We have seen that God created man and woman in such a way that they may find their authentic humanity together. Now we realize that a man can find this total participation and unity with only one other in marriage. The total being of one goes out to the other in a way that is unique, different from that which happens to any other two people. Something unique which cannot exist apart from them is fashioned out of this particular couple.

In Christian marriage a person shares a covenant relationship with another person and with God. Together, within this sacred agreement, they promise to forsake all others. This means that they not only take leave of parents and relatives by leaving the home physically; they transfer their emotional loyalty as well, which is a much more difficult task. As they make their vows to each other, this man and this woman pledge themselves to love each other irrevocably. The minister does not ask, "Are you in love?" He asks, "Wilt thou pledge . . . in all love and honor, in all duty and service, in all faith and tenderness . . ." That is, *married love, Christian style, is resolute love, shot through with decisions that run deeper than momentary feelings and a faithfulness more sturdy than mere pleasantness in relationships.*

This unity which God brings into a couple's life is not always pleasant. It is a unity, more robust than natural romantic love, which can persist in plenty or want, in joy or sorrow, in sickness or health. Each of these states, even those which are positive, can threaten the relationship of husband and wife. Realistically facing these conditions as a part of marriage and not as an excuse for leaving it, one can realize what the unity of God means. G. K. Chesterton lampoons:

> That dear, dreamy old bachelor notion—that notion that the unity of marriage, the being one flesh, has something to do with being perfectly happy, or perfectly good, or even with being perfectly and continuously affectionate! I tell you, an ordinary honest man is part of his wife even when he wishes he wasn't. I tell you an ordinary good woman is part of her husband even when she wishes him at the bottom of the sea. I tell you that, whether two people are for the moment friendly or angry, happy or unhappy, the Thing marches on, the great four footed Thing, the quadruped of the home.[5]

What if we should become convinced that God has called us into this unity, that he has given us these particular people—our mate and children—to live with intimately, to learn from, and to

---

5. Maisie Ward, *Return to Chesterton* (New York: Sheed & Ward, Inc., 1952), p. 90. Used by permission of Miss D. E. Collins.

teach in the school of discipleship? If this sense of calling, and not merely our personal satisfaction, is the basis of our unity, we might see marriage differently. We would not expect gratification from each other which can come only from God, and we might not be so hopeless about our quarrels. But if our home life always ran smoothly, our ultimate loyalty might be to each other rather than to God, who can heal our brokenness and the hurts we inflict upon each other. What is more fatal to a robust marriage than the I-live-only-for-you and you-live-only-for-me contract so common in American life? God's gift of unity is deeper than any feelings we may have toward each other; it is realized by our affirming him together.

Unity Without Uniformity. God does not intend this unity to mean that the two individuals in a marriage be carbon copies of each other. A woman was once asked on a TV program if she and her husband ever had a serious difference of opinion. Her thoughtful reply was, "We figure that if we always thought and acted alike, one of us is unnecessary." God intends us to be real people, not people who always lean upon each other, or who psychically swallow each other so that differences disappear. A marriage in which both people have to be alike and cannot tolerate or even enjoy differentness, has missed an essential Christian teaching about the relation of God to men and of human beings to each other. God does not absorb our wills into his. He wants persons united to him but as individuals. So it is to be in marriage, distinctness within unity.

Each spouse must also work out his own identity as a sexual being, as a man or as a woman. God created us as two radically complementary beings—male and female. If we lose that sense of polarity, we deny creation itself. It is easy to confuse what a society sees as "feminine" or "masculine" with the genuine differences between the sexes. In the light of anthropologists' findings about the various male and female patterns throughout the world, it would be impossible to state in parallel columns the precise differences between the sexes.

No outside authority, scientific or religious, can say with

certainty, "This characteristic is universally male, and this always female," except in speaking of the most obvious biological functions. *It may be that only in intimate relationship with each other can the particular couple find out what the essential differences are!*

To assert that there is a difference between men and women is not to claim that one is superior to the other. Even Paul, who shared the patriarchal, male-centered view of his day, softened the usual Jewish claim to masculine supremacy by his admonition that wives and husbands be "subject to *one another* out of reverence for Christ" (Ephesians 5:21). He illustrates this by referring to the sexual relation in which he says *both* the husband and the wife have a legitimate claim on the body of the other in love (1 Corinthians 7:3–4). When he states that the husband is head of the wife as Christ is head of the church, Paul certainly does not mean to say that husbands should be "bosses" of their wives and children. While upholding the father's authority in family life (which is always answerable to God), this passage (Ephesians 5:21–30) sees that authority transformed by Christ into sacrificial care. Just as Jesus Christ does not dominate the church, but takes the initiative to love and serve her, so husbands are to go ahead in anticipating the needs of those under their care. Thus, arbitrariness and domination in the family have been put away by Christ, whose love for the church serves as a pattern for the husband's love for his family.

There *is* a difference between husband and wife, and between parents and children in the Christian family. But it is not the difference that the world, with its principle of the strong "lording it over" the weak, often assumes it is.

A respect for the privacy and freedom of persons is also essential. Parents are not to break down the doors of personality to get their own way. They are not to "provoke [their] children to anger," but are to bring them up in "the nurture and admonition of the Lord" (Ephesians 6:4; K.J.V.).

The Renewal of Unity. American life, through its mass communications media, tells us that marriage is a unity which is kept alive by the mutual interests of family members, by togetherness in what we do. Christian faith affirms that this might be true on one level of life but holds that, more basic still, it is the grace and forgiveness of God which keeps marriage a living unity.

Christians claim it is unrealistic to settle for a harmony which must be purchased at the expense of genuine encounter and integrity. The rhythm of family living is one of alienation and reconciliation. We know this is so if we live without running away from each other. In no other human relationship do people live together as closely as in marriage. In that terrifying yet comforting closeness no secrets can be hid for long and no faults can be shut out of sight. The rub and wear of life upon life reveals horns as well as halos. Our life together both hurts and heals; it often builds our self-esteem and sometimes robs us of it.

What will keep us from running away from marriage when an inevitable negative manifests itself? This is not an academic question; most married people have asked it at some time in their lives. If marriage is just a commitment "until death us do part," a couple might as well be cell mates. But the Christian has more than a stark pledge of fidelity. While it is sometimes seen only as a deterrent to divorce, this pledge can be the reminder of God's faithfulness to us, the knowledge that God in his covenant never gives up on us, which keeps a marriage afloat for a while.

No union which is held together *only* because an unbreakable pledge has been made can be a marriage. To be sure, this basic decision to live together lifelong can furnish the stability and foundation for a good marriage. But Christian marriage is not meant to be an endurance test, holding something together which has no warmth, which is merely cold form without substance. Faithfulness, emptied of loving care, is but an empty and cold shell.

There are two deliberately linked words in the marriage service: "in all faith *and* tenderness." Tenderness is also the manifestation of grace. Comradeship outlasts passion in marriage, but tenderness infuses both with a warmth that none of us can do without. God knows there is competition and threat in any marriage at times. The book of Genesis continues the story of creation in chapter 3 by saying that when sin, meaning our trying to become God, enters the picture, a strain enters the unity of man and woman. Their innocent delight in each other is gone and shame appears in their relationship. Woman becomes not only man's complement, but also his competitor and he, hers. This biblical picture is, to some extent, the story of Everyman and every marriage.

But "in Christ" we are renewed creatures. Were it not so, we would constantly be in hopeless despair or at least quiet desperation. We are reminded:

> . . . all things were created through him and for him. He is before all things, and *in him all things hold together* . . . For in him all the fulness of God was pleased to dwell, and through him to reconcile to himself all things, whether on earth or in heaven, making peace by the blood of his cross (Colossians 1:17–20; author's italics).

Or as J. B. Phillips translates the "good news": "He came and told both you who were far from God and us who were near that the war was over" (Ephesians 2:17). If we can appropriate God's forgiveness, we can stop fighting ourselves. Then tenderness toward our spouse, called by Luther "the nearest and dearest neighbor," becomes a possibility for us. Our outlook can change so that we are able to see others, not merely as cantankerous and mean, but as suffering, too. In spite of our hurt, we can be filled with a desire to see what life looks like through the eyes of the other, and with God's grace we are able to accept his difference from ourselves. Tenderness, to paraphrase Paul's words, is "bearing one another's burdens," "by love serving one another," "weeping when they weep," "rejoicing when they rejoice," forgiving because we realize that we have been forgiven. Grace allows us to say, in the words of André Maurois:

> I bind myself for life; I have chosen; from now on my aim will be, not to search for someone who will please me, but to please the one I have chosen.[6]

---

6. André Maurois, *The Art of Living* (New York: Harper & Row, Publishers, Incorporated, 1940), p. 56.

This is what it means to live "in all faith and tenderness."

It is doubtful that such a way of life can be achieved by a couple themselves without the external support and encouragement of others—the larger family, friends, and above all the community of faithfulness, the church. Each of these outside forces can be a strain in an interfaith union, but when a compatibility of faith and values are found in a home, they can strongly support a marriage.

Failure in Marriage

"What therefore God has joined together, let not man put asunder" (Mark 10:9). This is the basis for the Christian contention that marriage is designed by God to be the lifelong union of one man and one woman. Many Americans, having committed themselves to the doctrine that happiness is the principal object of marriage, write it off as an interesting relic. The right of self-expression now reigns, and freedom has come to mean the absence of binding ties and constraint in any form. The arguments for divorce and remarriage boil down to this: our generation tends to think that if anyone wants very much to do a thing, he ought to be allowed to do it.

In contrast to this point of view, the New Testament regards marriage as a binding lifelong commitment on the part of the Christian husband and wife. That Jesus was unalterably opposed to divorce can be seen from the previously cited quotation from Mark, chapter 10. Lifelong, monogamous union is the intention of God. The exemption in the case of "adultery" or "unchastity" (as in Matthew 19:9) is now recognized by biblical scholars as an editorial softening of Jesus' absolute requirement which was added later (about A.D. 80 in Antioch) to bring his words into line with the Shammai school of rabbis.

The Recognition of Divorce. Jesus recognized that people were being divorced and would continue to be divorced. Indeed, provisions for divorce are nearly universal in the more than 250 societies which have been studied; it is found among all peoples in all centuries. The first written code of divorce regulations was incorporated into the Assyrian code of Hammurabi as early as 2500 B.C. So, marriages do break down, and for a variety of reasons.

What are we to say when the spirit of a marriage dies? Should divorce ever be considered by a Christian couple? Christian people are divided on this point. Most Roman Catholics and many Protestants say that marriage can be broken only by the death of a partner. This union is created by God and is indissoluble. Some go on to say that if a pair are divorced, no remarriage is allowable. When two people find their relationship intolerable they must, of course, try to seek help for the relationship. But if that does not work out, according to this position, they must bear their hardship with fortitude. If the pair think that they cannot go on living together, they must, nevertheless, remain as man and wife. This law, it is believed, best preserves the sanctity and indissolubility of Christian marriage.

The source of this position is the Roman Catholic view of marriage as a sacrament. According to that view, the speaking of the vows *causes* the grace of God to come into the union in a special way. The miraculous efficacy of the sacrament is the cement which holds together what would otherwise split apart. Hence marriage is indissoluble; separation is the only resort for those who cannot live together. The exception is that a Roman Catholic *can* secure a divorce from a non-Catholic mate who interferes with his religious duties.

Not all Christians or churches share this belief that a marriage is to be held together at all costs. In many Protestant groups, divorce is accepted, but as a very last resort and a regrettable necessity for some few persons in marriages. It should be utilized *only when all else has failed,* only when, by all fair assessment, that particular marriage has "died" and is irreparable. It is always a risk to judge any marriage as hopeless, but sometimes there is no other answer. Divorce is seen as the discontinuing of a hopelessly broken and hostile union. Both John Calvin and Martin Luther attributed divorce to the persistence of sin in human life. Calvin allowed divorce for desertion, for adultery (which was spiritual desertion with a physical expression) and for utter incompatibility of religious views. But divorce was hard to come by in his day.

One can dip into the Bible and find support for both of these positions on divorce and remarriage. But the real issue cannot be settled by a proof text; no single verse can be a guide for the Christian. The center of the New Testament is the justification of the sinner by God's love, and his love weighs more heavily than any deed we can commit. Divorce is obviously a sign of weakness, of sin. But, unless we are to turn the gospel into a law, we must allow that sometimes situations can arise in which no divorce would be the greater sin.

In our day, the highest honor must go to those who continue to work at solving their problems, who endure anguish rather than escape into the easy divorce which our culture supports and even encourages. But God wants truth in the inward parts, not mere appearance, so what are we to do when the relationship of a couple in marriage is "dead"? If a couple has ceased to be one, keeping them together by law will not, of itself, create a oneness between them.

Divorce and Realized Forgiveness. God can forgive the sin of divorce. The word of forgiveness, the new opportunity, the compassion of Jesus upon those who have failed, are also a part of the gospel which cannot be ignored. In the case of a broken relationship in marriage, compassion should be exercised, help rendered, and divorce, and even remarriage, permitted. The prerequisite for remarriage, however, must be "realized forgiveness," says James Emerson in his helpful book, *Divorce, the Church, and Remarriage.*[7] This is the awareness of God's forgiveness to such a degree that a person is free from the guilt he feels *and* from the tendencies in himself which contributed to his failure in the first marriage. With realized forgiveness there may be hope for any subsequent union; without it, an unrepentant man and wife (for one partner is never totally innocent or guilty)

---

7. James Emerson, *Divorce, the Church, and Remarriage* (Philadelphia: The Westminster Press, 1961), pp. 21ff.

will go from one failure to another in their marriage ventures. Only when forgiveness has been accepted and the personal responsibility for the divorce is understood, can a particular remarriage be blessed. For it is nonsense to believe that every couple in marriage, no matter what the circumstances or the age and maturity of the couple at the time of the wedding, represents God's calling two persons to be joined for life.

The Idolatry of Marriage. The modern American says, "Marriage is the most important thing in life. It is the reason for existence." Popular songs proclaim this creed *ad nauseum.* At this point the New Testament brings us up short by declaring that the family is not the ultimate. If the family becomes the center of our existence, it will not stand.

Sometimes the idolatry of marriage in our society is expressed by a vote against parenthood. Numerous couples have decided that they do not want children to tie them down. They cherish the time to develop individual talents and the freedom to pick up and travel as they will. They relish the opportunity to devote endless hours to private whims, causes, and projects and to continue a prolonged honeymoon without the nagging guilt that a child is being neglected.

Children do restrict one's freedom. Most fathers and mothers realize that parenthood is the severest test of maturity. They often feel the burden that children impose. Yet they also realize the joy of their presence and delight in their growth and development. Children can be the necessary antidote for the self-concern that besets many an immature couple who have not yet emerged from adolescent irresponsibility.

However, a family with children can also be self-centered. As Luther put it so picturesquely, it may be "curved in upon itself." Jesus would shock us out of our idolatry: "If anyone comes to me and does not hate his own father and mother and wife and children and brothers and sisters, yes, and even his own life, he cannot be my disciple" (Luke 14:26). These searing words jar our sensibilities. They are harsh words designed to repel and to shock and not to win followers to him. This very Son of God whom we have come to regard as a companion, a friend to whom we can come when we are weary and heavy laden, wrenches us out of our complacency with these words. How can a man who bid us love our enemies, who blessed little children and the marriage from which they came, who took joy in wedding feasts, who arranged for the care of his own mother while suffering on the cross, say this? How can he require us to hate those closest to us, those for whom we are responsible?

Not a few who read the Bible have been disquieted by this passage and have turned with relief to the parallel sayings in Matthew where "loves . . . more than me" is substituted for "hate." But there is a reason for this extreme word. He had to shock those who wanted a bit of eternity, a touch of Christianity, one foot in the Kingdom of God. God wants a singlehearted man or woman for his service. Using the most extreme word available, Jesus was saying, "Count what it will cost you to be my disciple and see whether you are equal to it." What does this mean for us?

The gods that compete most for our loyalty, time, and energy are those which we see as good, not evil. In his own eyes, man is not tempted by something evil; our decisions are a matter of choosing between two things or relationships we regard as good. When a man is torn between more time with his wife and children and time devoted to work, is it not a matter of which will do the family the most good? But what is good by our standards *can be* the chief enemy of God. We may find this impossible to believe—and so Jesus jolts us with his words. In using the word "hate," which in Aramaic means "to love less," he stuns us who think that in being nice to our families we are satisfactorily serving Christ and his Kingdom. He is sounding an alarm bell to alert those of us who think that human affections and loyalty are enough. Jesus is saying: Look at your whole life in its most familiar relationships and see that it is not sin in its blatant forms which keeps you from an awareness of God. To be sure, your adultery, stealing, and lies do keep you from me, but you know that they do from your understanding of the Law of Moses. But do you not see that it is what you call your "love" for your mate, your child, your job, your future that can take my place in your life?

Unbelievable? Let us look more deeply. When one's whole life is invested in someone as close as a husband or wife, a child, or a parent, what happens? How do we really "love" then? Do we not see each of them as one who must be an extension of ourselves, as one who must grant us all our gratification? Do we not do for him what we would have liked to experience for ourselves? Think of the pressure, both outward and subtle, which we exert upon members of our families to become what they are not. Natural love enslaves; the love which is of Christ frees.

Do I each day bring my children and mate in prayer and thought to him who entrusted them to me? Do I see each as a gift of God to be set free to find his own real talents? There is a kind of love for family which can bring us closer to God, but there is also a kind of family love which will be seen as hate when we notice what it does to cripple persons.

Jesus is saying that if you do not seek first my kind of love and the meaning of each individual life within the family, you'll not be fit to love. When you love your family in your own natural, possessive, or neglectful way, you move further from me. Your love must be screened through my love.

The Transformation of Love. Jesus did not negate human love, but he knew it must be transformed or become hate when we live at close quarters. Interestingly, the apocryphal Gospel According to Thomas translates this same passage with three words added:

> Whoever does not hate his father and his mother *in My way* will not be able to be a [disciple] to me. And whoever does [not] love [his father] and his mother in My way will not be able to be a [disciple] to me.[8]

---
8. *The Gospel According to Thomas* (New York: Harper & Row, Publishers, Incorporated, 1959), Logia 97:32–35. Author's italics.

Whatever is closest to us can become the real enemy of God. We may be asked to love them less in order to love them with the freeing, caring love of Christ. That love can turn the mirrors of our homes into windows through which we are enabled to see a world in great need, a world of lonely people who may become a part of our larger family.

4
The Sexual Revolution: A New Challenge

The Christian standard for sexual expression is under direct attack from many quarters today. Historically, Christianity has said that sexual intercourse is to be saved for marriage and then to be expressed with one's mate only.

The biblical position thus rules out "fornication," the sexual relations of unmarried persons or prostitution;[1] "adultery," the sexual intercourse of a married person with someone other than his mate;[2] "homosexuality," sexual perversion preferred with a member of one's own sex;[3] and "beastiality," the sexual relations with animals.[4] The Bible is not delicate in its reference to sexual behavior. It has much to say about the proper use of sexual intercourse in marriage, and it also deals with the full range of expression which it regards as the misuse of a precious gift from God: premarital intercourse, prostitution, homosexuality, rape, divorce, incest, and masturbation. And if one looks deeply, he can find reasons for what it permits and what it prohibits.[5]

THE CHALLENGE TO CHRISTIANS

A pastor writes from an upper-middle-class suburban community:

> During the past eighteen months, at least five of our high school or recently graduated young people have been caught in the trap of premarital pregnancy. I am sure many

---
1. Such as, Deuteronomy 22:28–29 and 1 Thessalonians 4:2–8.
2. Such as, Leviticus 20:10; Hosea 2:2–3; and Romans 13:8–10.
3. Such as, Leviticus 20:13; Genesis 19:1–11; and Romans 1:18–28.
4. Such as, Leviticus 18:23 and Deuteronomy 27:21.
5. For three thorough books on the biblical view of these relationships, the reader is directed to William Graham Cole, *Sex and Love in the Bible* (Association Press, 1959); Oscar Feucht (ed.), *Sex and the Church* (Concordia Publishing House, 1961); and Helmut Thielicke, *The Ethics of Sex* (Harper & Row, Publishers, Incorporated, 1964).

more are bidding fair to follow in their footsteps. Although some of these young people are on the verge of trouble, or even come to us after they are in trouble, some are our leaders. I have talked with the Baptist minister and he says the situation is the same in their church.

A couple, advising a youth group in a local church, writes:

Last year we had a wonderful time with our twenty teen-agers, learning how to plan for fall. But the programs were a flop. We followed the furnished material—three sessions on baptism, three on the Trinity, and so on.

The kids said at our house, "Why can't we take up the problems that really bother us—like dating, drinking, smoking, cheating and petting?" We consulted the church officers who said, in effect: "This is not church business; parents must take care of that. The schools already teach too much."

But this summer a bomb exploded. B., one of the officers of the county fellowship and daughter of our high school assistant principal, was quickly married one Saturday. She was seventeen and pregnant.

Reactions in the church were strong. Some contended that we should be glad we did not talk about sex; or we would have been blamed for it. Others blamed the high school. But our own son and daughter brought us up sharp with: "Mom and Dad, you might have prevented this. If the program had been interesting enough, they might have come. Too many people around this church think that sex is dirty, but nobody tells us what Christianity says about it."

This increase in sexual activity outside of marriage and among our youth reflects a new attitude about sex. A great many people see little sense in confining it to marriage. And even people who hold a stricter standard for themselves are not likely to be too distressed to find their own code of behavior being broken all around them. Some careful studies show that, in contrast to the attitude of a few decades ago, relatively few men or women today would hesitate to marry a partner who has had premarital or extramarital sexual experience.

Christians can no longer bury their heads in the sand. If our faith has nothing positive to say about *this* crucial, animating drive of life, some will wonder if it has *anything* to say. In this chapter we will examine the continuing sexual revolution in America in order to understand what Christian parents must speak to if they are to be heard by the young people and adults of this generation.

It is not enough simply to reiterate the "ideal" as if repeated mention of it will somehow make a dent in the changed sexual ethos of our day. Modern people of all ages are curious to know if the church can justify a standard that appears to be a code given by ancient lawgivers whose only motive was to take the joy out of life. William Genné reports one young man at a church conference on sex as saying, "If you say 'wait' you must say why; and your answer must be real, valid, and concrete!"[6]

We, as the church, cannot fall back upon glib pronouncements or evade the full complexity of the problem confronting us if we would fulfill our vocation as Christian parents and children. Christians, it will be seen, need not be given to prudish moralism nor to easygoing tolerance of the status quo in their efforts to uphold God's intention for sex and marriage.

There is no doubt at all that, in the past, the church itself has contributed to the problem rather than to the answer. Until recently, it has not articulated clearly and convincingly its reasons for holding to chastity, fidelity, and monogamy. It has often spoken in vague terms of "sin" and "purity" which no longer carry much weight with modern youth or adults unless they are translated quite specifically. Generally speaking, the church has been generally speaking. And this is not enough. It is a way of burying its head in the sand while pretending that it is not doing so.

THE BREAKDOWN OF THE MORALISTIC VIEW OF SEX

When we ask why this permissive attitude toward sex has developed in our society, no one easy answer can be given. A

---

6. Elizabeth and William Genné, *Christians and the Crisis in Sex Morality* (New York: Association Press, 1962), p. 37.

dozen answers suggest themselves. The great wars in which this country has engaged were major battering rams which exposed our young people to the more permissive practices of other cultures and isolated them from the normal heterosexual associations of their hometown. Loneliness frequently looks for its antidote in illicit sexual liaisons.

The attainment of educational, political, and economic equality of opportunity for women has eaten through the double sexual standard. Once liberated from their status as chattel to their husbands, from powerful community opinion, and from the fear of pregnancy, they have sought equal freedom in sexual expression.

Furthermore, city life has depersonalized us so that neighbors cannot influence us with gossip as they once did. As we move from one place to another with disruptive frequency, we may also move away from the values of the community in which we lived. Free of neighborhood and larger family ties which once supported us, we are set down in a strange area and adopt new ways of life in our new surroundings.

The "new morality" is a product of many influences which represent general social change. These are only some of the changes responsible for the shift in attitude and behavior which represents a *rebellion* against the older, moralistic, repressive view of sex that some people still confuse with a Christian attitude.

The moralistic view held that sexuality itself is bad and sinful, regardless of the relationship in which it is expressed. Taken in its extreme form, the aim seemed to be to eliminate sexual intercourse from life as completely as possible without committing race suicide. A well-trained conscience, conditioned by a taboo on the discussion of sex, the horror of adults, and punishment for any sign of normal curiosity, would see that sexual intercourse, at least on the woman's part, was saved for marriage. And even in marriage sexual relations were usually something to be ashamed of, to be put up with, the "worse" part of the "for better or worse" of the marriage vows. It was hard to believe that sexuality is God's creation. When a baby was born of this sexual union, he might be considered a bundle from heaven, but there was certainly nothing heavenly about the process which God ordained to produce it!

In line with the double standard, it was generally thought that men were more interested in sexual intercourse than women, an assumption disputed by almost every modern study of women's attitudes. Consequently, the male was expected to break with the formal codes occasionally and to "sow his wild oats" outside of marriage. One way to avoid a breakdown of the formal code of chastity was to control as tightly as possible the "nice" girl's activities. If this was done by rigid chaperonage, by education designed to produce fear of sex in the hearts of the young, and by the irrepressible gossip of a small town, both sexes could be controlled. Men were moral because women were, and they, because of necessity. Three great fears—conception, infection, and detection—were powerful educators in the society of Protestant rural America. Little else was needed to control effectively the behavior of most marriageable young women before World War I.

The decreasing effectiveness of this code may not be immediately evident because so many still give it lip service while acting otherwise. This view of sexual behavior and life has broken down almost completely in modern America, but it has left its mark on our psychic life. That more than fifty percent of middle-class children today are told nothing about sexuality or reproduction by their parents shows that the "sex is dirty" attitude is far from dead in our thinking.

Surprisingly, one study of youth indicates that the more devoutly religious their parents are, the *more* students have received from them sex information and values regarding sexual expression. Those without a religious orientation are less likely to feel responsible for their child's sexual education. This brings us to an important observation: *the moralistic, love-without-sex viewpoint is not to be identified with a Christian, biblical understanding of the matter* (see chapter 3). These views do have something in common. They both speak in defense of chastity and they both admit to the profound social, and not merely individual, consequences of sexual intercourse. But beyond these affirmations, the similarity ends.

Prevailing Philosophies of Sexual Expression

Natural Expression and Romantic Love. Into the vacuum created by the banishment of a moralistic code of sex have come two main contenders for the public mind. Neither of these emphasizes the social implications of the sexual act, and neither sees it as bad in itself. In the latter attitude they seem to be in agreement with the Old Testament's appreciation of God's creation, but without its sense of fidelity and covenant.

The first school of thought, more popular among men than women, sees sexual intercourse as a *natural expression* having little or no connection with love; it is merely physiological release, a way to find pleasure. Sexuality is regarded as an irresistible urge which reaches the peak of its urgency in the teens. This view sometimes compares sexual intercourse with the need for a drink of water. When you are thirsty, you partake of it. It is strictly a matter of personal thirst, taste, and inclination. Its exponents, and many are highly educated people, see sexual expression as a purely private matter, *but this it can never be.* One older teen-ager represents the naturalistic philosophy well when he challenges:

> Prove that sex is harmful when precautions are taken against pregnancy, venereal disease, and openly teasing the public. Let the repressed busy-bodies stay out of my personal life. Look, whenever you moralists try to get rid of sex, it gets more expression. You're fighting a losing battle. Sex is obvious; it's natural, so it's moral.

According to this view, the word "natural" has a peculiar ring of authority. The libertines go on to remind us that the Samoans and people of many other cultures do not go through the struggles and tensions with which we have to contend.

Underneath their vigorous defense of sexual expression as a natural, irresistible urge that is lots of fun, they seem to be saying: "This is where the meaning of life is found; it's not apparent elsewhere. Let the boredom of life be punctuated periodically with the zest that sexual stimulation brings." For these disciples of "naturalism," the sex act is a kind of primitive mystical experience. Nature itself is deified; it becomes their god. The *person* of the partner is relatively unimportant.

There is nothing wrong in pleasure-seeking, according to this view, and there is no greater pleasure than sexual relations. Why not seek for these pleasurable experiences if you do not intend to hurt others? After all, life today is so precarious and so filled with tribulations. Such a "back to nature" view emphasizes the sheer goodness of physical vitality and pleasure in an otherwise meaningless life.

Many people in our society, while rejecting the biblical standard, want something more than this naturalism. They look for the meaning of sexuality in the context of *romantic love*. According to this position, sexuality in its serious expressions is acceptable—even right—when you have found *the* person with whom you are in love. The key is knowing when you are "in love." Because of the accent on emotion, the choice of a partner is often sudden and automatic—"When it hits you, you'll know."

An important ingredient in modern romantic love is sex appeal. A woman, at least before marriage, becomes as stimulating as possible in order to gain an emotional relationship with a man. The man in our culture both likes sex appeal in a woman and feels trapped by it. Often a kind of sparring takes place. According to an unwritten code, the woman lures the man with dress and appearance, the man goes as far as he can sexually, and the woman stops him as soon as she can. As a result, each partner may be threatened by feelings of jealousy, possessiveness, exploitation, and emotional desertion if the relationship does not work out. If they intend to marry, the romantically inclined couple see sexual behavior as the frosting on the cake of a lifelong honeymoon, the assurance of being wanted, and a way of keeping life from growing dull and boring. Too often they build their relationship on the superficial feeling of being "in love"; after marriage, when the romantic veneer has worn off, they may find, however, that they do not *like* each other.

To many romantic young women, the idea of extensive lovemaking with just any boy is met with horror. But, feeling that their relationships will develop into marriage, many girls engage in premarital sex relations with the person they hope to have as a future mate. However, there are also those who refrain from premarital sex relations because they do not want to jeopardize their possible marriage.

Christians have an understanding of love and marriage which tempers the emotional elements of romance with the realism of in-laws, bills, babies, haircurlers, and the art of living together and serving each other as real persons.

What can a discerning person say to the champions of these prevailing philosophies? Those who take the Christian position are often accused of repeating "moral ditties" in answer to the "facts" of those who advocate sexual freedom. To be sure, the arguments that would be convincing to an already committed Christian who is trying to do God's will would be quite different from the arguments of those who are not so committed. To the Christian, the principle of creative fidelity and of loving personal relationships is uppermost. Most Christians would agree with the theologian Karl Barth:

> Coitus without co-existence is demonic . . . What are you, you man and woman who are about to enter into sexual relations? What do you really want of each other? What is your business with each other? What do you have in common? Is there any meaning in it? Is it demanded and sustained by your real life together? . . . This is the challenge of God's command in relation to this particular human activity.[7]

Christianity affirms that coitus finds its basic meaning in a truly *personal relationship*. This kind of love depends upon the ability to give and receive the kind of affection and care which brings out the potentialities of the partner. Yet many sexual

---

7. Karl Barth, *Church Dogmatics*, eds. G. W. Bromiley and T. F. Torrace, trans. Harold Knight (Edinburgh: T. & T. Clark, 1961), Vol. III, Part 4, pp. 133ff.

episodes are not a part of a personal relationship. This is the major weakness of the naturalistic point of view. It is not love but *lust* which motivates the act. Lust is impersonal sexuality, pleasure or security sought for its own sake.

Many diverse motives are channeled into the sex act. The girl who reports, "I'm so hungry for love that if a boy shows me even a little tenderness, there is nothing I will not do for him," may be seeking affectional security. The fraternity or military man who is compulsively building up his sex record may be seeking status with his brothers and attempting to prove his own masculinity about which he has doubts.

Morality must find its roots, not in the "thou shalt nots," but in the positive quality of personal relationships if it is to get a grip on modern young people and parents. In other words, morality is related to loving God with the whole self and the neighbor as oneself. Youth want good relationships; they look forward to successful marriage. A dogmatic *No* concerning sexual expression will not satisfy them or us, but an examination of what sexual behavior *does* in and to our relationships is a subject of great interest to youth, even to the sexual athletes of our time.

When intelligent people feel called upon to defend their premarital sexual relations, they usually fall back upon two main arguments: the "marital adjustment" idea and the "testing" argument. These people seem to be as concerned about the quality of the relationship as Christian faith is. They want a good marriage and they accept as fact the assertion that couples who have had premarital intercourse make a better marital adjustment than those who refrain. A traditional argument denies that this is so because of the feeling of guilt that is built up. But fewer people today actually do feel guilty; a much more common reaction to premarital intercourse is *resentment.* This is especially true when a marriage does not materialize for the woman or when the man feels trapped by his erotic involvement before he is ready to commit himself to her.

It is *not* true that women who indulge in premartial coitus make a better overall marriage adjustment than those who remain virginal. There are many reasons for this research finding, only one of which will be noted here. Wives who have engaged in premarital intercourse are much more likely to engage later in adultery than premarital abstainers. Apparently there is something that can be said about the consistency of character. If a woman is willing to break the bonds of chastity *before* marriage, she is also more willing to break the bonds of fidelity *after* marriage.

The argument for "testing" one's compatibility by sexual experimentation before marriage also falls apart when closely examined. A few premarital episodes taking place under less than ideal conditions of security and social sanction can hardly be a fair test. Many studies have shown that it takes a good deal of time to adjust sexually to each other even within marriage. In any event, sexual intercourse is overrated by these couples. They think that smooth functioning in the sexual area of life will guarantee a smooth marital adjustment; but this also involves coming to terms with money matters, social life, in-laws, religion, and many other crucial areas of relationship. The "testing" argument is most often a convenient rationalization for what the couple wants very much to do for the excitement and pleasure involved. As such, it cannot be taken seriously by Christian young people. To use sexual relations simply to "test" one's relationship may prevent him from ever experiencing its meaning and purpose.

Homosexuality. Another problem of growing concern to Christians is the rise of homosexuality among both males and females in American life. Christian standards are not only upset by the philosophies which urge our people to go back to nature or get swept up by romantic love, they are also challenged by the homosexual perversion of the sexual function. Such perversion is directed toward the same (homo) sex rather than one of the different (hetero) sex.

Of the various deviations from sexual normalcy, homosexuality is the most often encountered. It has existed from earliest times and in every society. Sometimes it has been encouraged, sometimes tolerated, sometimes heartily condemned and punished. The Christian's opposition to it has biblical roots: The conviction that "male and female he created them" is deeply imbedded in the Judeo-Christian understanding of Creation. There is no in-between, no bisexuality acknowledged in the Bible. God made male and female to relate to each other sexually in an ordained way. To do otherwise is to turn one's back upon Creation and to accept a distorted understanding of oneself as a human being of a definite sex. Both Paul (Romans 1:18–28) and modern psychotherapy recognize homosexuality as the manifestation of a confusion about personal identity and a disturbance in relatedness rooted in family maladjustments.

Most investigators in the field of homosexuality find it more common among males than females. They estimate that more than one out of every three males has had some overt homosexual experience between the onset of adolescence and old age. About one in four females in the U.S. has so engaged. Homosexuality, then, is not a rare phenomenon, although those adults in our society who have an *exclusive* interest in their own sex are a small minority.

That small minority, which includes respectable people in all walks of life, works diligently to convince people that homosexuality is a way of life rather than a disease. Rarely do they seek professional help for this condition. They establish their own communities and institutions such as bars, streets, parks, baths; formal and informal associations such as The Mattachine Society and ONE, Inc.; living arrangements, including "homosexual marriages"; and magazines and a special language. This effort to form a society is the natural reaction of a condemned and persecuted group which clings together for support, and may also be motivated by the desire to persuade each other that they do not need help.

While biochemical or constitutional factors play an indirect predisposing part in adult homosexuality, most of the evidence points to its roots in disturbed family life. In a disturbed family the child tends to model himself after the opposite-sex parent or after a same-sex parent who tends to act more like the opposite sex. Every effort should be made to help the child form strong, friendly relations with the parent of the same sex who understands what it is to be a man or a woman.

While the causal factors are discussed diligently by professional workers in the field, in the light of biblical faith the Christian must regard homosexuality as an aberration with tragic consequences for the individuals involved. We must, therefore, regard the questions of prevention and treatment as important ones for the covenant community to consider in cooperation with professional helpers.

The Results of Sexual License

No human society is without its particular restrictions on unlimited sexual behavior. We look in vain to find a completely promiscuous society, in spite of the wishful stories in today's erotic magazines. Complete sexual freedom has not been countenanced because it has not worked satisfactorily anywhere. Each culture has its rules—but here the similarity ends. Some societies are quite permissive about sexual relations both in and outside of marriage. And there are those societies whose stringency would put a Puritan to shame. Generally speaking, however, it is only in cultures deeply influenced by the Judeo-Christian view of life that we find a very high premium put upon premarital chastity. And when we find this view of life losing its hold among the people, we also find a developing laxity in sexual behavior. The naturalistic philosophy and the romantic way of life may be contributing to the changed picture of sexual behavior, or they may simply reflect the behavior of more and more people both in and outside of marriage for reasons of pleasure and expediency. In any event, we find enough evidence of increased sexual promiscuity to call the change a "sexual revolution."

For example, illegitimate births have reached an all-time high with about one-quarter million babies being born out of wedlock in 1963. Many teen-agers are involved, but it is surprising to know that women between thirty and thirty-four years of age bear an even larger number of these children than do teen-agers. One out of every six American brides is pregnant at the time of the wedding, according to our best studies. And among high school girls one-third to one-half are pregnant when they marry.

Venereal disease is spreading like wildfire among teenagers in spite of (or because of) the availability of quick medical cures. The more than 200,000 cases reported in 1963 account for only a fraction of the actual number of diseased youngsters.

Illegitimacies, pregnant brides, and venereal diseases are the usual public signs of sexual relations apart from marriage. And since relatively few of those who engage in sexual intercourse incur these results, we must assume that there is even greater incidence of such activity in the American society as a whole. It is to just this conclusion that the many recent studies of sexual behavior in American society force us.

Christian people need not condemn the sexual behavior studies, of which Professor Kinsey's is the best known, as the machinations of evil. To be sure, some of the research methods and conclusions are questionable. But *those who turned the spotlight on the sexual problem did not create it;* they simply reveal its startling proportions.

According to the findings of the best research studies, more than seven out of ten males in the United States engage in sexual intercourse before marriage. About one-half of American women so indulge before marriage, most of these with their future husbands. These studies reveal that, *while the American male's sexual practices before marriage have not changed much in the last fifty years, the American woman's behavior has shifted tremendously.* Looking at women as a group since 1910, each decade shows a steady decrease in virginity before marriage. The average woman has apparently been far more deeply affected by the change in the American outlook than has the average man.

Infidelity, expressed by sexual intercourse outside of marriage, is as old as the biblical record and is now found in abundance among us. Marriage trades and temporary sexual adventures among married couples are the newer types of unfaithfulness reported in the tabloids. Some observers report a growing tendency for separated or divorced women to attempt to wrest married men away from their wives through sexual liaisons. According to the Kinsey reports, about half of the husbands and one-quarter of the wives in the United States have had extra-marital sexual relations. As we have already seen, infidelity is seldom the cause of a marital breakup; more often, it is but a symptom of an already unsatisfactory marriage.

All of these expressions of sex outside of marriage are attempts to take this gift out of its intended context as part of God's creation which he gave to mankind in order to further the unity of husband and wife and to beget children.

GUIDANCE FOR CHRISTIANS IN THE SEXUAL REVOLUTION

We have not really understood the Bible's view of sexuality if we think it consists of tiresome and ineffective moralizing. Christians are called to discover the meaning of sexuality in the light of a biblical understanding of creation and redemption. That understanding is portrayed in the previous chapter. Truth about the sexual dimension of life can be grasped by both adults and youth if they are willing to study the Bible with steadfastness and intellectual vigor. Such a view of life can become a genuine part of the Christian, a lens through which he sees the relationships of men and women in our world.

Responsible Sex Education

It is not enough for Christians in families, faced by the sexual revolution, simply to preach homilies about the old-fashioned virtues of chastity, monogamy, and fidelity. There are too many vital forces active around us to take such a deceptively simple approach. We are not living in or speaking to the simple, church-going, small-town society of two generations ago. Bolder steps must be taken.

1. *Christians in families must inform themselves of the best studies that support chastity before marriage and fidelity within marriage.*

The reader has been introduced to the subject in chapter 3 and in this chapter. But beyond these, very thorough guidance is available in comprehensive new writings by dedicated, informed people. Helmut Thielicke, *The Ethics of Sex* (Harper & Row, Publishers, Incorporated, 1964); Evelyn and Sylvanus Duvall, *Sex Ways: In Fact and Faith* (Association Press, 1961); Seward

Hiltner, *Sex and the Christian Life* (Association Press, 1957); Elizabeth and William Genné (eds.), *Christians and the Crisis in Sex Morality* (Association Press, 1957); and Sherwin Bailey, *Common Sense About Sexual Ethics: A Christian View* (The Macmillan Company). All are worthy of study by parents and young people. The contributions of such books should be shared together in groups within the church.

2. *Christians in families must experience in healthy husband-wife relations the kind of love which manifests the love of God, in order that children may be equipped to enter marriage with the essential ingredients.*

Some children of the church come from homes in which such relations do not exist. They must be given the opportunity to meet such families in a congregation. Adults who really care for children can help them find the kind of love which keeps them from being victimized by the inner hunger for affection or for the power to exploit which leads to sexual adventures. Chastity can no longer be safeguarded by fear. A positive example of good marriage and a positive Christian view of sexuality are essential. If a child has sexual identification problems, a husband and wife might well examine their own relationship with the help of professional people, especially in the light of the fact that children learn more from how mothers and fathers treat one another as members of the other sex than we have ever imagined.

3. *Christians in families must learn to temper their judgment with mercy and understanding as they look beyond sexual misconduct to its meaning in the lives of the persons involved.*

From Christ's teachings we learn that we must look beyond a person's action to its *meaning* and *motive*. "Out of the heart come evil thoughts . . . adultery, fornication . . ." (Matthew 15:19). Again and again he warns us not to be misled by appearances. He spoke frequently about those who do their works to be seen of men, of "whitewashed tombs . . . full of dead men's bones" (Matthew 23:27); of those who look upon the external appearance while God looks upon the heart. Just as one can appear right without being right, one can also appear wrong without being wrong. We are inclined to deal with externals, with symptoms, with "sins" rather than with sin, the inward disposition to make one's own life secure at the expense of others. Not that conduct is unimportant; of course it is. Right behavior *is* crucial in the Kingdom of God (see Matthew 25). It is in our *response* to God's love that we try to live exemplary lives.

There are good reasons for standing firm on the Christian standards of premarital chastity and marital fidelity. But we must give far more attention to the inner life out of which sexual misconduct springs and to the relationship in which such acts are expressed. Only then can we intelligently serve those who need the Christian witness and ministry. That ministry, which belongs to *all* Christians and not merely to those ordained, recognizes that people need much more than external restraint, or moralistic exhortations, or new laws; they need that inward transformation which will make the misuse of sexuality seem both foolish and unnecessary. To moralistic church folk, who may love their ideas more than they love people, it is always a shock to see that Jesus spent little time belaboring harlots and adulterers. He knew their inner lives were warped and miserable. He knew that the exhortations of the law were no substitute for the healing grace of the Good News.

What does Christ's attitude mean for us as we face the sexual revolution of our time? It means, at least, that we must look beyond a person's outward sexual behavior to its *meaning* for him and to the *situation* in which he finds himself. It is so easy to judge behavior by either-or standards yet miss the *person* completely.

Not all adulterous affairs are alike; the attitudes of people who have been unfaithful to their spouses differ radically. Some attempt to conceal; some are open. Infidelity may be confined to a single repented episode or may be a long-standing deliberate pattern of life. Can these situations be judged by the same standard? Do we minister to each the same way? Who would be most willing to receive help?

In order to minister to persons who have experienced premarital relations, we must recognize that the *kind of relationship* in which a person becomes involved has a bearing on the outcome. Few of us would be willing to equate the meaning and the consequences of sexual intercourse with prostitutes with those with a fiancée for whom there could be much affection and sense of responsibility. For that matter, not all sexual experience *within* the legalized relationship of marriage can be seen as having equal meaning for marital partners. In some unions, sexuality is an expression of love and tenderness; in others it amounts to legalized prostitution, a payment for services rendered.

Christ's way of understanding the motive and the situation has within it the hope of genuine inner transformation. As John Oman reminds us, we must be life-understanders before we can be life-changers.[8]

Adults need to be much more realistic than they have been about the terrible conflict in which youth often find themselves and remember their own struggles in adolescence. Perhaps it is the pain of that anxiety which prompts some parents to "lay down the law" in a harsh, nonunderstanding manner. We can explore with youth the consequences of their actions which they may overlook when caught in the "passions of love." Parents and teachers can affirm that the argument that "everybody's doing it" really is no answer to the ethical choice of the individual.

Christianity is very realistic about human nature; it looks squarely at our brokenness, our self-centeredness, our separation from self, others, and God. We are all estranged from our authentic selves, from others. This is the meaning of the Fall of Man depicted in Genesis. It is because of this estrangement that we *use sexuality,* not for the Creator's purposes, but merely for alleviating anxiety, for releasing tension, for seeking security, and for exploiting others. And in spite of our misuse of this precious and awe-full gift of God, Christian faith assures us of his forgiveness and his grace for new life if we realize that we are living contrary to our creation. Of this Christian parents and their youth can be absolutely sure: *our past and even future mistakes need not enslave us.*

We may remember how Jesus responded in the presence of the woman taken in adultery (John 8:3–11). When the men who

---

8. John Oman, *Concerning the Ministry* (New York: Harper & Row, Publishers, Incorporated, 1937).

regarded themselves in charge of the morals of the community were about to stone her to death, he turned on them: "Let him who is without sin among you be the first to throw a stone at her." He had already taught them that sin has as much to do with the inner life as with the act. He that ". . . has already committed adultery . . . *in his heart*" (Matthew 5:28; author's italics) included all of them, but he did not condemn them for their sin. And he turned to the woman and said, "Neither do I condemn you; go, and do not sin again." We are called upon to be witnesses to God's mercy to ourselves and to others in sexual relationships.

4. *Christians in families must attempt to transform the conditions in society which provide the soil in which sexual misconduct grows.*

We may not want to face the hard truth that many Americans have traded in their traditional moral codes in the pursuit of the goals of acquiring, possessing, and competing successfully. Sexual attraction is now used as a means of achieving those goals. Success and prestige are hammered into the child and adult by TV, press, schools, and even by the home. These influences speak more loudly than moral codes which have frequently been robbed of their theological undergirding. So we find the advertising industry using sexual attraction to sell almost every product by openly advocating and subtly suggesting images of secret delight. It does not seem to care what being constantly stimulated sexually does to a culture. But the Christian family does care.

In pursuit of vicarious success, many parents push their children into heterosexual *social* relations long before they are emotionally ready. In some communities dances and nylons are common in the fifth grade. As a consequence, "going steady," which often implies sexual behavior privileges, may begin as early as twelve and thirteen years of age. This early sexual sophistication is yoked with emotional and spiritual immaturity. The combination is lethal. But parents and economic interests have conspired to get the children "socialized."

The automobile has made it possible for young people to escape chaperonage almost completely. Most teen-agers who have engaged in sexual intimacy confess that it started in a car.

Contraceptives, now easily available to most, have made great inroads upon premarital chastity, promising, but not always delivering, immunity from unwanted pregnancy. One is forced to conclude that the effect of the sexual revolution will not reach its peak until use of an oral contraceptive removes for many the probability of unwanted pregnancies both inside and outside of marriage. Oral contraceptives are invisible to the partners and easy to get. They appear to be medically safe and psychologically desirable.

Perhaps the Christian view of life and destiny has never been the philosophy of the majority in America. But its by-product, an ability to postpone immediate satisfactions for future goals, has become deeply rooted in American life. Advancement in education, profession, and business depends upon our capacity to take the long-range view. But keen observers of the American scene see signs of the loss of the ability to hold to the long-range goals. They point to the increasing number of early marriages, to the shortage of first-class students who are willing to take the arduous route to the professions, and to other vocational objectives which require lengthy training and delayed, if not modest, monetary reward.

Life cannot be lived in a value-vacuum; some way of organizing and understanding experience is always necessary. The reigning ethical deity in American life is fun. According to Martha Wolfenstein, who coined the suggestive phrase "fun morality,"[9] fun is no longer the prerogative of the rich. The rise of this new ethic may mark the passing of the belief that the future, either in this life or the next, is worth working and waiting for. If the present life is the only life one can count on, why not have fun now? Thus, the modern hedonist lives for "kicks"; he must experience everything in life before it is too late, sexual relations included. Paradoxically, the pursuit of fun becomes as compulsive and rigid as the most inflexible of the old Puritan codes.

It may well be that *we lack a sense of adventure and destiny in our lives;* this is why the fun morality reigns and the search for

---
9. As quoted in Max Lerner, *America as a Civilization* (New York: Simon and Schuster, 1957), p. 675.

thrills and excitement dominates the young person and adult alike. We long for a way to escape from the stuckness of life. We yearn for a dimension of meaning to cut through the boredom of the days. We can sense the low-keyed monotony of the newer suburbs in which gardening, entertaining, and community participation become a matter of expectation and duty rather than joy. Life becomes predictable and boring; even work no longer provides the central focus and excitement of life. Sociologist David Riesman reports comments by business and professional men who actually *create* anxieties and emergencies in their work in order to give it drama and bite![10] Since we are not really attached to anything wholeheartedly, we look for spurs when life no longer automatically provides them. For many, illicit sexual relations is one of those spurs.

Man is created for an experience of performing to the limit of his capacities; he needs the comradeship and meaning that develops under such rigorous conditions. Yet this opportunity is often lacking in our affluent society. For this reason many men remember their war experiences as the greatest time of their lives, regardless of the dangers involved. And many couples look back with nostalgia to the Depression of the early 1930's or to their early years together when they attempted to live "on a shoestring." For *it was when they underwent their severest struggles that they meant the most to each other.*

Christian faith and fellowship can renew that great adventure in a sick world. It continually demands the best and most rigorous performance of which persons are capable in the risky service of the Kingdom of God. For want of heroic goals, even the most respectable families may turn to distorted forms of risk taking—to gambling, overspending, speeding, sexual adventures, and shoplifting—in order to capture some of the missing zest of life. This may be one key to the moral confusion of our time. Responsible families must work with other homes in the church to bring order out of the confusion and a sense of certainty to the restless search of the human spirit for significance.

---

10. David Riesman, "The Suburban Dislocation," *The Annals* (of the American Academy of Political and Social Science), Vol. 314, November 1957, pp. 123–146.

Responsible Parenthood

One of the technical discoveries most closely associated with the sexual revolution is effective contraception. Like most inventions, it can be used for both good and evil. On the one hand, it eliminates the fear of unwanted pregnancies that was once a major obstacle to sexual intercourse outside of marriage. On the other, it can make possibly truly responsible parenthood within the framework of marriage.

By giving us the gift of sexuality, God makes it possible for male and female to be partners with him in his creative activity. In such creativity God is present. Our word *pro*-creation means to create *in front of,* or to bring *forth*. Over and above the pleasure and the re-creation of their love that a husband and wife confirm in sexual union, children may be an added divine blessing.

The Bible does not see procreation as the chief and only purpose of sexuality in marriage. It is *one* of the chief purposes to be sure, and only extreme selfishness and immaturity would fail to recognize that the Creator expects children to come out of marriage. Protestants believe, on the basis of the biblical witness, that a husband and wife are free to choose whether a single act of sexual union shall be an expression of love and pleasure only, or whether that act will also be for procreation. This is what the concept of *responsible* parenthood means.

The couple have a responsibility to the expected child. He has a right to be wanted, well-born, and well cared for. They also bear a responsibility to the mother of the child whose health, both mental and physical, may be affected by the birth of one child, or of several in quick succession. Beyond the immediate family there is the wider community to be considered. The "population explosion" demands an answer. Not only will unlimited procreation produce a threatening lack of food, but there will also be a problem of insufficient space for all on the face of the earth. In contrast to that period in history which needed the admonition to "be fruitful and multiply, and fill the earth," we now find ourselves in danger of overpopulating it. In the light of this, many Protestants feel that it is their duty to be fruitful in the *quality* of their relationships rather than in the quantity of their children.

Sometimes children come unexpectedly. It is estimated that more than half of the married couples in this country did not plan one or more of their children. On the other hand, there is a considerable number of infertile married couples (about fifteen percent) who decide to have offspring but find that they cannot. Both of these groups undergo serious strain. The latter are often deeply disappointed and frequently must turn to adoption agencies. Some need medical help to achieve conception.

In the case of couples with unplanned pregnancies, the reactions of husband and wife are often traumatic. The first few months often find one or both of the partners with regret, or in despair, or even engaging in mutual accusations. Usually the later months bring them to accept the thought of new life in the family, and even to anticipate the event. After the baby comes, surprisingly, they may recall the conception of the child as having been "planned."

Increasingly, unplanned pregnancies are due to ignorance, carelessness, or religious objections to medically effective contraceptive means. The controversy of whether or not there should be control over conception no longer rages among various faiths; it is a matter of what *kind* of controls are acceptable. While Roman Catholics forbid mechanical devices and chemicals as being unnatural, the Protestant feels that these are no more unnatural than medicine in general. To the Protestant, the major question is, "What is the most efficient and ethically sound way of planning parenthood, of spacing one's children?" There are now thoroughly responsible statements from the churches which deal forthrightly with the knotty questions of contraception, abortion, sterilization, and artificial insemination.[11]

Each Christian couple must personally decide the most ethical, aesthetic, and efficient method suitable to the planning of their family with the help of a responsible physician. The

---

11. See, for example, James Pike, *If You Marry Outside Your Faith* (Harper & Row, Publishers, Incorporated, 1954); Alfred Rehwinkle, *Planned Parenthood and Birth Control* (Concordia Publishing House, 1959); and the report to the 174th General Assembly of the United Presbyterian Church in the U.S.A., entitled *Responsible Marriage and Parenthood*.

medical profession must have freedom to give advice about birth control in all communities. In order to assure this, the church must give its political support to the theological gift of God to all men to be free—*free to be responsible.*

To "subdue the earth" means that man is to have dominion over the forces of nature. The general Protestant conviction is that *motives,* rather than methods, with the exception of those which destroy or maim human life, form the major moral issue, provided the methods are used for responsible parenthood within marriage. For example, the destruction of life already begun (abortion) cannot be condoned, except when the life of the mother is jeopardized by the pregnancy. The complicated issues of voluntary sterilization and artificial insemination are now being studied by responsible Christian scholars and physicians. As these issues are clarified, Christian responsibility indicates that aid for family planning within marriage should be made available to all peoples at home or abroad.

From the Christian point of view sexuality is intended to occupy an important, positive place in the life of mankind. We see the distortion and exploitation of this aspect of human personality as an expression of sin in human life. When men and women have new being in Jesus Christ, they alter the focus of their lives in all aspects, including the sexual aspect. In the midst of a world which is confused, frightened, and overstimulated, Christians are called to find again the true meaning of sexuality and to convey its significance to their children and to those with whom their lives are cast.

5

The Vocation of Parenthood

"Is it better to impose your will and insist that your way be done than to let the child make a decision for himself? . . ."

"We keep forcing them all the time; it's the same proposition."

"If you want your child to attend Sunday school, should you insist he go?"

"Occasionally."

"Should I insist that my child practice her music lesson?"

"I think we tend to insist but not necessarily force, but we do insist. I am most certainly against this situation of letting children do as they please either at home, at school, at church, or wherever. I think it's up to the adults to sort of guide the child, lead them perhaps gently, but lead them."[1]

Such a dialogue between parents would not have taken place two generations ago. When unquestioning obedience was the mark of a good child, knowing what one must do as a parent was a simpler business. Children were considered naturally full of idle deviltry and mischief. The job of parenthood, in its sterner aspects, was to subdue the child's will by reason if possible and by birch rod if necessary.

Today confusion reigns among us. Parenthood has become an arduous, problem-solving task instead of a natural process. When a battle of wills flares up in the home, fathers and mothers are deeply afraid of inflicting damaging guilt or fear upon the personalities of their children. Several decades of mental health

---

1. Roy W. Fairchild and John Charles Wynn, *Families in the Church: A Protestant Survey* (New York: Association Press, 1961), p. 141.

advice have made parents understandably cautious about exerting the too heavy hand. Seeing the child as a person in his own right, not as passive clay to be molded, they are torn between giving in to him and dominating him. Today's parents are often plagued by a paralyzing self-consciousness which asks, "Am I doing the right thing?" They are not unlike the centipede that got along quite well until someone asked him how he managed to synchronize all of his legs. Then he lay in a ditch paralyzed, considering how to run!

WHAT PARENTHOOD REQUIRES

It is hard to imagine a Christian home without children. Ideally, they are the fruit of a good marriage, the "product" of a husband and wife who have willed them into existence as an expression of their love. But it takes courage to accept the "calling" of parent these days. The estate of parenthood calls for changes in the couple's own relationship. It has been said that parenthood, not marriage, is the greater adjustment.

No matter how well integrated a wife and husband have become before their first baby arrives, the addition of a third party will force a reorganization of their relationship. The addition of a member can affect a family unit as profoundly as the loss of a member. In many homes the coming of the first child actually constitutes a crisis. The husband and wife may have romanticized parenthood. They simply did not know that babies required so much care.

When they were only a couple, husband and wife could bask in each other's companionship. Now they find that child care, housework, and other cares have usurped the time they had for joint recreation and other activities. A part of their attention must now be diverted to the child and his extensive needs. There is not as much energy and attention to go around, and with each child it is spread a bit thinner. If the young parents have been rather self-centered before, they will find the new baby demands a change in their way of life. But while they may both resent this, they can begin to mature because of it. As the small child begins to respond and grow, their own capacity to love and give may also grow; they can become larger persons because of the child. But at first it will not be easy—achieving maturity never is.

The new couple is tied down more than previously. Night feedings, lack of money for baby-sitting and entertainment, and sheer fatigue prevent them from going out as much as they used to. Social life may be severely curtailed unless a cooperative grandparent or neighbor is willing to step in.

Household routines are upset and responsibilities increase abruptly with the new child's arrival. Feeding schedules, a new and intensified regimen of laundry, as well as the continuing responsibility for the husband's well-being, almost doubles the new mother's work load. Into such a situation a wise husband will project himself as a helper in the many chores to be borne, including the care of the new infant. This is the time for him to begin in earnest the "fathering" which will prove to be so important later on in the lives of his children. The new father need not fear that much housework and parenting will feminize him. On the contrary, his leadership and his practical concern for the family is one way of expressing his masculinity.

While the new mother will need help in the physical care of home and child, she needs the love and understanding of her husband even more. Having some time off and help with the chores can boost feminine morale, but nothing can give her the strength to carry on more than a concerned and loving husband. If he can put aside temporarily his need to relax when he comes home, and instead listen to her experiences, and help to fulfill her need for adult companionship and a little excitement, he will find that she will respond to this kind of love more than to any number of household gadgets or new dresses. Few men realize that the mother of preschool children is probably the most chronically fatigued person he can find. If she is to fulfill the life needs of those persons who are almost completely dependent upon her, she too must have someone who can nurture her life needs and thus renew her strength and heal her discouragements.

The husband and father, therefore, is of greater importance when the children are quite young than he is usually aware of being. His chief service to *them* is to give his wife and their mother an extra portion of love and understanding; he loves them best by loving her.

The realistic Christian couple called to the vocation of parenthood knows that life will not be the same. New life in the family need not separate them. They can grow together on a new and deeper level as they share the responsibilities and joys of bringing their own flesh and blood to maturity. In this new responsibility they become " . . . heirs according to [the] promise" (Galatians 3:29).

WHAT CHILDREN CAN DO FOR PARENTS

Our attention is so often directed to the grave responsibilities of parenthood that we may fail to note what God can do to our lives through the gift of children.

When one shares in the procreation of a child, he is likely to think of himself as a complete man or woman. Remember the glow of pride that came with the birth of the first child? But the child is an asset in many other ways as well. A child can often draw parents together as they work for his well-being, care for his ills, and plan for his future. Great joy may come to parents with the realization that their own flesh and blood will be perpetuated. One has only to watch parents with their children at an amusement park or on a bright Christmas morning to know that one of the benefits of parenthood is the opportunity for parents to enjoy again their own past life in their child's fun, discoveries, and adventures. And for parents who had painful memories of their early life, a child is seen as a "second chance," an opportunity to correct past mistakes by the proper guidance of their child's future.

All human beings need a sense of significance. The parent often feels a sense of importance both because he is regarded as important by his child, at least until adolescence, and also because he must guide, protect, and be responsible for this relatively helpless creature.

Children enlarge their parents' world as they compel them to stretch their minds in response to searching questions. Sensitive parents are forced to broaden their social and political responsibilities for the health and welfare of all children everywhere.

The parent's spiritual response is also deepened. By facing his own inadequacy as a parent, he can begin to learn the meaning of God's love in spite of failure. Children help parents to grow up as persons, to learn to love as well as to seek love, to order their values according to new priorities. When a parent lives with his children for a while he may become aware that he probably receives far more from them than he gives to them.

If we are open-minded and still able to learn, we come to know ourselves better because of our children's intimate life with us. Our offspring are sensitive to both our unspoken and spoken communication. *Often their reactions are a guide to what we are saying without knowing it.* For example, sometimes we think our children are disobedient "just for spite" or that there is no cause for rebelliousness. But a closer look may reveal that the messages we send to them at times ("you are not able to accomplish anything" or "you are not worth loving") are related to their unpleasant behavior. A child's mood is often a clue to his parents' own unrecognized state of mind.

Children can also reintroduce to parents the delights and wonders of the world that they have too long taken for granted. A child's capacity to create, to learn, to try new things can lift them from their ruts and allow them to see the world anew. Parents can have a larger, richer world if they allow their children, in some measure, to be their teachers.

WHAT PARENTS CAN DO FOR CHILDREN

No parent is perfect and no marriage is without its flaws. Yet, within an understanding of Christian faith, it is necessary to see that even imperfect people can be God's servants in their child-rearing efforts. This is not to say that we can ever guarantee the outcome. We deal with persons, not with clay. We do not do as well as we intend for "we have this treasure in earthen vessels" (2 Corinthians 4:7). Christian parents are "earthen," completely human. Often discouraged, frequently not knowing what to do, they nevertheless are God's chosen way to produce and rear children who will be a part of his servant people. Parents are "vessels" because they are useful in spite of their mistakes and immaturity. In calling them into marriage and parenthood, God also promises them strength and insight for the next steps ahead.

There is a story attributed to an English author who sat on the beach one holiday with his young son just as the sun was going down. He pointed to it dramatically and said, "Going . . . going . . . gone!" And the sun disappeared from view. With the great faith that small boys often have in their fathers, the child demanded with all expectancy, "Do it again, Daddy!" We cannot claim such power or wisdom even though our offspring often think that it is ours to command. We will make many mistakes; at times we will be downright stupid in our child-rearing efforts. There is so much pressure for us to succeed as parents from every magazine we read and every expert we hear. Consequently, haunting doubts clutter our thinking about what it is that we are attempting to do.

The gospel assures us that we can always start anew, that it is never too late for a fresh beginning. In fact each new day can be another start. Waiting upon God for strength and insight, we are not imprisoned within a history of past failures. It is a future of grace which God grants us.

The Need for a Mature Faith

"Today's parents are at a loss to know how to understand the Christian faith, much less how to teach it to their children." This opinion was voiced by an active churchman in a discussion group on "The Parent's Responsibility for Christian Education in the Home." Perhaps most candid church parents would agree with him. They are genuinely confused about the meaning of faith and ethics in today's complex, scientific world; so confused that many have given up trying to understand it. It is easier for them to stop studying and thinking and simply equate Christianity with the

"American way of life" or to see it as "idealism" composed of one part democracy, one part mental health, one part congeniality. When a major denomination asked its parents what they hoped their children would someday remember about their early home life, eight out of ten church parents wanted their children to remember above all "loving and happy relationships." Only two out of ten parents wanted their children to be able to recall first of all the essential meaning of the Christian faith. Apparently, when there is hurt, failure, misunderstanding, and estrangement, Christianity has nothing to say. But the Christianity of the cross is most relevant precisely at these points—when reconciliation is needed, when resurrection from a living death is what we yearn for, when forgiveness is crucial.

Christianity has a content and its content is Jesus Christ and his life, death, and resurrection. Here is the point at which God stands in judgment and mercy on every attempt man makes to be self-sufficient and to create a god of his own. As William Lee Miller has said, religion for Americans is so often belief in believing, faith in faith.[2] This is exemplified by the former radio program "This I Believe" which had plenty of "believe," quite a bit of "I," but not much of "this." So God becomes the divine inkblot into which we read our wishes or our fears. If Jesus Christ is the human life of God revealed in a way that human beings can grasp and be grasped by him, then we must know this Person who gives us the clue to the meaning of God's life and ours.

The Christian is frank to say that without the person of Jesus, he knows nothing at all about God, even from the wonders of nature or from his dearest human relations. Our present dilemma as parents is that we do not know this story or its implications for the basic experiences of life and for familiar fields of thought. As the college boy said, "God, for me, is just a big oblong blur." If this is the situation in a home, how can parents expect to be teachers of their children in matters of Christian faith and life?

Parents are asked to expose themselves open-mindedly to the most thoughtful interpretations of the faith to see if it does not

---

2. William Lee Miller, *Religion and the Free Society* (New York: Fund for the Republic, 1958), pp. 5ff.

make more sense for their mixed-up lives than any other option. The communicators of this faith ask only that a *genuine* decision be made; that it be accepted or rejected with eyes wide open. *If faith has never been a matter of doubt, perhaps no real decision was ever made.* It may have come to such parents by habit, or custom, or social persuasion. They may be Christian only by heritage and inertia. Such parents will find it hard to interpret Christian faith meaningfully to their children whose penetrating questions will quickly challenge their platitudinous answers. To begin to teach one's own children about God is to test the foundations of one's own understanding of the faith. And the parent who is not willing to submit to such a trial cannot teach them much of anything.

The normal child asks many questions about life, birth, death, God, right, and wrong. Unlike the adult who has learned erroneously to compartmentalize his life into the religious and the secular, the child's faith includes every aspect of life, or nothing. Anyone who reads the Bible can surely see that God must be at least as interested in the other aspects of our lives as he is in our religion.

Religion is not a course of study that can be given in the family. It cannot be a scheduled, classroom affair, although there may be regularity in some of our attempts at home teaching and worship. Just as the relationships of Jesus, the disciples, and the world furnished the "curriculum" for that first group of followers, so it is with informed, perceptive parents. They learn to think theologically about life. They school themselves to look at relationships through their faith in Christ. When this becomes a natural part of parents' thinking, their children will begin to look at the many events of the day, whether close at hand or across the world or into space, in the light of God's providential care. Such parents do not simply "use" crises and crucial events in the life of children to teach about God. They do not stand around waiting to say, "Ah, now I'll have a chance to make that point." If the Christian interpretation of life and death is real to them, parents are bound to share it; if not, the artificiality of their words will show through.

The reality of the parent's faith is prior to any consideration of his teaching it in the home. It is not enough to teach because it is a nice thing to do for them. The need of the parent is as great as that of the child.

It may seem strange to us that in his plan, God has given to rank amateurs the most difficult and important task on earth. Fortunately, we can work at our understanding of the faith and our ability to articulate it to others as we enter into a serious quest for biblical understanding with other adults in the community of faith, whether it be found in the parish church building or in the neighborhood.

It is fortunate, too, that we teach not only through words, concepts, and doctrines, but also through our relationships. This, in the last analysis, **is** our only authority. Children see parents as the church of **Christ** long before they can understand the language of the **church.** Later, the theological concepts they learn will be *understood* **as they** are combined with a loving relationship through which growing lives receive their Christian nurture. This revealing conversation was reported between a small boy and his father:

> "What did you learn in Sunday school this morning, Jimmy?"
>
> "Well, I learned that God loves me. That's **what I** learned," Jimmy replied.
>
> "That's very interesting. Did you learn that God loves **me** because the Bible tells you so?" asked the father, remembering a familiar Sunday school song.
>
> "No, not because the Bible tells me so, but because **Mr.** Martin says so."
>
> "So then, you know God loves you because Mr. Martin says so."
>
> "Not just because Mr. Martin *says* so," replied Jimmy, "but because Mr. Martin loves me. *That's* why **I** know God loves me."

The confidence of Christian parents lies in the conviction **that** God will use the power of their love, limited and sinful though it is, to prepare their child to consciously receive that greater love of God and find his real purpose in the world.

In the sacrament of infant baptism, faithful parents stand with their baby in their arms in front of the pastor and in the midst of the congregation. They are asked three questions:

1. Do you acknowledge your child's need of the cleansing blood of Jesus Christ, and the renewing grace of the Holy Spirit?
2. Do you claim God's covenant promises in (his) behalf, and do you look in faith to the Lord Jesus Christ for (his) salvation, as you do for your own?
3. Do you now unreservedly dedicate your child to God, and promise, in humble reliance upon divine grace, that you will endeavor to set before (him) a Godly example, that you will pray with and for (him), that you will teach (him) the doctrines of our holy religion, and that you will strive, by all the means of God's appointment, to bring (him) up in the nurture and admonition of the Lord?

The congregation is then asked:

Do you, in the name of the Church, undertake responsibility for the Christian nurture of this child?[3]

They have studied the meaning of these words carefully and thoughtfully answer, "I do." Two small words, yet what a panorama of history lie behind them. Christ's church is being perpetuated; new life is coming into being.

This promise made by parents sets the tone for our discussion of the Christian nurture of children. It is not our own love or wisdom or omnipotence upon which we have to rely for this enormous job; it is the grace of God.

In the sacrament of infant baptism we are commissioned to "bring them up in the nurture and admonition of the Lord." What

---

3. *The Book of Church Order of the Presbyterian Church in the United States,* revised edition, 1963, § 209–5.

does this mean? *Nurturing* means giving to the child that which will nourish him. It is a deep caring for all aspects of the child's life and his development, the feeding of the whole person. When we hear the word *admonition* we think of correction, or a warning which attempts to put the child back on the right path. In its deepest sense, admonition refers to the parental responsibility for providing direction or teaching in the life of the child. Caring for and teaching offspring are the basic functions of parenthood, biblically understood. The reason for our caring and teaching is also clear to us: to provide the conditions of life that will help the child decide to become a disciple of Jesus Christ. This is the Christian's greatest dream and the expression of his deepest love for his child.

The Nurture of the Lord

"The nurture of the Lord" means providing for children physical care and emotional protection, as well as the development of a sense of identity and an awareness that life and grace are undeserved gifts of God.

Physical Care and Emotional Protection. All children come into the world helpless and if not given the essentials of food, warmth, and protection, they could not live long. Parents intervene between the world and the newborn to keep him safe and to insure his proper growth and development. Christian parents do not need to be reminded that the physical abuse of infants that we read about more and more frequently these days comes at the hands of the mentally ill or of those who are angry at the very existence of the child. In contrast to harshness, the term "tender loving care" used in medical circles, while not in the Bible, is an idea which is consistent with the scriptural definition of love.

Parents cannot anticipate how exhausting the process of providing for the feeding, medical care, and comfort of their child will be in the early years, especially for the mother. Two o'clock feedings only hint at the heavier demands yet to come. A source of confusion for parents is not knowing what is required to foster optimum growth and development. As parents, how much should they, and how much can they meet their children's needs? Beyond the minimum standard of care and feeding, we are at a loss to know when to meet the child's demands. All children are essentially helpless and whatever is required for survival will have to be given to them or taught to them.

American children seem to expect far more than they actually need for sound growth and development. Parents are perplexed. They are constantly having to decide how much to give their children. Many parents tend to take their standards from the neighbors and are almost crushed by the accusations of their youngsters that they are not giving enough. If giving their children what they themselves never had becomes a necessity, parents do them a disservice. If parents are sure in their own minds about what is right to give and to withhold, a child can adjust to it healthily. But the bewildered parent prompts the child to push and pull and express himself in various forms of anxious behavior.

In protecting the child, how can parents shield him from danger and at the same time encourage him to cope with his own troubles? No one wants his child hurt, but neither does he want him to grow up helpless. What should one do about the neighborhood bully, the difficult teacher, the possibility of physical hurt in competitive sports? If the parents have strong fears themselves, these are bound to influence their decisions. The parent who is always expecting disaster needs to explore these deep-seated anxieties or run the risk of inflicting crippling fears on his children. "God did not give us a spirit of timidity," says Paul in his letter to young Timothy, "but a spirit of power and love and self control" (2 Timothy 1:7). Irrational fear needs the purging of Christian faith.

A Sense of Identity. The fact that none of our children are alike makes nurturing difficult. Parents often express amazement when they realize that their children are really individuals. Individuality is what God intended. One child may be quiet and serious, more interested in reading and daydreaming. Another **might be a happy extravert with great enthusiasm for social**

contact, full of energy, and interested in sports. Parents should not assume that because their children have the same biological parents, they also have the same family environment. Brothers and sisters conceived at different times do not receive the same genetic composition from their parents. They may have some common characteristics, but they are far from identical. Neither do they have the same family environment. A firstborn child, for example, always has relatively inexperienced parents. Further, he has them to himself for a while, even if he later has a younger sibling, or perhaps several. The second-born child never has the experience of being an only child; there is always someone ahead of him. The differences are almost endless. It is a fallacy, therefore, to suppose that children born to the same parents and reared under the same roof are going to turn out alike. They react with unique responses to food, light, noise, or pain. Is it so surprising that later they should react differently to parental love or discipline, or even to God?

Nurture and care of the child give him a sense of who he is. We do not deliberately teach him, "Now, this is who you are and what you can do," although encouraging the signs of growth is important. How nurture contributes to a child's concept of who he is—his strengths, limitations, abilities, and potential—is a very subtle process.

Notice how the child comes to know and value his own sexuality: One important thing that a father and mother living together can give to a child is the sense that his particular sex is valuable. How does he get this confidence? A child can get a relatively clear picture of the place of male and female in his world from his observation of his parents with one another. Or he may get a confused picture.

By observing his father and mother, a child learns what it means to be a man or a woman. He learns very quickly that people come in two genders, male and female. "And God saw that it was good." But some parents do not act as if it were good, and they pretend that all members in the family are the same. In other families the contrasts are pronounced and sometimes unjustified. One mother says, "If you walk into a boy's messy room, everyone will say, 'Oh, a typical boy's room.' But if you walk into a girl's room that looks like a wreck, everyone is disgusted." Such a statement reveals immediately the double standard we hold, and it also reveals clues to what is believed to be "masculine" and "feminine." Many of the distinctions are learned, and a great many children become confused about the differences.

We owe our children, as part of our belief in the goodness of God's creation, a consistent and clear picture of *how we believe males and females are different and yet valued for their differentness.*

Caring for the child physically and emotionally so that he may one day possess confidence, strength, and faith are some of the ingredients of nurture. No one really knows what gives a parent the gift of sound nurturing. Thousands of parents without much formal education have reared wonderful sons and daughters, drawing upon their warmth, their native intelligence, and their good humor in their efforts. To be sure, they make their quota of mistakes, but God can do something even with these. *There are no formulas, no rules for successful parenting that compare with a capacity for loving deeply and enjoying the growth of those in one's care.*

In every activity of nurture, a recognition of God's presence can be cultivated. It is not formal teaching alone from which the child learns. One mother tells of her approach:

> We try to bring God into our family life every day somewhere through our discussion. Whether it's when we're washing the dishes, or making beds, or just talking about what the kids have done, or in saying their prayers. But we make out of it an everyday conversation so that God is not just "The Man Upstairs," but someone who is a part of our life. . . . I want my children to gain a close feeling to God so that when they grow up they will know they have a God to depend on. That's my highest ideal; and I want that for my family, no matter what else we do.[4]

---

4. Fairchild and Wynn, *op. cit.*, p. 185.

Life and the Grace of God. Embraced with warmth of Christian nurture, a child learns that life and the grace of God come as undeserved gifts. He learns, bit by bit, how to venture, how to be free responsibly within the protection of loving concern and watchful care. In such an atmosphere children learn what mercy and judgment mean; they learn that where one suffers pain, all share common grief and love. They learn that forgiveness is a reality, that they are valued without regard to their success or failure. In the home of responsible Christian parents, a foundation is laid for the story of the gospel which will later speak to the deepest needs of the child's soul.

The Admonition of the Lord

Admonition, correction, discipline, direction—all of these words point to the *teaching* task of parents. It is necessary to go beyond the care and nurture of the child, physically and emotionally, to help him become a complete human being. Firmness as well as feeding is necessary; direction as well as care.

In recent years, students of the family have decried the removal of the educational functions from home to school. To be sure, a great deal of the formal education which was earlier dispensed at the hearthside is now the responsibility of the school. As knowledge advances and becomes more complex, parents simply cannot, even if they wanted to, keep up with the vast areas of discovery and the teaching methods to convey this knowledge. But we must not assume that this leaves nothing to be taught at home. Whether or not parents recognize their responsibility, much education is still almost exclusively within the province of the home. Some of what must be taught to children includes the need for self-discipline, the development of conscience, and a system of values which is in harmony with a Christian interpretation of life.

The Need for Discipline. Parents are the child's first "socializers." They teach the child that he is not the center of the world. He must learn to balance his wants with those of others. At birth the child is not at all aware of the needs of other people in his world. Measured by adult standards, he is an unsocialized horror who snatches at your watch even while he is being tenderly talcumed.

He is insistent, demanding that every desire be instantly gratified, oblivious of the value of property. Obviously, some of these characteristics must be modified or he will be a monstrous adult. For his own safety, as well as the welfare of others, not all self-expression can be allowed. Even though children may complain loudly, discipline is a part of growing up. The impulse-ridden child is not safe, happy, or pleasant to be around.

Discipline is a subject which confuses the modern parent more than almost any other feature of child rearing. The word "discipline" has a long history. Basically, it means "learning" and comes from the Greek word *disceo*. Thus, we speak of "professional disciplines." It denotes deep, significant learning as implied in the word "disciple." There is, therefore, a close relationship between discipline and Christian faith as practiced in the family.

Unfortunately, the word "discipline" has taken on other meanings which are foreign to its original sense. It has often come to mean "punishment" or enforced conformity through pain, deprivation, and hostility. There is no doubt that spanking, whipping, and other practices that inflict pain will, for the moment, cause a child to stop his misbehaving; it may even prevent his doing it again in your presence. Punishment can enforce obedience, but obedience is not the goal; it is but a first step in parent-child relations. *Self*-control and *self*-discipline is the goal for Christians. We want discipline to get *inside* of the child, so that it will not always be necessary for an authority to be standing by. It is only when discipline is *internalized* that children can become *disciples*.

The Development of Conscience. When guides for behavior have been made one's own, we say that he has a "conscience." We are not born with a trained conscience; it must be developed through proper relationships with parents and others. By taking the restrictions or ideals inside and by modeling himself in the light of a person's behavior he admires, the child develops inner controls that go with him wherever he goes. In most children one sees the beginnings of a trained conscience between three and five years of age. At first, conscience is a simple thing for the child: what Daddy and Mommy approve of is "good"; what gets him into trouble with them is "bad." In later life this changes as he sees that his parents are not God.

Conscience is not automatically the voice of God. What is good or bad is defined very differently by different people and various societies. What was good to a Nazi conscience is bad to a Christian conscience. Our consciences must be tutored by Jesus Christ. *The Confession of Faith* (XXII:II) puts the issue clearly when it says "God alone is Lord of the conscience." And in Paul's letter to the Romans we read the words, "Do not be conformed to this world but be transformed by the *renewal* of your mind" (Romans 12:2; author's italics).

Discipline, then, is related to the growth of conscience. And the parents' "ultimate aim . . . is to produce the love which springs from a . . . good conscience" (1 Timothy 1:5; Phillips translation). Discipline is an essential gift of the parent to the child. But why are parents confused about discipline? (1) They do not want their children emotionally hurt by their discipline. It is difficult for some parents to distinguish between firmness which is necessary and the anger which often accompanies their disciplining efforts. They are rightfully concerned about what their anger will do to the child's sense of confidence and trust. (2) The modern parent wants to stay on good terms with his child; he wants the child to be a friend. He suspects that restrictions will somehow ruin the relationship. It is so important that his children have what he did not have, and a parent who suffers from memories of a lack of closeness with his own mother or father would like to have a better relationship with his children. One often gets the impression that many modern parents are cowed by their offspring and earnestly seek their goodwill and approval. Some say that, if they have to choose between cringing obedience and warm companionship, they would not hesitate to choose the latter. One father says:

> My parents would just have to speak softly with a stern look (and the ever-present threat of the switch) and we obeyed. We were very frightened . . . With the children

now, we yell and they don't listen to us, and our voices get louder, and *still* they like us. There is really a genuine affection and they talk to me about things I wouldn't have discussed with my parents.[5]

Fortunately, one does not have to choose between the permissiveness which often drives both parents and children to distraction, and the harsh, arbitrary enforcement of former times. We do not want to produce children who are constantly demanding and without social awareness, but neither do we want children who cringe in servile obedience or strike out in rebellious hate.

Since this is not a "how to" book on discipline and child-rearing, let us list four of the conditions known to be related to the development of "good conscience" from which love springs:

1. Good conscience develops when each parent honors the child's needs for both correction and companionship. Without a backlog of fun, adventure, and learning with parents, a child is likely to resent the disciplinary efforts and refuse to make the restrictions his own. When parents enter the child's world only when he steps out of line, he will begin to see adults as those to whom he must sacrifice his selfhood on the altar of unjust demands. On the other hand, if the relationship between the child and his father and mother is liberally sprinkled with opportunities for companionship and delight together, he can take deprivation in his stride. When a mother or father irritably turns off the TV set after asking the child a half dozen times to get his homework, he might think, "That old killjoy." But this resentment will not last if he has an abiding conviction that these two people love him and really are trying to guide him wisely. Without this, resentment will simmer and he will strike out in retaliation. The parent who has little love for his child, or who spends little time with him except when he needs reprimanding, is likely to receive less love as a result of discipline. Perhaps this is one meaning of the enigmatic saying of Jesus: "I tell you, that to every one who has will more be given; but from him who has not, even what he has will be taken away" (Luke

---

5. *Ibid.*, p. 142.

19:26). A parent who has strong love for his child will find that proper discipline can strengthen his own and the child's love still more.

2. Good conscience does not come overnight, but grows as the child is given the opportunity to learn to make his own decisions. Through the exercise of choice under guidance, the child learns to become responsible and to trust his own judgment. One cannot expect the child to suddenly grow to maturity when he reaches the age of twenty-one. Like all other growth, growth in decision making—and so of conscience—must be gradual, starting with small inconsequential choices and going on to those of increasing importance. If a child has been guided to think through the consequences of his choice, parents need not be so anxious when adolescence arrives. A child can learn to make intelligent choices within the range of his experience if he has been given plenty of practice in helping the family to make its decisions about vacations, schedules, and household arrangements.

3. Good conscience needs firm boundaries of behavior for both children and parents. Reasonable restrictions give both the child and the parent security. A group of people must learn to live together so that the needs of each member are respected and allowed expression. This calls for regulations.

Children also need protection from their inexperience. No parent would think of arguing about whether or not little Johnny should rush into a busy street. A few rules, *clearly understood by all*, help the family to work together as a team. It is natural for children to rebel sometimes at restrictions, but they will also feel a certain safety if parents hold fast. Older children will test the restrictions and try in many ways to get parents to let the bars down. To be sure, restrictions *do* need changing as children grow older and more responsible. However, not a few adolescents, having fought the fight, are greatly relieved when they cannot talk their parents into something about which they, themselves, have some fear and doubt. It is often a great relief for a teen-ager, whose friends are pressuring him to enter into questionable activities to be able to say, "Sorry, but my parents have lowered the boom on me. They are so old-fashioned. But that's the way it is." As children grow more mature, they might well be encouraged to help make the decisions for the family. Then, at adolescence, they feel personally responsible for the regulations regarding, for example, their curfew and use of the car. They are far more likely to follow these regulations if they have had some significant part in creating them.

4. Good conscience is formed by experiencing a consistency between actions and words. The Christian parent and child both have an obligation to family regulations. The parent knows that his authority is a limited one, deriving from God's own authority to which he, too, is responsible. This leaves no place in the Christian home for the arbitrary tyrant. For example, in the matter of teaching manners, abstract lessons in courtesy and good manners and punishment for infractions are not likely to take without a parental example to follow. "Never interrupt a conversation" can be preached by a parent, but when the child is playing with friends and talking excitedly with them, a mother might not think anything of breaking in to say, "Come here this instant and set the table." If a wife, having a conversation with her friends, were interrupted with, "Get to the kitchen and prepare dinner," we could predict the outcome! When the example contradicts the verbal teaching, a child may conclude that manners are just "kid stuff." When you are grown up you do not have to pay attention to them. "Love has good manners and does not pursue selfish advantage," says Paul (1 Corinthians 13:5; Phillips translation).

A System of Values. The teaching of a system of values is a byproduct of the correction and guidance that parents give children in everyday matters. In the process of disciplining, the child learns what his parents regard as right and wrong, good and bad, better and best, desirable and undesirable. Children are constantly absorbing these opinions because they have a great need for some basis upon which to make judgments about the events and people they see outside the home. The parents' values cannot be hidden; the observant child quickly learns what is important to his mother and his father, which of his interests and attitudes bring approval, disapproval, or indifference. We have discovered that relationships teach more than we had thought.

Some key questions can often furnish clues to a family's values: How is the salary used after spending for essentials—for a new car, furniture, recreation, books, travel, entertaining? How does the family spend its spare time—with in-laws, in gardening, education, church work? The use of extra *time* and *money* are very sensitive indicators of value and the child catches on quickly. Thousands of such choices add up and enable him to form a notion of "who we are" and "what we do about it."

Some unchurched parents, speaking in the name of democracy, maintain that a child ought to be given the opportunity to choose his own values, especially his religious values and his church affiliation, when he reaches his majority. These people often fail to recognize that parents' values are revealed in their everyday living and absorbed, at least in part, by the child. How much freedom do they expect the child to have after he has been "indoctrinated" by a hundred daily choices made without the awareness of God and his will? A child *learns* what to value even though he is not explicitly *taught* what is considered the good life.

Leaving until later the crucial question of whether or not there is a definable Christian style of life, we assert here that it is necessary for the parent's own maturity as well as for the nurture and teaching of the child for the parent to make explicit his values, goals, and intended way of life. Tracing the growth and development of persons from four years of age to the age of thirty, one study showed a striking difference between children whose parents were not definite about their own standards and a comparable group of children whose parents had a clear understanding of what they believed and how their children should be reared. Both groups of parents extended approval and love to their children. Those children reared by parents who were not afraid of demonstrating their values and the way they felt about personal and social issues became adults who were more responsive to the feelings of others, who were more satisfied with their jobs and home life, who used their minds more efficiently and who were more trusting of others.[6] *Parents need to explore their own system of values and make their commitments clear to the child.* The child will not always follow the parent and, indeed, the parent will sometimes modify his own point of view. A child may learn decision making by making his own decisions but, in the process, he needs to know where his father stands and where his mother stands. In the long run, this will be the child's strength even if his parents' standards are unpopular with him at the moment.

Teaching a system of values is not an easy business. Parents may discover that they are teaching words without meanings. Once in a while they are jolted to discover that a child is able to parrot back a sentiment to the mother or father, but has not caught its intention at all.

In one family, the parents had earnestly tried to teach their children that sharing with the unfortunate was a Christian thing to do. Their son quickly acquired the habit of giving to all sorts of causes and dropped pennies and nickels into the many containers found in stores these days. He was generous, from his small allowance, in his church pledge. But one day as he walked out of a store unwrapping the candy bar his mother had bought him as a reward for his charity, a neighbor's child asked for a small piece; the boy snarled, "Go buy your own candy." It was easy enough to get a parental reward for sharing with those he did not know, but very difficult to express himself charitably in a face-to-face relation. The lesson had been lost; the meaning had been interpreted as "how to get the approval of mother and father."

This particular family found that donating money to people in need instead of giving of themselves and their talents was not a way to teach charity effectively. And the whole family worked out imaginative ways of filling the needs of people that they could see, ranging from the donation of blood and hospital visitation to collecting good used clothing for a children's home which they had come to know firsthand. If our children are not learning the values we cherish, perhaps we ought to ask ourselves what kind of *messages* we are getting through to them.

---

6. Dale B. Harris, "Stand Up and Choose," *Presbyterian Life,* May 17, 1958, pp. 18–21.

WHAT FAMILY WORSHIP CAN BE

There is no subject relating to the Christian family about which pastors talk more, and parents do less, than worshiping together as families. Consequently, any discussion of the subject is likely to arouse guilt feelings on the one hand and grandiose claims for the practice on the other. We will limit this discussion to some reminders of the limitations and possibilities of family worship in the home.[7]

1. It must be recognized that, though extolled in hundreds of magazine articles, sermons, and references each year, regular worship as a family group is seldom found in the modern church home. Most parents confess that they just do not know how to go about it—how to assemble their family long enough for this ritual, where to turn for adequate resource materials, and how to hold the attention of children of different ages. Most parents are not really interested in learning what worship is expected to accomplish and how to go about it in their home.

2. It must be admitted that many claims have been made for family worship in the home which just cannot be substantiated. When it is promised, for example, that "the family that prays together stays together," one might remark in all candor that the kind of family which prays together might very well stay together anyway. When it is suggested that "prayer stops quarrels," or "binds a family together," the fact that in many families the insistence on family prayers together causes quarrels or intensifies animosities already present is overlooked. The claim is sometimes made that family worship will make us honest with one another. We know, however, of homes where the pretense of religiousness covers up real feelings.

Most serious of all errors is the assertion, whether stated openly or covertly, that the practice of family worship will *cause* the grace of God to come into our life as a family. In the Protestant view, this is a misunderstanding of the way God comes to us. No practice ever *guarantees* a new infusion of grace from

---

7. The reader is referred to John F. Jansen, *The Nature of Christian Worship* (Richmond: The CLC Press, 1966).

him; no ritual we may choose to go through controls his action toward us. To regard family worship as such is to make it magic and not an expression of faith. Let us be cautious of *any* claims made for family worship, whether they be the creation of togetherness, the alleviation of our discipline problems, the solution to our quarrels, or, as one often hears it, "putting us in direct touch with God." We must not expect of worship in the home that which may not happen.

3. We must avoid making family worship a form of education for the children. In some ways worship and teaching are intimately bound up together. Often when one learns about God from the Bible, he is moved to worship him. Conversely, the experience of worship often leads one to inquire more deeply into the nature of God and his relationship to us. But education or teaching is *not* worship. We might say, although this may be too sharp a distinction, that education involves knowledge *about* God while worship is a knowledge *of* God. In Christian education we talk about God; in worship we listen to God himself and talk to him as "Thou."

Now here is the temptation of the parent: When he sees worship as education of the children, as a way of teaching them something, the adult may exchange *his* role as a worshiper for that of a *teacher*. Adults might "hear" the prayers which children "say," but there is a great distinction between "saying prayers" and actually praying, for both child and parent.

In the Christian nurture of children in the home, there is no substitute for the parents' function. If family worship is held (and it will not endure without an adult to nourish it), it is because the *adult* is moved to rely upon the grace of God for his life. Regardless of how much parents and children are separated by age or understanding, they have this need in common.

What we *do* attempt in worship is simply to pay attention with all our effort to God as revealed in Christ. We do recognize how God has acted and is now acting on our behalf through genuine prayer and Bible reading. In worship we are *responding* to One who knows all our needs before we ask him. In worship, following the example of the Lord's Prayer, we do pray for the revelation of God and his Kingdom and we do pray for the deliverance from the troubles which beset us—bodily concerns, guilt, temptation, and the power of evil. This is the way we praise God.

* * *

A Parent's Prayer

When a child lives in our family, whatever our dreams for him, whatever our joy or disappointment, we can rededicate ourselves to the vocation of parenthood. Our commitment may be expressed in the words of a prayer suggested by Dr. Marion B. Durfee, a psychiatrist of Pasadena, California:

Help me to the stature of good parenthood, O God. I pray I may let my child live his own life and not the one I wish I had lived. Therefore, guard me against burdening him with doing what I failed to do, and when tempted to seek his balm for old wounds, strengthen me against my self-justification.

Help me to see today's missteps in perspective against the long road he must go, and grant me the grace of patience with his slow pace, lest in my impatience I force him into rebellion, retreat, or anxiety.

Give me the precious wisdom of knowing when to smile at the small mischiefs of his age and when to give him the haven of firmness against the impulses which in his heart he fears and cannot master.

In time of needed punishment give me a warm heart and a gentle voice so he may feel the rule of order is his friend and clasp it to his soul to be his conscience.

Help me to hear the anguish in his heart through the din of angry words or across the gulf of brooding silence, and having heard, give me the grace to bridge the gap between us with understanding warmth before speaking my own quick retorts, and stay my tongue also from the words which would chill his confiding in me.

Still my voice and smooth from my brow all that mars infectious serenity and joy in living; rather let my face so shine that these later years will seem to him a promised land toward which to strive.

I pray that I may raise my voice more in joy at what he is than in vexation at what he has done; so each day he may grow in sureness of himself.

Help me to hold him with such warmth as will give him friendliness toward fellow man; then give me the fortitude to free him to go strongly on his way.

Then as I see him striding forward eagerly, self-sure, friendly, and in good conscience my grateful heart will swell with joy.

Amen.[8]

What does it mean to rear our child in "the nurture and admonition of the Lord"? It means first and foremost a father and mother knowing what it means to be accepted and forgiven by the working of God in Christ. It means the flow of life, full life, between the husband and wife as they accept this gift in gratitude and joy. As this happens there is a good chance of abundant life flowing between them and their children. And there is the possibility that through his parents the child will become aware of God's love. Yes, even through our weakness, our need for forgiveness, and our very spotty love there is the possibility, "for we have this treasure in earthen vessels."

---

8. Used by permission of the author, Marion B. Durfee.

Part II
The Family:
The School of Christian Relationships

6 Family Communication and Authentic Personhood........125
7 Family Unity and Personal Differences..................145
8 Christians and Creative Conflict.......................159
9 Decision Making and Discipleship......................177

6
Family Communication and Authentic Personhood

> How long will you torment me,
> And break me in pieces with words?
> These ten times you have cast reproach upon me;
> Are you not ashamed to wrong me?
>
> Job 19:2–3

Like Job, family members have all experienced the powerful impact of words—words that tear down, destroy confidence, make us feel less than a person. We also receive messages that build up, increase trust, and link us with another life. Two kinds of communications are present in Christian families—both healing and hurt. Our very presence in a family means that we cannot *not* communicate. Both our spoken and unspoken behavior send messages to other members.

A wife may say to her husband, "I wish you would fix that faucet." He may react in a number of ways to this communication. He may say that he will, but not now. He may answer with a grunt as he continues to read the sports page. He may become angry or make it clear that he has more important things to do right now. But whatever he does, he cannot *not* communicate; even his silence contains a message.[1]

In many modern homes, the record player or the television comes in handy to escape from talking to each other when family members must be alone together. Even with this diversion, however, they cannot not communicate something to each other.

If one were cut off from all communication with his fellows, past and present, he could not be a person. If no messages of any

---

[1] I am indebted to Dr. Paul Watzlawick and Mrs. Virginia Satir of the Mental Research Institute of Palo Alto, California, for this and other insights in this chapter.

kind came to him, he would not know who he was or have any bond with that which makes him human. For to understand himself, man needs to be understood by another. And to be understood by another he needs to understand the other. In a real sense, this is what family life is all about. Through communication we confirm each other's existence, sometimes pleasantly, sometimes painfully. When we are praised or spoken to with respect we come to regard ourselves as persons who are worthy and loved. When we are yelled at or ignored, our selves are not accepted or confirmed. But we need to understand the other person in order to get this message, whether positive or negative, about ourselves.

If a man needs to be understood by another in order to understand himself, and if he needs to understand the other in order to find out how he is understood, we can see the deep wisdom of Psalm 139 for the deepest level of family communication.

> O LORD, thou hast searched me and known me!
> Thou knowest when I sit down and when I rise up;
> > thou discernest my thoughts from afar.
> Thou searchest out my path and my lying down,
> > and art acquainted with all my ways.
> Even before a word is on my tongue,
> > lo, O LORD, thou knowest it altogether.
> Thou dost beset me behind and before,
> > and layest thy hand upon me.
> Such knowledge is too wonderful for me;
> > it is high, I cannot attain it.
> Whither shall I go from thy Spirit?
> > Or whither shall I flee from thy presence?
> If I ascend to heaven, thou art there!
> > If I make my bed in Sheol, thou art there!
> If I take the wings of the morning
> > and dwell in the uttermost parts of the sea,
> even there thy hand shall lead me,
> > and thy right hand shall hold me.

If I say, "Let only darkness cover me,
   and the light about me be night,"
even the darkness is not dark to thee,
   the night is bright as the day;
for darkness is as light with thee.
. . . .
Search me, O God, and know my heart!
   Try me and know my thoughts!
And see if there be any wicked way in me,
   and lead me in the way everlasting!

THE INDIVIDUAL AND FAMILY COMMUNICATION

The quality of community, in the home and elsewhere, depends upon the character of the communication among its members. Communication in the family, both verbal and nonverbal, is the means by which family members come to know each other, to live and work side by side with high morale, and perchance to love each other. Merely because we are of the same "flesh and blood" does not mean that love is automatically included in the genetic package. Because people are related is no guarantee that genuine warmth toward each other exists. This must be created largely through communication. Such community comes not by words alone but through other avenues as well:

- by playing together, using mind and muscle in recreation and laughter
- in eating together, creating a basic bond to which the Bible gives liberal testimony
- in the sexual relationship, in which husband and wife come to "know" one another
- while worshiping together, attending and responding wholeheartedly to God's address to us
- by working together, focusing our energies in changing the earthly terrain or map of the mind
- through suffering together, sharing the dangers and anxieties which life thrusts upon us.

Each of these avenues has enormous possibilities for a Christian family. People need people, but in order to achieve any needed relationship with them we must be able to communicate honestly. And in order to communicate meaningfully, we must establish a bond of trust. Experienced parents know that sitting up all night with a desperately sick child can often heal their many ego wounds and build an irreplaceable love. The family can be "a school for living," as Martin Luther titles it.

Good communication can be learned in a family that senses its importance and, looking at life around us, we can sense what a witness such a home could be.

The Search for Genuine Intimacy

Numerous observers of our society have spoken of the painful loneliness in American life. They are impressed by the emotional isolation of modern man. In spite of his gregariousness, he avoids that creative solitude, that "apartness" which can bring some substance into togetherness.

There is little in the American culture as a whole that encourages genuine communication with another. The mechanized model of industry has also invaded our personal relations. We content ourselves with just enough contact to carry out our business; we frequently see the people we deal with as "functions" to be manipulated, persuaded, counted, or categorized. Our frequent moving patterns make us wary of establishing deep roots with people whom we may soon leave. Social mobility, our desire to move onward and upward in our work and social life, militates against any relationships which would soften our competitive drive and standing. We speak to impress.

Life is more and more an impersonal jungle with anonymous, unanswerable, and frequently electronic voices resounding inside and outside our homes. If this is our experience, the Christian family with its promise of renewed love in Jesus Christ, of freedom for genuine personal existence, is all the more imperative for us. It must be a place where we can be more than "part-people" fragmenting our lives into the social roles we play. We would like that family to give us the freedom and love to be able to "unpack our emotional suitcases," to be what we are rather than what we feel forced to be in the competitive striving which saturates our work, our school life, our neighborhoods and sometimes, God forbid, our churches.

It is not superficial "contacts" we hope to find in the family; it is an *intimacy* in which, in the words of Psalm 42, "deep calls to deep." If we find this genuine *communion* (not the "union" of two persons in which one absorbs the other), we lose the feeling of loneliness, yet are truly able to be who we are in the presence of the other. The "new being" as seen in Christ enables us, in Paul Tillich's words, to balance participation and individuation with others.[2]

With these high hopes for our homes (often too idealistic in the light of a Christian understanding of man), one realizes how necessary good communication is in this arena of life we so wistfully see as our refuge against a depersonalized world.

Because the family can be the most intimate, the most fully engaged in of life's relationships, there is an understandable temptation to seek our total fulfillment here, as we have already recognized. Succumbing to the romantic-idealistic view of marriage, we may unconsciously assume that family life *by itself* can create authentic personhood in us. So great are the aspirations of young married people for a perfect home that every quarrel may become a crisis, and each misunderstanding an evil portent of loneliness and failure. Thus we forget our finite humanity and lose our perspective and sense of humor about the human situation. We forget the necessity and the meaning of forgiveness upon which Christian faith stands or falls.

Two facets of life illuminated by Christian faith stand to correct our unrealistic hope that in the family we will find perfect understanding and communication. One is *the fact of our created individuality and finiteness;* the other is *the fact of our sin and self-protectiveness* which continues in us even though we have

---

2. Paul Tillich, *The Courage to Be* (New Haven: Yale University Press, 1952), pp. 86–90.

been restored to an awareness of our relationship to God in Jesus Christ.

The Mystery of the Individual

As Christians we are unique, individual persons and will be throughout eternity. (Each man is called by a name, and in the Bible that is a stamp signifying the particularity of his character.) We live within different skins. We are utterly unique when compared with the other members of our families. Even though children may imitate or identify with their parents and thus resemble them to some extent, there remains a mystery in each of us which only God can fathom, indicating that one cannot find God except through his self-revelation. Paul says this is also true ultimately of man: "For what person knows a man's thoughts except the spirit of the man which is in him? So also no one comprehends the thoughts of God except the Spirit of God" (1 Corinthians 2:11).

What does this mean for family communication? We must assume that we are always going to be to some extent strangers to one another; we will never understand each other completely. That we should is an unwritten demand of the modern man or woman which should be crossed off the Christian's list. As separate islands, we can only guess at the feelings that move in another's heart, the thoughts that stimulate his mind. Only God knows who we really are.

As I face my mate and children and in-laws, I am bound to say: "I am not you. You have your own memories, loves, talents, fears. We each live in our own private worlds with our own ways of seeing and feeling and thinking. (Notice this the next time you watch a television drama together.) You have your own fortress of decision and assent—and I have mine. If this were not true there would be no need for communication. Either of us could see and feel and act for both. In genuine communication something within each of us is awakened which we come to have in common and understand alike. But still you are not I and I am not you. God's will for you may not be the same as his will for me."

Realizing that there is an inevitable mystery in those persons to whom we are closest, we know there will always be a certain incompleteness in our understanding. Who has not discovered in family relations that the message he intended to convey was not the message received? A family member may have been preoccupied and heard only a part of what we said. Even when we have been heard, words have different meanings for different people in our homes. "I told you to come home *early*," says a mother to her child. "I *am* home early," the child replies, having quite a different idea of time.

Even when we are tempted to complain, "He doesn't understand me," or "I can't understand her," we know that, in the final analysis, we will never completely understand one another; but we can work toward better ways of sending messages. Each family member has a responsibility to see that a message is reasonably clear.

Because we cannot live within another's skin, or read his mind, we can never take another for granted. Christian husbands and wives can find an adventure in living together because even after decades, they are required to reach out, to inquire, to discover what is on the other's mind. Thank God for the mystery of individuality.

HUMAN SIN AND FAMILY COMMUNICATION

The Christian basically understands sin not as immoral behavior (which can be identified in different ways depending upon history and geography), but as man's desire to become the god of his own life and universe, thus turning his back on the real source of his being (Genesis 3:5ff.). All sinful acts stem from a person's inward disposition to enthrone himself, to determine for himself what is good and what is evil, rather than to see the real good and evil of human life as it is revealed in Jesus Christ. For most of us, "good" equals "convenient" or "pleasurable" and "bad" connotes that which is "inconvenient" or "unpleasant." "He's such a *good* baby," we say, speaking of the little trouble he has been to us.

The Cross, demonstrating the cost of divine forgiveness to

God, turns our lives upside down and confounds our "natural" values. We have built our lives on a "pleasure-pain" principle since birth. As an indication of this reversal of our values, we call that Friday "good" in which he bore the full cost of our inhumanity. As we participate in the drama of the life, death, and resurrection of Jesus Christ as the human life of God, we learn that his will determines what is good. Whether or not we think this is pleasant or unpleasant is more and more beside the point for the Christian. Regardless of the pleasure or pain, *knowing and being known by him is the chief good.*

As sinners who have been forgiven, we will *continue* to live in a self-protective way (see Romans 7:14ff.). It may not be the body we protect so much as the image which we have constructed of ourselves. This self-portrait may be either flattering or derogatory. There is an expression of a person's sin in thinking of himself both more highly than he ought to think and more lowly than he ought to think. Constant self-criticism is an effective way to avoid repentance! We can see this in the family member who always runs himself down and takes the blame but who will not change. We protect ourselves most often by getting into a position in which we cannot be hurt. "Sin" can be manifested in the family by our dominating the lives around us, by letting ourselves be absorbed by the life of another, or by moving away from others emotionally—not letting them really touch us. Our communication with each other will reflect these basic postures.

As a result of our self-defensiveness, language becomes distorted and conceals as well as reveals. Language is ordinarily the instrument with which we meet and know each other. But it can also be the source of misunderstanding, disruption, and deceit. Our words become barbed and are slung to hurt and destroy. Chapter 3 of the Letter of James speaks of the tongue controlled by self-protective impulses as "a fire . . . a restless evil, full of deadly poison," and a very small rudder which can guide the largest ships—and, we might add, the largest families.

The Bible sees our communication with each other as indicative of our spiritual condition. It makes it quite clear that when the original communion between God and man is broken and disturbed by sin, communication between man and man is, consequently, in disorder. And our lack of understanding in the family betrays this.

The Bible expresses this important fact in the famous tale of the confusion of languages and the tower of Babel. (Read Genesis 11:1–9, noting that the people's chief motives in building the tower were to invade the "heavens," the province of God, and to "make a name" for themselves.) When people are in harmony with God, the ground of their lives, the whole earth is of one language and one speech; but when disharmony and pride appear, people's language becomes confounded and they cannot fathom what their brothers are saying.

The sequel to this dismal tale is found in the New Testament in Acts 2:1–11. Here we see understanding restored. When the full power of the Holy Spirit comes at Pentecost, when man becomes *aware* that his sin is forgiven and that he is loved as ever by the Father, the confusion of languages disappears. Full communication, even across the natural barriers of cultural life, becomes possible again.

As Christians we see, then, that our family communication problems are not basically the semantic problems of what words to use or even whether or not we mean what we say, important as those considerations are. Rather, the problems are centered in our reluctance to realize forgiveness. When we can accept God's acceptance of us we are released from the need to "harden our hearts" and close our ears to others, or to hurt others with our indifference or our barbed syllables.

One of the continuing expressions of sin in Christian families is to talk about the evil in others. It seems so natural to us to "keep account of evil or gloat over the wickedness of other people" (1 Corinthians 13:6; Phillips translation). Read this familiar parable to your family:

> He also told this parable to some who trusted in themselves that they were righteous and despised others: "Two men went up into the temple to pray, one a Pharisee and

the other a tax collector. The Pharisee stood and prayed thus with himself, 'God, I thank thee that I am not like other men, extortioners, unjust, adulterers, or even like this tax collector. I fast twice a week, I give tithes of all that I get.' But the tax collector, standing far off, would not even lift up his eyes to heaven, but beat his breast, saying, 'God, be merciful to me a sinner!' I tell you, this man went down to his house justified rather than the other; for every one who exalts himself will be humbled, but he who humbles himself will be exalted (Luke 18:9-14).

The tax collector threw himself on God, knowing he needed forgiveness. The Pharisee needed God too, but only as an audience for the recital of his goodness compared to obvious, socially unacceptable sinners. With ease he discovered the evil in them. Many Christians are like turkey buzzards soaring over hill and dale, looking, not for delicious morsels to eat, but for a corpse.

A common sin in many families is a preoccupation with the evil of others—whom we can scarcely judge since they are mysteries to us. This is a sign, not that we love ourselves too much, but that we know deeply that we do not know we have a self worth loving and so must cut others down to our size. In short, our preoccupation with the evil of others is an indication that we have not heard what God has said to us. We have failed to hear what we should *do* about what we are and always have been in Jesus Christ, namely, his beloved children.

What does our family conversation reveal? The late James Bossard of the University of Pennsylvania studied dinner time conversation of families over an extended period of time.[3] With the parents' permission, he placed tape recorders unnoticed near the dinner tables and recorded more than 200 samples of table talk which fall into five main groups, three of which will be described here.

First, there is the conversation at hurried meals where

---

3. James H. S. Bossard, "Family Conversation's the Key," *Presbyterian Life*, January 25, 1958, pp. 7ff.

members of the family seem to be engaged in a refueling process. Food is gulped down as if eating were a waste of time. Conversation is blunt, sparse, and direct. There is a liberal sprinkling of "yes," "no," "salt," "butter," "uh-huh," "more," and other monosyllabic extravagances.

The second kind of dinner conversation illustrates a sensitivity to the evil in others: There are those family meals that seem to be dedicated to the proposition that the dinner table is a battleground for current domestic warfare. The atmosphere is jagged and hostile. The children are taken to task for past and present misbehavior. Parents nag at each other. The food may be criticized and its preparation disparaged. Table manners, so often a source of embarrassment to parents, are brought to the attention of everyone. Frequently anger explodes and tears stream, and the hurt person "excommunicates" himself from the family group.

The third type of family conversation is focused upon the evil in people outside the family: Criticism is expressed in "talking about" the neighbor's child who is in trouble again, or the teacher who is too demanding and not fair. In this family, habits of dress, peculiarities of speech, and just plain differences from ourselves are targets for St. James' "tongue of fire." Yet, says Dr. Bossard, some of these same parents wonder why their children have no friends at school.

This kind of conversation suggests that the participants, particularly the parents because they set the tone, believe that they do not need to be forgiven for anything they do and are. Because they cannot accept forgiveness, these "righteous ones" are hard and warmed by very little love. Their condemnatory attitude will boomerang; often the very lessons a strongly moralistic parent would teach a child are rejected by that child when he becomes an adult, if not sooner. *High standards, taught without an atmosphere of forgiving love, may produce a long-faced, humorless moralism, but not the freedom with which Christ makes us free.*

Paul Tillich asks some searching questions about this matter:

Why do children turn from their righteous parents and husbands from their righteous wives, and vice versa? Why do Christians turn away from their righteous pastors? Why do people turn away from righteous neighborhoods? Why do many turn away from righteous Christianity and from the Jesus it paints and the God it proclaims? Why do they turn to those who are not considered to be the righteous ones? Often, certainly, it is because they want to escape judgment. But more often it is because they seek a love which is rooted in forgiveness and this the righteous ones cannot give.[4]

The biblical message of forgiveness has relevance for the most common element of our life together—conversation.

CHRISTIAN FREEDOM AND FAMILY COMMUNICATION

As a Christian is freed from self-preoccupation, as the realization dawns upon him that he can put his confidence in God alone, the chains which bind him to his self-defensive life are broken. He will return to the security of his shackles many times in his life; he will attempt to find safety in bondage. But his freedom in Christ is a reality. He is free of the need to pretend; free of what others think; free, finally, to enter the lives of others with love. And it is impossible to remain free without prayer and common worship and hearing again and again the word of him who sets us free. That Christians are so freed by the Holy Spirit is the persistent witness of the church throughout all ages. Men and women are changed toward the image of God by his Spirit, an

". . . obdurate pressure
Edging men towards a shape beyond
The shape they know."[5]

What is the new "shape" toward which men are persuaded?

---
4. Paul Tillich, *The New Being* (New York: Charles Scribner's Sons, 1955), pp. 13–14.
5. Christopher Fry, *Thor, with Angels* (London: Oxford University Press, 1948), p. 46.

For *what* are we set free by God's grace in Jesus Christ? We are released from bondage in order to care. We are set free to be neighbors to those who need us—the hungry, the imprisoned, the lonely, the self-righteous, the despairing, the helpless. Sometimes the neighbor may be in our own home. What might God's freedom mean in family communication?

The Freedom to Understand

We are set free to listen with understanding. Listening to men and listening to God are not basically different. As we read the New Testament, particularly the parables, we hear our Lord saying repeatedly, "He who has ears to hear, let him hear."

We can listen without hearing a family member; we may appear to be attentive without really entering his life and thought at all. We may give the impression of listening when actually we are just other warm bodies in the room with those talking; our minds may be a hundred miles away. We may be preoccupied with pressing matters on our minds, problems to be solved which capture all of our energies until we arrive at a solution. We cannot hear; there is too much noise inside. It is possible that we are occasionally preoccupied precisely to *avoid* the close involvement in another life that listening might bring.

Familiarity can also slacken our attention to another. If we hear the same expression again and again, or assume that we will hear nothing new, we may turn off our hearing aids to family members. Surely the teen-ager does this when he hears for the tenth time, "Now I want you to clean up your bedroom, Jim." When one of my daughters was quite young I read familiar children's stories to her most evenings. Soon I knew the words by heart and could read while pondering something else that concerned me. But my blank expression and obviously bored tone were caught by the three-year-old. "Where *are* you Daddy?" she asked perceptively. I had not reckoned with her response, her subsequent questions about the story, her need for my being *with* her; this was the communication she missed. How easy it is to give but a *token* of ourselves to a situation because we think we have been through it before. Yet no one situation is just like another. Who knows when a "visitation" might come, when a truly personal relationship will be brought into existence, when God might speak to us through that relationship? Perhaps we do not listen deeply enough when our family members talk.

The famous Jane Addams of Hull House in Chicago once listened to a group of immigrant mothers who claimed they could not get close to their adolescent daughters. She asked if they really cared about listening to their afternoon chatter even though they, representing another culture and generation, could hardly be expected to understand the world of their youngsters. She advised them to stop what they were doing when the teen-ager came home and try to listen to her attentively, no matter how trivial the conversation might be. She concluded sagely, "If you don't listen to the little things first, the big things won't come out."[6]

Are there ever any "little" things in the lives of persons if they are the means by which we bridge the gap between one mysterious life and another? Many a husband becomes "the silent one" in his marriage because his wife did not recognize how important were the "little things" that he started to tell her about work before he was cut off or ignored or condemned for something he had failed to do.

"He who has ears to hear, let him hear." Our Lord knew that without real hearing, we could not come to know the reality of God nor the world around us. Without attentive listening, we often live for years with *imaginary* persons instead of the real individuals with whom God has cast our lives. We build mental images of each other and of God and respond to those images instead of to the real persons. There are still some surprises in store for us. The person we have known for decades is a living, growing self to some extent renewed day by day. "Surprise," C. S. Lewis reminds us, "is the signature of grace."[7] *Thinking we know everything there is to be known about familiar persons, we lose*

---

6. As quoted in Douglas V. Steere, *Dimensions of Prayer* (New York: Harper & Row, Publishers, Incorporated, 1963), pp. 67–68.

7. C. S. Lewis, *Surprised by Joy* (New York: Harcourt, Brace and Company, 1955).

the sense of wonder, of anticipation in the encounter, and even of the newness of life which God promises. "Behold, I make all things new" (Revelation 21:5).

Parents can do much to move patterns of family conversation out of the old ruts and thus change our habits of listening. There are ways of enhancing listening and learning which parents can provide. Dr. Bossard reports a fourth kind of family conversation which has something to say to Christians.[8] The families in this category fill their meal hours with human interest talk. Members of the family tell about their experiences of the day—funny, sober, and embarrassing. Choice bits of news are saved for meal time. Good jokes are told. The personal triumphs, disappointments, and pleasantries of the day are related. Mother tells about her trip to the grocery store where she accidentally knocked over a stack of cans. A program on TV is discussed and evaluated. Even such high-level talk as a crisis in Southeast Asia is brought into the picture and the older members of the family try their hand at explaining it simply to the younger. Listening and asking are stimulated by the sheer interest in life around them. (This is often forgotten when quarrels among the children keep families obsessed with how the children are not getting along.) Frequently, such table talk is enriched by the presence of guests, selected with care to interest the younger members of the family as well as the more mature. Missionaries on furlough, people from other cultures, races, and faiths are long remembered by the little ones to whom we are introducing God's world.

By grace we are freed to listen. But the perceptive Christian parent listens to more than words. Certainly not all communication between persons in the family is verbal. The language of the body conveys much. This is the earliest language the child learns from his mother—touch, sound, and tension or relaxation of her body, facial expressions, and other signs indicating the fine nuances of mood and attitude she feels. When children are older the grimace, the frown, the clenched fist may convey far more than the artificial "Now dear, will you say goodnight to the

---

8. Bossard, *op. cit.*, p. 9.

company and get to bed?" when repeated requests have failed to elicit a response. The message that is conveyed may have little congruence with the words expressed. A wife may say about her husband, "It's not so much *what* he says that disturbs me, it's the *way* he says it," and we know what she means. "Little children," says the First Letter of John, "let us not love in word or speech but in deed and in truth" (1 John 3:18).

The late Harry Stack Sullivan used the term "emotional contagion" for the early nonverbal communication between mother and child.[9] Even though it is without words, he insisted, this "empathic" contact has great importance for the child's feeling of well-being in later years. Whether or not the mother conveys feelings of safety and care which will evoke trust in the infant depends heavily upon her own feelings of worthwhileness and the conviction that she is loved.

The potency of the subtle forms of communication of body stance and muscular variations is demonstrated by the response of nonseeing and nonhearing individuals such as Helen Keller. Her teacher tells of her sensitivity to the emotional reactions of other people in her presence even when words could not be heard.

> One day, while she was out walking with her mother and Mr. Anagnos, a boy threw a torpedo, which startled Mrs. Keller. Helen felt the change in her mother's movements instantly, and asked, "What are we afraid of?" On one occasion, while walking on the Common with her, I saw a police officer taking a man to the station-house. The agitation which I felt evidently produced a perceptible physical change; for Helen asked, excitedly, "What do you see?"[10]

We listen as Christians to the language of the body as well as to the language of words.

---

9. Harry Stack Sullivan, *The Interpersonal Theory of Psychiatry* (New York: W. W. Norton, Inc., 1953).

10. Helen Keller, *The Story of My Life* (New York: Doubleday & Company, Inc., 1954), p. 295.

The Freedom to Respond

As Christians we are freed to respond creatively to the one communicating to us. Communication is interaction, a two-way process which is reciprocal. How do we respond? Do we demonstrate that we have been listening? We may think we are good listeners, but do we listen in a way which really shows that we have grasped what the other is trying to convey to us? Dr. Carl Rogers, the well-known psychotherapist who sees much mental distress as communication breakdown, suggests an experiment by which we might test the quality of our listening. The next time we get into an argument with those inside or outside the family he suggests we stop the discussion for a moment and institute this rule: "Each person can speak up for himself only *after* he has first restated the ideas and feelings of the previous speaker accurately, and to that speaker's satisfaction."[11] This means that, before presenting our own viewpoint, we really have to understand that of the other. It sounds simple, but in the realities of family life, it is a most difficult discipline to learn. When we are able to do this, we frequently find that our own comments must be drastically revised. What we thought we heard initially was not what we understood finally—and the heat often disappears out of a discussion.

Given the mystery of the selves God has created, can we assume that we know what the other means with his words, his gestures, his actions? Instead of jumping to conclusions, *we can learn the art of asking*. Each of us can learn to ask husband or wife or child or grandparent what is meant, felt, or intended when misunderstandings have arisen or threaten to arise. Does not this response befit a Christian style of life in the family?

Understanding requires a positive response from one's partner. More people have stopped talking with one another because what they have to say is ignored or harshly criticized than for any other reasons. If a mate criticizes us, especially when we have made a mistake, we have little incentive to share the troublesome

---

11. Carl R. Rogers, "Communication: Its Blocking and Its Facilitation," *Social Progress* (Crawfordsville, Indiana: The United Presbyterian Church U.S.A., April, 1961), p. 33.

aspects of our lives with him or her. Criticism begets silence, withdrawal, or attack. At best it yields mere co-existence in the family; at worst, leaving the field of battle through divorce.

Robert Blood has made an intriguing study of the various responses of husbands to their wives who tell their troubles to them.[12] He finds that a husband may respond by noticing what she says or by disregarding it. If the husband notices, he can accept or repudiate her feelings about her difficulties with children, housekeeping, or whatever. If he accepts them, he can actively undertake an effort to make her feel better: (1) by working with her to prevent a recurrence of the difficulty; (2) by taking her temporarily out of the situation; (3) by expressing sympathy and affection; (4) by offering advice and discussing with her how she herself might work toward a solution of the difficulty; (5) by listening without apparent response. The responses designed to produce grateful, satisfied wives are also in that order: (1), (2), (3), (4). Passive listening (5) was not much more helpful than a clearly rejecting or scolding response. Paul refers to the sensitivity of those of the body of Christ who "bear one another's burdens," and who "weep with those who weep" and "rejoice with those who rejoice." Once again social science research has confirmed anew ancient gospel insights.

The Freedom to Be Real

The courage to be real with each other is another freedom Christians can have in family communication. Pretense is so often the response of the moralistic Christian even as it was of the Pharisees in Jesus' parables. Honesty with one another is one of the dividends of a life which knows it is graced by a God who loves us in spite of what we are. We have less need to hide our shortcomings since our guilt has been absorbed by his suffering love.

This courage can have an amazing effect in others around us. In a remarkable biography of a small boy, *This Is Goggle*,[13] we

---

12. Robert O. Blood, Jr. and Donald M. Wolfe, *Husbands and Wives* (Glencoe, Illinois: The Free Press, 1960), pp. 175–220.
13. Bentz Plagemann, *This Is Goggle* (New York: McGraw-Hill Book Company, 1955), pp. 79–93.

see this chain reaction occurring: Ten-year-old Goggle is a lively creature and all boy. On the Fourth of July he shot out the windows of a lovely French door from a dismantled house with a BB gun. When a friend is accused, Goggle broods about his misdeed to the point of appearing ill. Finally, he admits the shooting to an officer. His mother assures him of her love and helps him to work out a way of restitution for the destructive act.

Then a surprising thing happens. Neighbors begin to drop in unexpectedly, even those the family did not know well. They make it a point to visit when Goggle is there. And all confess to buried "sins." Gentle Mrs. Worthing tells Goggle of a church window she had broken when she was made to stay home from a church school picnic. She had never told anyone about it until now. Tom Mitchell, a member of the board of directors of the local bank, had once soaped the railroad tracks which brought a freight train to a stop for hours. He had not had the courage to admit it until now. And so it went. Imperfect people found realness through the courage of a small boy to "speak the truth in love." Grace, mediated through loving acceptance, gives the "courage of imperfection," to use a phrase coined by Alfred Adler.[14]

Good family communication is a practical expression of our love. It is not unrelated to our love for God. "For he who does not love his brother whom he has seen, cannot love God whom he has not seen" (1 John 4:20b).

Can we afford pretense in our spiritual lives and our lives with one another? Do we not hunger for authentic existence? Are we not relieved when we can say what we feel instead of its opposite, when we are given the grace to cease groveling before what we dislike and dishonestly rejoicing over that which simply brings unnecessary pain upon the world and ourselves? In Christ we *are* new creatures, and the problem of the Christian life is realizing and becoming what we basically are. We do not have to

---

14. As quoted in Rollo May, *The Springs of Creative Living* (Nashville: Abingdon-Cokesbury, 1940), p. 103.

prove anything to find his salvation. When we feel we must prove our wisdom, or our goodness, or even our ability as parents, we become the "righteous" one, the Pharisee.

When we are given the courage to admit our mistakes to our children, they will know we have a God above ourselves. Some may argue that we must be examples to our children and therefore can never show our seamy side, but there is no warrant in the Bible for this common assumption. To be sure, we want to set before our children the best pattern of Christian life of which we are capable. But we do it not to *teach* them something, but simply because we want to be faithful to Jesus Christ. Furthermore, we cannot hide our flaws from children or from each other. The only example worth communicating is our constant dependence upon God's grace for our lives. The Christian parent learns to say with Noah in *The Green Pastures:* "I ain' very much, but I'se all I got."[15] Paradoxically, in the acceptance of his own poverty and God's grace, comes the courage to be real.

---

15. Marc Connelly, *The Green Pastures* (New York: Rinehart and Company, Inc., 1929), p. 68.

7
Family Unity and Personal Differences

When the minister said that in Christian marriage "the two become one," one man was heard to mutter, "Which one?" In many homes, the unwritten and unspoken contract seems to be: "Differences are bad. If we love each other, we will be alike. If you love me, you'll be like me," or "Because I love you, I'll be like you." Whatever else the unity of marriage may mean, it does *not* mean that personal individuality is lost. If anything, true personal identity is enhanced and encouraged by good marriage.

THE NEED TO RECOGNIZE DIFFERENTNESS

The Discovery of Differentness

In the "falling in love" stage of a relationship lovers normally show only a part of their personalities to each other; when the masks are dropped the couple may discover that they do not know each other very well after all. They may be surprised to discover that a Mr. Stay-at-home has married a Miss Keep-on-the-move; a Mr. Daring has said his vows to a Miss Cautious; a Mr. Tight-lip has been linked with a Miss Talk-it-over; and Mr. I-don't-feel-comfortable-unless-I-run-things has become the husband of a Miss I-don't-either!

Differences, whether in such superficial habits as the way we squeeze the toothpaste tube, or in deeper attitudes such as the meaning of money, cannot be submerged for long. It is soon discovered that Betty may consistently burn the toast or come to breakfast with her hair in curlers. And to the disgust of his wife, Jim leaves his dirty socks strewn around the bedroom and regards his paycheck as his own to allot as he chooses. The imaginative anticipations of the betrothal must give way to a willing recognition that we are just imperfect human beings. Some of the annoying features of the other's personality can be softened by good humor and mutual agreement, but a reforming attitude, if pushed too far, gives birth to smoldering or open resentment. As we shall see, some differences can be a source of enrichment to Christians in families.

When early in marriage a difference of opinion and habit may spill over into the first quarrel, the newly married couple may congratulate themselves that their marriage is actually under way and beginning to perform one of its functions! They are beginning to discover that they *do* live inside different skins and that there is, at last, a place where two real people can be what they are—human beings. Though they are painful, these first quarrels are not a tragedy. The tragedy occurs when the couple cannot find a way to combine the inevitable differences that must arise into a workable way of life.

Differentness there will be. How will we deal with it? Consider the following family activities and interests: family finances, recreation, ways of demonstrating affection, a system of values, friends, community activity, religious faith and church affiliation, in-law relations, sex relations, child-rearing philosophies. It is an unusual, even rare, family in which members see eye-to-eye on most of these issues. When disagreements arise around these aspects of family life, what happens? Does the discussion usually result in the husband giving in? the wife giving in? no decision being reached? the children taking over? agreement being reached by mutual give-and-take? the subject being changed?

There is no greater problem in marriage and family living than trying to combine our need for self-fulfillment and separate identity with our equally strong need for love and belonging.

Every marriage which lasts must work out the delicate balance of inevitable individuality and the desire for belonging. This is also true of a whole family. If individuality always reigns among family members, anarchy ensues and with it comes a great insecurity in the children which they will learn to cope with in strange, unpleasant ways. Yet too much emphasis upon *uni-*

formity also prompts them to react with fight, flight, or many other bodily symptoms.

The expression of true and honest feeling can be positive evidence that the family is secure enough to give us the freedom and ease to be ourselves even when those selves are irritated with one another. Such expression is dangerous only when the marriage is otherwise so fragile that it can be kept together only by superficial good manners. Such a family believes only in appearances, not in the God who is the source of its unity. It lives not by faith, but by fear.

The Denial of Differentness

It takes maturity to live comfortably with those who are not like oneself. The mature person has learned to live comfortably with himself, knowing that he is adequate to do something useful in the world and that he is worth something to someone about whom he cares. For the Christian, that "someone" is supremely his Heavenly Father. In contrast, the person with low self-esteem feels he has nothing to give; he fears that if the other finds out what he is on the inside that person will not love him or stay with him. It becomes necessary for the person who feels "empty" to seek his source of self-esteem almost entirely in his mate or children.

Tom and Mary met in a church young adult group and were almost immediately taken with each other. They started to date, confident that since they met at church their basic convictions about life were the same. Friends who introduced them were happy about their matchmaking: Tom and Mary seemed "right" for each other. Sharing many common interests, they found themselves engaged in playing tennis, listening to classical records, and going to church groups together. After a whirlwind six weeks of dating and courtship all rolled into one, they were married.

They saw something in each other which seemed to fit their high hopes. Tom acted self-confident and strong on the outside. Mary liked the way he spoke up and contributed to the discussion in their young adult group. She appreciated the way he always knew precisely where they should go on their dates. She felt that he was a strong person who could take care of her. This was a satisfying thought because she often felt uncertain and frightened on the inside. Tom saw Mary as a vivacious and cheerful person, easy in social contacts in contrast to his seriousness and anxiety over casual meetings. He thought, "Here is a mature, confident person who can give me what I need in my relations with others."

After marriage each found that the other was not the strong person hoped for, needed, and unfortunately, imagined. Frustration, disappointment, and anger were bound to result. Six years and one child later they were ready to separate. A church friend suggested that they see a Family Service counselor who helped them to reconstruct their lives and hopes together.[1]

Such persons bring both high expectations and great fears to marriage. Tom and Mary wanted to find in each other characteristics which they felt they lacked within themselves and within their early family life. Above all, they wanted the other's unqualified approval. When it did not come, or when the other person could not fulfill the image in which he had been cast, they were crushed, or felt angry and betrayed. Why? Because they each hoped to realize through the other what they had never found in themselves. And further, they had never been able to accept God's acceptance of them.

Both an overdependent mate and a domineering mate lack self-esteem. They believe that there is little within them that is worthwhile and that the source of all good is in the other person. For such a couple, marriage is an unwritten contract saying two contradictory things: "I am nothing; I will live for you," and also, "I am nothing; therefore, you must live for me completely." "We must live on the same bloodstream; we cannot afford to live in two different skins."

---

1. For many of these insights on the acceptance of differentness by husband and wife, I am indebted to Mrs. Virginia Satir, Director of the Training Program for Conjoint Family Therapy at the Mental Research Institute of Palo Alto, California. Her book elaborating these thoughts is *Conjoint Family Therapy* (Palo Alto: Science and Behavior Books, Inc., 1964).

Differentness is another way of saying "individuality." We were created as irreplaceable individuals, different from any who have gone before or who will appear again. This is a frightening thought to insecure people who have not realized that God considers each person to be a talented individual of unique worth. Differentness paralyzes them because difference in tastes, characteristics, and values are likely to lead to *disagreements*. Disagreement is seen as the mate's withdrawing his love from oneself. When disagreements arise, one feels as if he were thrown back on his own, robbed of the support needed for life. Lacking trust in each other, such mates feel secure only when there is outward agreement between them, whether it is genuine or not.

In the marriage of people with *low self-esteem,* there is an attempt to avoid any issues which would bring out a *difference of opinion.* As early as the honeymoon the newlyweds may begin to *not* discuss what they do not agree upon. They may feel the relationship is not yet strong enough to take a difference between them. The areas they cannot talk about will multiply. It is safe to express themselves only here and there. Spontaneity ceases and the calculated life grows. No longer can they be open with each other. "I can't mention that subject to my husband. It makes him furious," says one wife. Some couples find so many areas they "can't talk about" that they are almost mute. Others quarrel about everything, even things which should be merely a difference to be dealt with and worked through. To them "difference" means a competitive "fight" for survival. Their marriage is one long game of uproar. In both types of families *differentness* is considered *dangerous,* not something God has ordained which can enrich their lives by the creation of something greater than either of them can give alone.

Perhaps the victim of this situation most to be pitied is the child. He must be so much more than a child to such parents. He must be, for example, an extension of their own frustrated desires. John was a boy with budding artistic and musical talents judged far above average. Yet his father would constantly make remarks about these "sissy" activities within his hearing and was crushed when his son did not make Little League. He showed his disappointment in many ways and soon John could turn only to his mother for support. One may find it hard to understand the father's behavior until he discovers that from childhood on he had had grave doubts about his own manliness. He had been taunted by other boys and by his own father for his weakness. Now he is trying to be an ardent sports fan, hunter, and fisherman, not because he has a genuine interest in these activities, but because he is still trying to make up for childhood hurts and the deficit felt within his own life. He also strenuously avoids doing anything women would do, including washing the dishes. When his son does not want what he wants he is not only disappointed, but angry. Such a child's individuality is crushed or he limps through life never able to affirm what talents God has given him.

THE NEED FOR A BALANCE OF INDIVIDUALITY AND UNITY

A Foundation of Unity

The balance of individuality and group spirit in the family does not come automatically. A deliberate effort is needed to avoid both the anarchy of individual interests and the suffocation of always doing everything together. Some families do not structure enough time together to find out what the members are doing when away from home. The children have their school activities, clubs, and personal friendships. Father is preoccupied with his work and mother is absorbed in housework and community activities. Their days rarely intersect. Parents sometimes feel hopeless about this state of affairs and resign themselves too easily to a scattered kind of living which turns the bedrooms into dormitories and the kitchen into a filling station.

The needs of individuals change as the family develops and then contracts when children leave home. One of the tasks of Christian parenthood is to be able to size up how these changes can be taken into account in the job of keeping a sense of unity in the home. In mature Christian love, a husband and wife contribute to the continuous development of each other and, later, of the children. Such love is dynamic, always ready to change the form of the relationship and consistently willing the good of the other as the realities of life change in the family.

Although we may deplore the overemphasis upon group activity today, it is true that a "we" feeling develops primarily from "we" activities. Without something of a common life we become strangers to one another.

Frances Fowler tells of a childhood experience in which the sheer excitement of kite flying drew both grown-ups and children into a common world.

> Even our fathers dropped hoe and hammer and joined us. Our mothers took their turn, laughing like schoolgirls. Their hair blew out of their decorous pompadours and curled loose about their cheeks, their gingham aprons whipped about their legs. Mingled with our . . . delight was a feeling akin to awe. These adults were playing with us, really playing! . . . Once I looked at Mother and thought she looked actually pretty! And her over forty!
>
> We never knew where the hours went on that hilltop day. There were no hours, just a golden, breezy Now. I think we were all a little beyond ourselves. Parents forgot their duty and their dignity; children forgot the combativeness and small spites. "Perhaps it's like this in the Kingdom of Heaven," I thought confusedly. . . . [The author goes on to tell about the day this memory made her alter her activities and come out of her private world:]
>
> A good many years had passed, and one day I was flying about a kitchen of my own in a city apartment. I was trying to get some work out of the way while my three-year-old insistently whined her desire to "go park and see ducks."
>
> "I *can't* go! . . . I have this and this to do first, and when I'm through I'll be too tired to walk that far."
>
> My mother, who was visiting us, looked up from the peas she was shelling. "It's a wonderful day," she offered, "really warm, yet there's a fine, fresh breeze. It reminds me of that day we flew the kites."

I stopped in my dash between stove and sink. . . . I pulled off my apron. "Come on," I told my little girl. "You're right, it's too good a day to miss."[2]

A family must also *plan* in the midst of busy schedules to do some significant or enjoyable things together. Without purposeful planning, these increasingly rare times are crowded out by life's claims upon us and our conflicting interests. "Why do I have to go on the old picnic? John and I want to ride bikes," whines ten-year-old Mac. It is no easy task for the family recreation organizer, usually the mother, to satisfy the desires of all. She knows that you can lead a horse to water, but you can't make him drink. But, she might also reason that, if he tries a bit of it, he might find that he is thirsty! Every family has found some things which almost always click with the majority. And this takes effort and imagination, key ingredients in Christian love.

Few things can unite a family like planning something together, whether it be a yearly event like a vacation or a once- or twice-in-a-lifetime-project like a new home. As all the members of the family pour their ideas, desires, efforts, and talents into a plan, the group morale can grow perceptibly. And into the relationship of people who have planned, played, worked, and created together can be cemented a foundation for handling disagreements. Basic trust of each other grows out of such endeavors. Only a family which has become a community and found some ways of enjoying each other can afford to let real disagreements be expressed and dealt with honestly. Without a backlog of constructive, pleasant experiences, a family will find its disagreements—and parents their attempts at discipline— exploding into crises again and again. If a husband and wife have cultivated their leisure life together and have refused to let it be submerged by the distractions and demands of their busy existence, they will have a firmer ground on which to work out the inevitable differences that arise between them.

---

2. Frances Fowler, "The Day We Flew the Kites," *Parents' Magazine*, May 1949, 24:142. Published by Parents' Magazine Enterprises, Inc., 52 Vanderbilt Avenue, New York, N.Y. 10017.

A family which develops a strong bond of mutual interests and continues to develop them and add new ones can afford to cultivate separate interests. Both mutual endeavor and separate leisure are necessary to keep married love alive. The poet Gibran has put it beautifully:

> But let there be spaces in your togetherness,
> And let the winds of the heavens dance between you.
> Love one another, but make not a bond of love:
> Let it rather be a moving sea between the shores of your souls.
> Fill each other's cup but drink not from one cup.
> Give one another of your bread but eat not from the same loaf.
> Sing and dance together and be joyous, but let each one of you be alone,
> Even as the strings of a lute are alone though they quiver with the same music.[3]

Differentness Within Unity

The picture of the body of Christ in Ephesians (and also in 1 Corinthians 12 and 13) is a clue to what the family that claims to be Christian might be. It is a portrait of a group with a variety of gifts and temperaments and with one Spirit cementing them together.

> I therefore, a prisoner for the Lord, beg you to lead a life worthy of the calling to which you have been called, with all lowliness and meekness, with patience, forbearing one another in love, eager to maintain the unity of the Spirit in the bond of peace. There is one body and one Spirit, just as you were called to the one hope that belongs to your call, one Lord, one faith, one baptism, one God and Father of us all, who is above all and through all and in all. But grace was given to each of us according to the measure of Christ's gift. . . . And his gifts were that some should be apostles, some

---

3. Kahlil Gibran, *The Prophet* (New York: Alfred A. Knopf, Inc., 1923 and 1951), pp. 15–16.

prophets, some evangelists, some pastors and teachers, for the equipment of the saints, for the work of ministry, for building up the body of Christ, until we all attain to the unity of the faith and of the knowledge of the Son of God, to mature manhood, to the measure of the stature of the fullness of Christ . . . speaking the truth in love, we are to grow up in every way into him who is the head, into Christ, from whom the whole body, joined and knit together by every joint with which it is supplied, when each part is working properly, makes bodily growth and upbuilds itself in love (Ephesians 4:1-7, 11-13, 15-16).

Here we see that the church, and therefore the church-in-the-home, is not a structure in which identical parts fit like cogs in a machine. Nor is it a loose aggregate of individuals, each going his own way without a central unifying relationship and Spirit. Rather, it is a remarkable balance of individuality and unity which Christ brings into his church. In the same way, the family is neither a body reflecting the ideas and will of only one member, nor a group of individuals whose personal preferences always take precedence over those of others. It is in the family that children and parents learn how to get along with human beings who differ from them in sex, age, and temperament, how to give-and-take, how to be a part of a complex whole and make a unique personal contribution.

Sometimes the importance of these disciplines is not recognized in the American home, where there is a strong emphasis on the rights of the individual child who must have his own room, his own toys, and his own radio or TV. Children are not given enough practice, for example, in sharing a room and working out compromises between the one who wants to play records and the one who wants to do serious reading. Parents who can avoid collisions by simply providing separate radios, television sets, and even telephones do not recognize how valuable it is to learn to come to agreements over the use of these things. If this valuable lesson in the art of growing to maturity is missed, will these youngsters be ready for the necessary compromises of marriage?

From this key passage on the nature of the church we learn that there can be an interlocking pattern of different individuals with various needs and talents *because they were bound by something in common*—"one hope that belongs to your call, one Lord, one faith, one baptism, one God and Father of us all . . ." In marriage, it is imperative that husband and wife achieve some agreement about their ultimate values and loyalties. Otherwise, they will be divided on many practical points, such as their use of time and money, their respective responsibilities in keeping the family group going, their goals for their children, and the purpose of their life as a team.

Agreement about basic values is closely related to marital success, but it must not be assumed that a husband and wife need to be alike in all aspects of their loyalty to ultimate values. The important thing is that they are working *toward* understanding their basic commitments and sharing them with each other. (We must not jump to the conclusion that "if only I can get him to go to church with me" the issue is settled. Religious activity may have a uniting effect, but it can also be disruptive as each clarifies his real convictions.) A couple must face Christianity, not as something they are related to because of their children, but as something which has meaning for themselves. And they cannot afford to wait until the "empty nest" stage to do this soul-searching; some degree of shared commitment is essential to their unity all through the years of their marriage and family development.

THE NEED FOR PARENTAL TEAMWORK

Parents come in pairs for a reason. A child needs the *teamwork* of a loving mother and father. Fathers and mothers bring different gifts to the arduous tasks of raising their offspring. A child with but one parent is robbed of more than half of his education in the family, and maybe more.

Agreement on how to raise their children is a crucial part of parental teamwork. What do they want their children to be like? What do they see as each other's responsibility in planning for and rearing the children? How do they set rules for the children to follow? Who enforces them and how? A lack of agreement on the answers to these questions can create a tension in or reflect an already existing tension in the relationship of the husband and wife.

When we ask why parents cannot agree on child discipline and other such matters, two possible answers suggest themselves:

First, fathers and mothers bring notions about rearing children out of their own childhood family experiences. More often than we realize, our memories of our parents' practices influence our present viewpoints and actions, positively or negatively. For example, Mary saw her mother as the "head" of the family, confidently directing all family members and extremely solicitous about their welfare. The children were considered frail little people, needing to be protected against the harshness of life. She and her sister were rigidly supervised, and it was difficult for them to do things on their own and to "stretch their wings" as they matured. Mary may not think much about the effect of her mother's practices, but it is almost inevitable that she, too, will be overprotective of her children. Her husband, Tom, on the other hand, had a father and mother who both worked outside the home. As a boy he often took care of himself. He, too, knew that life was rough, but, unlike his wife, he had to make his own way through it. He feels his youngsters, especially his boys, should fight their own battles and not be protected from them. Tom is amazed that his wife seems to want their children to become sissies or at least hothouse plants—and says so. Mary is shocked that Tom would let the children be exposed to the dangers of life so early. Is he a sadist, she asks? Truly, our own childhood experiences do form our ideas of child rearing.

Coming as we do from such different backgrounds, the task of integrating our concepts of child rearing often is not easy. In courtship or early marriage it may appear that we are compatible in our ideas about rearing children, but the real test comes when the children arrive. Our deepest thoughts and values come into play then, often revealing more differentness between us than we had suspected. It was this kind of discovery that led Thomas

Fuller to warn, "Deceive not thy self by overexpecting happiness in the married estate. Remember the nightingales which sing only some months in the spring, but commonly are silent when they have hatched their eggs!"[4] Yet two married people who respect each other and are warmly in love can, by open communication and patient effort, come to basic agreements which are not mere reflections of their own early home life, but a product of their own thoughtful discussion and unique aspirations for their children.

If husband and wife are on good terms and tend to see life in the same way, their intelligence will lead them to adopt common standards and rules of behavior as well as consistent means for enforcing that behavior. They try to avoid those situations that would belittle their mate in the eyes of their children. They cooperate with each other in working out what they genuinely feel is best for their children.

Problems of parenthood frequently represent problems in the marriage. Once again we can see the Christian emphasis upon the husband-wife relationship as crucial to the life of the family confirmed in our daily living. If father and mother quarrel frequently about the discipline of the children, there may be a deeper problem. What seems to be simply a difference of opinion may be a marital struggle between the husband and wife. They may be hitting out at each other by differing on what the child should be allowed to do and how he should be disciplined. Without being aware of it, they are making the child a scapegoat in order to express their mutual disappointments in each other. In severe marital conflict, the child may develop "sick behavior" or "problem behavior" in order to take the attention off of his parents' conflict and focus it upon his own. When a couple solves the more basic problem, this conflict over child rearing generally clears up.

One can understand why attempts at Christian nurture of children in the family go amiss, why parents who are noted for their individual piety fail in the religious training of their

---

4. Thomas Fuller, "Of Marriage," *The Wit and Wisdom of Thomas Fuller* (London: The Religious Tract Society, n.d.).

children. Parents may be ever so diligent in taking the children to church school, and in carrying out religious practices at home, but something does not ring true to the child. The sacred name of Jesus Christ may be uttered frequently, but somehow the *language of relationships* in the family does not match the language of words. A father and mother may think they can hide their own disappointment and dissatisfaction with each other from the children, but they cannot. Perhaps the parents' most important gift to the child is their own willingness to first "be reconciled . . . and then come and offer your gift" (Matthew 5:24). Fortunately, one mate with enough courage can start the process. The New Testament affirms that one "believing" member sanctifies the whole household. That is one of the most tremendous things that the Bible says about marriage.

8

Christians and Creative Conflict

Vera: "Look at that ad, Ted. I had no idea they were that expensive. Even on special, they're expensive. That's Logan Brothers for you.

Ted: Well, then, that ought to settle it.

Vera: Settle what?

Ted: They're too expensive.

Vera: I didn't say they were *too* expensive. I just said they were expensive.

Ted: Then that's too expensive.

Vera (*voice rising*): We seem to have enough money for the things you want! And when I want to make our home a real family place, then it's too expensive.

Ted: Now Vera, I don't think that's fair. We can't just go out and buy curtains for the house like this without considering where the money is coming from. In my home, Mom and Dad used to work out the major purchases together.

Vera: I know, Ted, but if *we* did that, I'd never get any of the things I want.

Ted (*trying to change the subject*): Vera, let's talk about this after dinner. What are we going to have?

Vera: Well, it won't be much. I'm not in any mood to cook.[1]

Disagreement is inevitable at many points in marriage and family living. Anyone who observes life closely or studies the

---

1. This episode was contributed by the Rev. James C. Huffstutler.

Bible will be aware of this. But unlike many modern people who think of "harmony in living," the Bible speaks of *alienation and reconciliation*. In its doctrine of the Fall of Man, Christian faith, when applied to marriage and family matters, means that family members will sometimes be *competitors* as well as helpers and complements to one another.

Such a realistic observation does not mean that we must rest easy with this state of affairs. The loneliness which comes from self-imposed distance can crush the human spirit. We are eager to know how we can reduce the personal hurt, recrimination, retaliation, and cleavage in the relationship. When hurt does come, we want to discover the meaning and dynamics of reconciliation.

The person whose understanding incorporates the biblical view of life is not dismayed by the presence of hurt and hostility in human relations. The author of Ephesians, who gave us his profound concept of the body of Christ, also knew that there would be stress and strains in the body. He dealt with both the reality of hostility among the members and the new reality of reconciliation in Jesus Christ. Writing from prison, Paul was well aware that a difference in views could land one in trouble!

The earlier chapters of Ephesians tell of the new family of God which comes into being through Christ's reconciliation. The old barriers which divide us are broken down. (For the Ephesians, these were chiefly the barriers dividing Jew and Gentile.) We are now one in Christ. We know, therefore, what it means to pass from the living death of separation from God and each other to the new life which unites us. Only the love of God toward us makes this possible; we cannot bridge the gap. In response to God's acceptance of us, we are to continue this ministry of reconciliation with each other and with the stranger (Ephesians 2:1–16).

This letter which so completely links faith and practical action speaks to contemporary family tensions. The last three chapters are devoted to the matters of home life. Let us look at how intensely practical this theological understanding is for our own family affairs.

THE REALITY OF ANGER

The Need to Express Anger

Angry reactions are inevitable in a Christian's life. Those who say, "But Christians are not supposed to be angry" may be shocked by the words, "Be angry but do not sin; do not let the sun go down on your anger, and give no opportunity to the devil" (Ephesians 4:26-27).

Until the Kingdom comes in its fullness, anger will be a part of our lives, especially in the closeness of the family. It inevitably emerges as a group of people seek to build a common life. Personal intimacy is not possible without some conflict, and occasionally this conflict spills over into angry words of heat and rejection.

Some people are so afraid of anger that they cannot recognize it in themselves. If we think that we are above this emotion and have denied it, we must remember that it was said of our Lord, "And he looked around at them [those who would prevent him from healing a man on the sabbath] *with anger,* grieved at their hardness of heart" (Mark 3:5). Our anger does not often have its roots in this kind of altruism; we most often get angry when personal goals are thwarted, when we are deprived of self-direction, when we have our pride wounded and our self-picture shattered, and when our self-esteem is threatened.

There is probably nothing in the family which disturbs parents as much as fighting and dissension between brothers and sisters. "Sibling rivalry" is as old as the human race. We are aware of the poignant stories of Cain and Abel, Joseph and his brothers, and Jacob and Esau in the Old Testament. We cannot miss seeing and feeling the resentment of the older brother in Jesus' parable of the Prodigal Son. The jealousy of brothers and sisters is a continuing theme in the world's literature. Even after they are adults, people still feel the pangs of resentment toward brothers and sisters which was built up in childhood.

So anxious are parents about the relationships between their children that they may overlook the constructive features of some anger and quarreling. Perhaps parents are too conscious of what an ideal home "ought to be" to be able to see what a service siblings might render each other in fighting. We all have negative feelings at times and one of our problems is finding the right outlet for them. Personally frustrated, we look for a target for our anger—another person, group, race, or country. Brothers and sisters serve each other by being available objects for temporary anger. The child soon learns that hostility expressed toward a sibling is less dangerous than an expression of hostility toward an adult. Furthermore, he feels safer when his anger toward his brother or sister is protected by parental limitation. He knows he can be stopped and feels safety in this. Parents should look upon these quarrels and fights among children as growing pains and learning experiences instead of breaches in relationships. It is possible to "be . . . angry, and sin not" (Ephesians 4:26; K.J.V.). Parents should try to discover what follows the quarrels. Do the quarrels help the children to know how they are different from one another and thus encourage a sharpening of individual identity? Do they teach the value of settling conflict by compromise? Do they lead to long-time estrangement, or are they followed by periods of friendliness and mutual helpfulness? Does the friction extend to many areas of living or to only a few? If a child is in constant conflict with his brothers and sisters in *all* areas of childhood experience, parents might well seek help from child guidance counselors.

Living with a sibling can teach one many lessons. One of the most important is learning to get along with someone you may at times strongly dislike, although there are some things that make you fond of him. "Idealism" has perpetuated the myth that one must either like a person completely or dislike him entirely. This is an illusion that Christians, understanding the doctrine of the Fall of Man, should be able to see through more easily than others. No matter how much we like someone, there is always something about him that can irritate us. The problem is learning to live with *both* kinds of feelings at once, positive liking and annoyance or even anger.

It is tragic when Christians feel that there is no room for anything but strictly positive feelings toward spouse, aging parents, or children. They fail to realize that anger is universal, and all human beings express it at times, either directly or indirectly.

As human beings, we have to find expression for both love needs and aggressive needs; they are often manifested together. After a particularly frustrating evening in which a little girl was forbidden something she wanted, she placed this note on her mother's pillow:

> Dear Mommy,
> I hate you.
> Love,
> Nancy

Here is healthy honesty.

The normal quarreling of children can teach us something about anger. Although parents may be overwhelmed by the competitive struggle, children often regard it much less seriously. One college girl, looking back on her quarrels with her sister, tells us what it was like:

> . . . We would just argue about little things like that, and I know when mom or dad would go away somewhere, we used to sit there all night and argue—and love it! . . . Sometimes mother would yell from the kitchen, 'Stop arguing over nothing.' We'd try to tell her we weren't arguing, we were just fooling around or were just kidding each other . . ."[2]

Quarreling is usually only a *part* of the relationship. If, when they are not fighting, children do something together which is fun, or gang up with each other against some threat from the outside, such as a neighbor or parent, then it is possible that they are learning, in a stormy fashion, to get along with someone they do not like all of the time.

Parental attitudes and practices may have much to do with sibling quarrels. The favoritism of a parent for one child over

---

2. From the author's case records of counseling done at Mental Research Institute, Palo Alto, California.

another (remember the Jacob and Esau story); the intolerance of any aggression in family relations; and the feeling that one is failing as a parent can make the situation worse. If it were not for adult horror at such strife, children would forgive each other and start over sooner than most parents think. To remember that children are learning to handle aggression in a fairly safe relationship would be reassuring to the anxious parents. But if quarreling is serious, and persistent, and the children never have any good times together, it is time to find out what the trouble is.

Anger can have causes which have little or no connection with our "targets." If we have had a tense day at the office or at school, we may displace that anger to the safety of our homes. The recipient of such wrath will be justifiably puzzled and ask, "What did I do to deserve this?"

When we are angry with ourselves for some failure or are ashamed of our behavior, we are like sore toes ready to be stepped on. When our threshold is low it does not take much to make us angry. We must find out what makes us feel uneasy with *ourselves*.

The basic reason for anger is what we see as an attack, through action or word, upon the picture that we hold of ourselves. We all want to keep an image of ourselves as *people who are worth loving and who can achieve something*. When we repeatedly hear or see others say and do things that deny this image, we want to destroy that which would destroy us. Because we may see or hear what was not intended by the communicator, we must learn to find out what was really meant. We can absorb occasional barbed jokes and sarcasm if we are confident of a solid relationship which includes expressions of endearment and the enjoyment of many things together.

The biblical author admits the inevitability of occasional anger in saying "Be angry but do not sin; do not let the sun go down on your anger." Do not let it disrupt your relationship; find a way back to each other. And do it quickly, before the day is over.

When we let resentment grow and simmer, it builds up day after day until, in some situations, even the cause is forgotten and the devil gets a foothold on us. Once we let go of the pride which lets us think that we never feel anger, we can come to recognize it in ourselves. And once we recognize it, we can learn to tell those who have made us angry how we feel and to ask why they feel the way they do toward us. Never go to bed angry. Evening prayers might well be accompanied by mutual confession of mate with mate, parent with child. Such an act can clear the air and bring us together again in warm expressions of love.

The Need to Resolve Anger

Separation and Silence. God in Christ keeps us together when we want to run away. "But now in Christ Jesus you who once were far off have been brought near in the blood of Christ" (Ephesians 2:13).

It is natural for human beings who sense a difference between them to separate. We naturally come together with those who are like us and are naturally distant to those unlike us. This is true in politics, religion, and race. So it was with the Jew and Gentile until they realized the reconciliation brought by Jesus Christ.

In family life, too, when the differentness of individuals spills over into disagreements, there is a tendency to move apart and keep out of contact, at least emotionally. We may grow silent, or change the subject, or not even "hear" what has been said that disagrees with our position. We also run away physically. In spite of all the talk of "togetherness," in times of tension, our tolerance for being close lessens. We get very "busy"; we attend a great many meetings and are preoccupied with important issues in order to avoid confronting the one closest to us. We are ingenious in devising ways of staying away from the very conversations which might see a problem through. As Charlie Brown of the *Peanuts* comic strip concludes: "There's no problem so big that you can't run away from it."[3] In-law tensions, differences in the

---

3. From Peanuts. By permission United Feature Syndicate.

handling of money or children, sexual maladjustments (which usually *reflect* other strains and hurts rather than *cause* them) are all painful topics. We escape them by pulling apart. We often say that we do not discuss these things because we do not want to hurt our mate, when *we* are the ones who do not wish to be hurt, and who expect to be hurt if a difference of feeling or view is raised. For some families, this avoidance becomes a rule of life which is passed on to the children: "When you feel a real difference don't express it. Gloss it over or move away; it's safer." In families who are afraid of their differentness and do not know that in Christ they can learn to use that differentness creatively, there is a tendency for each member to live in a separate sphere of life. A mother's "living for her child" and her husband's complete absorption in his job are only two ways people try to avoid this problem.

The Christian should know that facing issues squarely is the only way to live in unity and that in Christ even extreme differences need not break our love. He died that the natural barriers in our lives might be overcome by his love for each of us as we are now and for what we will become.

Speaking the Truth in Love. In an honest relationship of love, real issues between us must be raised. "Speaking the truth in love, we are to grow up in every way into him who is the head . . ." (Ephesians 4:15). "Therefore, *putting away falsehood,* let every one speak the truth with his neighbor, for we are members one of another" (Ephesians 4:25; author's italics). One wife says, "It's exasperating. He'll go into his shell and not say much to me for a week. But he'll never tell me what he's got against me. It's hard to live with that kind of sulkiness." How false it is to pretend that everything is all right when it is not, to convince ourselves that our annoyance is only a trifle which will pass, when it keeps gnawing away at our feelings of well-being.

Irritated with a member of the family, we will inevitably express our annoyance, directly or indirectly, in various ways. If one undiscussed "trifle" is added to another until one day an explosion occurs, it will be quite out of proportion to the initial offense. Anger might also be expressed outwardly by a lack of enthusiasm about plans made, by neglecting the usual expressions of affection, and by apathy and fatigue, or it may be turned inward to break out finally in a variety of psychosomatic disorders, including ulcers, headaches, and asthma. In these situations the nonverbal behavior of a family member *contradicts* his verbal response. When he said "Let what you say be simply 'Yes' or 'No'" (Matthew 5:37), Jesus was saying that love means what it says and says what it means. We are to *speak the truth* in love. This is the opposite of contradictory or indirect or incomplete communication. A noted family therapist reports that many families who are troubled or have an emotionally disturbed member are also unable to communicate fully the "truth" that is within them. They have inside thoughts which never get into words. The following excerpts are examples:

Mother: "They never help around the house."
Therapist: "You mean the kids?"
Mother: "Yes."
Therapist: "Have you told them what you want them to do?"
Mother: "Well, I think so. They're supposed to know."
Therapist: "But have you *told* them?"
Mother: "Well, no."

* * * * * * * * * *

Husband: "She never comes up to me and kisses me. I am always the one to make the overtures."
Therapist: "Is this the way you see yourself behaving with your husband?"
Wife: "Yes, I would say he is the demonstrative one. I didn't know he wanted me to make the overtures."
Therapist: "Have you told your wife that you would like this from her—more open demonstration of affection?"
Husband: "Well, no, you'd think she'd know."
Wife: "No, how would I know? You always said you didn't like aggressive women."

Husband: "I don't, I don't like *dominating* women."
Wife: "Well, I thought you meant women who make the overtures. How am I to know what you want?"
Therapist: "You'd have a better idea if he had been able to *tell* you."[4]

The way we raise issues with one another is important. "Speaking the truth *in love*." The second half of the statement is as important as the first. It does not imply that we must raise every issue with a smile on our face; that would negate the truth we feel inwardly.

Christians are called to discuss their disagreements in such a way that the relationship is not disrupted although they may sometimes be hurt by the charges made. Can they be communicated in a spirit which will give the promise of a better relationship among us?

Some ways of communicating are guaranteed to bring trouble. One of these is accusation without an opportunity for explanation. A tone of voice which conveys personal vindictiveness or a feeling that the other person is without worth is an attack on his self-image and will almost always bring retaliation or withdrawal or both. Wounded pride quickly brings a fight with, or flight from, the attacker. Nagging and constant complaining is also destructive to our relationships. To "gnaw" at a person without letup, to fight a war of attrition does not face an issue fully and forthrightly. When nagging comes high on a husband's list of complaints about his wife, at least part of the reason for her nagging may be his failure to give her a full and thorough hearing about matters which concern her.

Christians need to learn the fine art of interpreting their own feelings to each other: "I'm annoyed at the way you are always late for dinner" is infinitely better than "You inconsiderate beast!" "Something is wrong with our mealtime schedule, I think," can get further toward resolution than "You'll just have to make more

---

4. Virginia Satir, *Conjoint Family Therapy* (Palo Alto: Science and Behavior Books, Inc., 1964), pp. 72–73.

of an effort to get home on time," or "You'll have to give up that after-school activity." Love gives us the courage to listen to another's personal situation and the willingness to understand how he feels about it. Blaming, exploding, and attacking prohibit an understanding and clarification of the problem, as well as the making of good decisions.

"Walk in love, as Christ loved us" (Ephesians 5:2). As God in Christ experienced our human life from the inside, so Christians are to empathically sense the situation of another. We may be tempted to indulge in wild guesses about the other person's behavior. Almost nothing can strain relations like assuming you know the "why" of the other's behavior and then hurling your interpretation at him. When we try to understand what he thinks is happening *from his point of view,* we are on safer ground. Can we dare understand the pressures, anxieties, and possible suffering we would feel in his position? That kind of courage is born of Christian love.

Humility and Patience. A Christian response to disagreements includes a willingness to be patient in working out a solution. ". . . With all lowliness and meekness, with patience, forbearing one another in love" (Ephesians 4:2). Or as J. B. Phillips translates this verse: "Accept life with humility and patience, making allowances for one another because you love one another."

Humility does not mean that we should doubt our own worth or grovel in the dust of another's opinions. In thinking about disagreements, humility means that one is willing to entertain both the idea that he is not always right and the idea that one is never *all* right in a complex personal struggle. To be humble is to be teachable. The opposite attitude is demonstrated in this verse:

>In matters controversial
>My perception is quite fine.
>I always see both points of view—
>The one that's wrong—and mine.

The willingness to exchange information, feelings, and ideas with one another leads to mutual understanding. Our first idea about a problem will not always be the same as our later understandings of it. As new ideas are expressed and the discussion develops, the issues may change.

In the authoritarian pattern of decision making, one partner makes the important decisions about major purchases, family plans, or jobs, and expects the other to acquiesce to him. When the subordinate member gets the message, "Your ideas are of no worth to me," from the autocrat, resentment will grow and be expressed in many indirect ways. Humility calls for most basic decisions to be made in collaboration with each other.

Money management, for example, always calls for genuine partnership in marriage. Until husband and wife get together on what they value, they will have difficult going. Many couples have difficulty because one regards the money he (or she) earns as private property instead of a joint trust. They may even keep separate bank accounts. To this extent, they are living private, not married, lives. Collaborating with each other in trust about overspending problems, a husband and wife can agree to put up with a good deal of privation *if one does not accuse and blame the other.* If one mate feels deprived by the other there is little room left for feelings of love and respect.

Patience is the other ingredient of which the book of Ephesians reminds us as we struggle to reconcile our differences. In the New Testament, one Greek word translated "patience" speaks of endurance, standing in the face of difficulty without losing heart (James 5:11; k.j.v.). We might ask ourselves, "How important will this be five years from now? Do I want an immediate victory which would vindicate me or a solid long-term relationship?"

The word "patience" is also derived from another Greek word which means waiting until the appointed time without a flurry of excitement and panic. We know that we cannot hurry our children's growth, yet how often do we expect a three-year-old to act as if he were eight and an adolescent as if he were thirty? Patience is the ability to allow them to be children and not expect them to be adults. Christian parents often expect them to be wiser and better behaved than is the nature of a child. And so we nag and find fault and criticize. How wise Paul was when he wrote, "Fathers, don't overcorrect your children, or they will grow up feeling inferior and frustrated" (Colossians 3:21; Phillips translation). This does not mean that there should be no guidance. Rather, the parents must balance their correction with encouragement.

Very often our anger is an expression of our *impatience with ourselves*. Disenchantment is often the plight of the young couple a few months or a few years after their marriage. It is not primarily the result of the unromantic facts they learn in the course of their daily lives together. More often, the source of disillusionment is the recognition that they are left with the same old selves that they have lived with for years. They had hoped that marriage would change them radically. Sometimes it does, but more often they find the same faults they had before and become discouraged and disgruntled.

We are told to "grow in . . . grace" (2 Peter 3:18). Growth is slow spiritually and emotionally even as it is in bodily development and mental grasp. It is our business to go on quietly learning how to better develop our competence in working through our controversies as we give him time to do his work in us. If we try to make haste, in our impatience we may regress instead of grow as loving persons.

THE REALITY OF GOD'S FORGIVENESS

God's forgiveness enables a Christian to find his way back to the one from whom he is alienated. "Let there be no more resentment, no more anger or temper, no more violent self-assertiveness, no more slander and no more malicious remarks. Be kind to one another; be understanding. Be as ready to forgive others as God for Christ's sake has forgiven you" (Ephesians 4:31-32; Phillips translation).

The grace of God's forgiveness can be grossly misunderstood and misused by families. A person may say to one who has hurt him, "I forgive you." But his attitude may reflect superiority and hostility, so that he is actually communicating, "It is I who have been hurt and it is you who are to blame. I will be an unselfish person and condescend to let you come back to me." This kind of "forgiveness" can generate more anger than was present before!

No one who understands himself and a Christian view of man can regard himself as one without guilt and responsibility for alienation. The honest woman may begin to realize that her own coldness was at least a part of the reason for her husband's adultery. The courageous husband will find out how he is involved in his wife's constant unhappiness. The discerning parent may begin to see that in some very subtle ways he has contributed to his child's inability to concentrate or make friends in school. We are members of one another and we are each involved in the other's life. To label one partner in a divorce "guilty" and the other "innocent" is a denial of the Christian understanding of man. We need mutual forgiveness which acknowledges that both people are guilty, that both must forgive and be forgiven. Such forgiveness comes only from God. This is a hard fact to accept. But the realization of our own sin and God's forgiveness enables us to forgive one another.

Real forgiveness costs; it hurts. He who forgives, *gives himself for the other* in spite of hurt and sin. He regards the act with dead seriousness. He does not make light of the sin or say that it does not matter. If one can talk lightly of forgiveness he is not forgiving; he is condoning something that he does not take seriously. When we love one whom we know has hurt another and himself and God, we are tempted to excuse rather than forgive. It is impossible to be forgiving without acknowledging both the seriousness of sin and our involvement in it, and the forgiveness of God for both ourselves and the other.

Christ went to the depths of suffering in his forgiveness. No one saw so clearly how we hurt one another and God. Yet, through the cross, bearing the pain of our self-centeredness, he made it possible for us to be forgiven. To realize his cost enables us to bear the cost of forgiving one another. It will continue to cost us. God's forgiveness restores those who are alienated. It does not take away the fact of sin or its consequences. It does not take away the memory of sin; the Prodigal would never forget his exploits in the far country. God reestablishes the relationship which has been broken by our sin. When we experience this reconciliation, we are able to share it with those who are separated from us.

Reconciliation is what we want at the depth of our being. This is affirmed in all high religion, all good fiction, all psychiatry, and is confirmed in personal experience. From infancy on, we are engaged in the long process of conflict and reconciliation. As lovers, we assert ourselves against the beloved and wound each other. Then, in the moment of making up, of accepting mutual forgiveness, we find more keenly than before the joy of losing ourselves in the love of another. We have been restored to each other. How can we accomplish this miracle without first appropriating the miracle of God's forgiveness of us in spite of our unworthiness? "For he is our peace, who has made us both one, and has broken down the dividing wall of hostility" (Ephesians 2:14).

Realized forgiveness creates a growing desire to upbuild each other in love. "Let no evil talk come out of your mouths, but only such as is good for edifying [building up], as fits the occasion, that it may impart grace to those who hear" (Ephesians 4:29).

When one has realized forgiveness he will offer support to other human beings who are suffering. They, too, are struggling to maintain their integrity and confidence and to defend themselves against hurt. Can we enter into their lives and try to understand them and with them find the reasons for their unpleasant behavior? Can we encourage them by emphasizing their strengths instead of their weaknesses? In working with "under-achieving" school children, or with children who lean toward delinquency, I have been impressed with the attitude of their parents. They usually correct, blame, or accuse the child far more than they encourage or praise or express hope. Everyone needs the presence of persons who discover the good in us and will say so. Some parents feel that it will "spoil" a child to compliment him for something well done. However, it is often the demanding child and the one who brags who are *not* nourished with "upbuilding talk" and so must struggle to find their self-esteem.

Keeping married love alive is not difficult for those who

refuse to take each other for granted. When we begin to expect what our mate does for us as a "right," we sometimes forget to thank our spouse for a good meal, for her constant care of the children, for his steadfastness at his bread-winning job, and the multitude of helpful actions on our behalf. Were it not for our covenant of love, we might have been tempted to quit at times. A word of thanks, a thoughtful act of kindness, a habit of appreciation by mates or children is never amiss. Little things like these help us feel that our cup is running over and that married love is worth all the sacrifice it may involve. The endurance of family members, the steadfastness of their love, is increased a hundredfold by "upbuilding" speech.

WHEN PROFESSIONAL HELP IS NEEDED

There are families in which the members become so alienated from one another that all of their energies are given over to self-defense instead of creative conflict. Husbands and wives can be so threatened by each other that almost any issue becomes a battleground for them. Parents can become so exasperated with their children, and children with their parents, that their relationship has become one long uproar. When family members are compelled to run away from each other in order to get along, it is wise to turn to competent outside guidance before things reach the point of permanent disruption and a loss of all affection. Sometimes it is difficult to know whether a marital problem or a child's problem is one that time can overcome or whether it will continue to plague you and the family. When one is really in doubt, neighbors, friends, and relatives who are so free with advice cannot be of much help. It is the better part of wisdom to seek out professional assistance.

Many parents who are overwhelmed by guilt about their child's problem and confusion about their own problems are amazed to discover that trained, professional people do not think in terms of blaming someone or something for the difficulty. People brought up in an extremely moralistic atmosphere may find it difficult to believe that they will find sympathy instead of harsh judgment. But professional people have as their only aim the alleviation of the distressing behavior and the fostering of self-understanding.

Christian people may be reluctant to seek help outside of the family because they feel that their "faith" ought to bring them through any problem. Genuine faith *does* play a part in the solution of all problems. Such faith, however, should not be confused with the pride that makes us reluctant to admit that our dilemma is quite beyond our understanding or management.[5] It is the Christian understanding of life that we are members of one another, that we need one another, and that none of us is self-sufficient.

If we suspect that our family needs special help, whom should we see? Most people first see the pastor or family physician to get ideas about the problems and information about whom they might go to for help. Many pastors and most doctors have made a study of the available resources of the local community, the county, schools, or public health service. Because it is so easy to fall into the hands of "quacks," it is important for the pastor and parent to be able to make a judgment about existing services. But it is not the parents' job to discover what *kind* of treatment is needed; that is the task of the professional. If there is a Family Service Agency in town, it is usually the best place to go.

How can we judge a good counseling service?

- It makes a careful study before expressing a judgment about the problem.
- It does not promise quick results or tell you precisely how long it will take to alleviate the difficulty.
- It uses only professionally trained workers who have specialized in such fields as psychiatry, sociology, psychology, or pastoral counseling. They have a master's degree and often a doctor's degree in the area of their competence.

---

5. One can find warning signs which indicate that professional help is needed in an excellent pamphlet by Greta Meyer and Mary Hoover, "When children need special help with emotional problems" (New York: The Child Study Association of America, 1961). It is available from the Child Study Association of America, 9 East 89th Street, New York 28, New York.

- It charges nominal fees which are always frankly and openly discussed with the patient or parents.
- It is affiliated with reliable local and national organizations designed to keep high standards and ethical practices in the respective professions; for example, the National Conference of Social Work, the American Psychological Association, the American Association of Marriage Counselors, or the American Association of Pastoral Counselors.
- It does not advertise its services, but relies upon referrals from established professional people and its own former clientele. However, the agencies and personnel may be listed in the telephone directory.

Difficult as the step might be, seeking professional help can be a sign of love and an expression of faith in God's provision of people who can help with distressing family situations. Many friends and relatives will not understand one's decision to get help. But this is not their decision. It is his who is a steward of God for the family's well-being and the child's happiness and usefulness in God's world. To see each family member grow as a mature man or woman with a capacity to love and work productively and serve his Lord will be compensation enough for the embarrassment and opposition which might have to be faced. But then, Christians have never been promised immunity from suffering—or from joyful victory.

9
Decision Making and Discipleship

Consider a husband sitting in his favorite living room chair on a Sunday afternoon. As he glances through the Sunday newspaper, he is stopped by a full-color advertisement of the new model of his favorite automobile. Entranced, he reads every word beneath the picture and leans back, wondering to himself about the possibility of such a pleasant purchase for his family this year. If one could observe Mr. Adam's mental processes, he might see a cerebral tug-of-war taking place—pushes toward the purchase of a new car and pulls away from such an investment.

Encouraging Mr. Adam toward the dealer's showroom is his awareness that his neighbor, Mr. Jones, has just purchased a new car. He is sure that if Mr. Jones could handle such a transaction financially so could he. Furthermore, pressure from his children has not made living next to the Jones' and their new car any easier. The two families take turns transporting the youngsters to church school. When it is the Jones' turn, the children come home talking excitedly about the new pushbuttons and the smooth ride. In a tone of disgust his teen-ager compares the new car's power with the difficulty of getting their "old clunk" to move. Mr. Adam has to admit that this is a point worth considering. When the car was new he could not be passed on the highway or at a stop light. Now he finds it rather intolerable to be poking behind most cars on a super highway. The old bus really isn't up to it, he muses. Perhaps it ought to be retired. The car will need new tires and a valve and ring job, at least, before the year is out. And he could get more on a trade-in now than next year. Mr. Adam's mental adding machine starts to work and soon the sum of tire and repair expense plus the loss in trade-in value looms large enough to make him look again at that advertisement. Power steering would make it easier for Mrs. Adam to park, he thinks, and she never did like the color of their present car.

But there are some things to be said against buying the new car, too. No matter how he juggles the figures of car expense and trade-in, the new car would mean a greater outlay of money. Mr. Adam's family, like most, have to ration both their money and their energies; they have to choose among many alternatives. He can think of half a dozen expensive items that he and Mrs. Adam have considered in the past. They have felt the need for new living room furniture. Looking around him, he knows something must be done soon about replacing it if they are to entertain at all. The children have been agitating for a recreation room in the basement, someplace to bring their friends to play Ping-Pong, watch TV, and hold parties. Mr. Adam knows this would cost several hundred dollars even if he did the labor himself. While he is at it, he smiles inwardly, he might build that workshop he has always wanted. After all, they could live with the old car a few more years if they'd get a little work done on it. If good transportation is what the family needs, they have that now. Let the kids complain. They don't pay the bills. We've spoiled them enough by catering to so many of their whims.[1]

We leave Mr. Adam with his decision, not knowing what his choice will be. Even if he makes up *his* mind about a course of action, there are *other* people to reckon with in his home. He cannot ignore their desires or feelings. His musings are just the first step in the complicated process of balancing and weighing his own desires and needs with those of the other family members. Those few times he chose to ride roughshod over their feelings and made a "family decision" on his own he was not particularly successful.

Families differ widely in their decision making ways. Some families plan ahead and try to anticipate the needs of the future. Others live for the present, letting the future take care of itself. Most of us are somewhere between these two extremes, some-

---

1. Adapted from Robert L. Kahn and Charles F. Cannell, *The Dynamics of Interviewing* (New York: John Wiley & Sons, Inc., 1957), pp. 29–30.

times careful and calculating, occasionally acting spontaneously with an inspired dash of carelessness, yet things seem to work out all right. Families obviously hold different values. Travel and education are cherished by some families over the more durable goods such as houses, cars, and appliances. Families differ in their ability to express their thoughts, feelings, and preferences and to combine them into a workable family choice. Some families have worked out effective means of reaching agreement on the major decisions of their lives. Others find each decision an occasion for confusion or even conflict.

THE ACTIVITY OF RESPONSIBLE DECISION MAKING

Biblical insights about decision making have a relevance for the most practical aspects of family living. When we come to the crossroads of a major decision, we have to face up to what we really want most, what counts with us. This feature of decision making is the key to Christian nurture in the family. For if we really consider what we value as we make decisions, we may discover the gods we are serving. This can be embarrassing, but it is also an indispensable step to Christian discipleship and joy. Until we discover what we *do* want and value, we cannot see what God's intention is for us as a family. What does the Bible say about the problem of making up our minds?

Choice

To be uniquely human is to choose responsibly one's course of action from among the many which are available to man. "Choose this day whom you will serve" (Joshua 24:15). Choosing means reflecting upon and assessing the value of the possible goals for which one can strive, courses of action one might take, attitudes one might adopt. Decision making is an *active* process of the human mind. It is the opposite of passively allowing ourselves to be molded by our surroundings, the loudest voices of propaganda, or the convenience of the moment.

Unlike the lower animals which are fixed in their development through instincts and the unfolding of a preordained pattern, man has imagination. He can "image" in his mind what he wants to be and accomplish and work toward that image. He has some degree of freedom from irresistible instincts and from external stimuli. Through the distinctly human gifts of imagination, memory, reflection and foresight, he is able to pause and consider the future consequences of his acts. He is able to measure possible (never *certain*) future satisfactions against the promise of immediate pleasure. If this is a measure of maturity, some people never grow up. "They want what they want when they want it."

Both impulsiveness and drifting are ways of avoiding a genuine human existence. Drifting is a form of dependence, waiting as a small child might wait for his mother to take care of him. "Something will come along," this person thinks. "Time will take care of things." A decision not to decide is to drift, *to be decided* by events and outer pressures. If a person is constantly unable to make choices, he is spiritually ill. Sometimes life seems easier this way; sometimes it seems safer. We remember the parable of the Talents (Matthew 25:14-30) in which the man of one talent, probably neither happy with his gift nor confident that his efforts to use it would do any good, apathetically let his talent lie buried in the ground. He lost even the one talent he had. He was passive, an indecisive personality.

The person who cannot make up his mind may be a person whose imagination is undisciplined, who has never learned his limits as a person. Limits may have been lacking in his early home life. If he was psychically overfed by admiring parents who believed he could do anything, this person may imagine that everything is possible for him. So many possibilities may be conjured up mentally that it is almost impossible to choose a direction in life. Handicapped by a lack of self-knowledge, he makes little effort to define what is possible for *him*. He cannot sort out the possible, the merely probable, and the utterly unfeasible according to *his limitations* of body, mind, and circumstances.

No one can have or achieve everything he imagines. This is pointed out in one of the first stories of the Bible. In Genesis, chapter 3, we read the dramatic parable of the Fall of mankind:

Man (male and female) wants to be everything; man wants to become God instead of accepting the limits of his created life. This is one meaning of his eating of the "tree of the knowledge of good and evil." Man did not decide to be *himself*, one person, with limited time, energy, talents. He wants to know and be everything he can imagine. He assumes that he can know the full range of good and evil, as God does. Martin Buber, the well-known Jewish philosopher, claims that this misuse of imagination, and the consequent unwillingness to be a real and limited person, channeling one's efforts where they can count, is the basic evil, the "original" sin of the Genesis story.[2]

This tendency to drift and avoid decision is contrary to the biblical injunction to "have dominion over" the subhuman elements of our lives. The misuse of television, for example, can produce a passivity which makes us unprepared to face life actively. It is not so much the content of TV that should concern us, but what persistent watching can do to our ability to be self-activating. A child may learn to relate to unreal and uncomplicated TV personalities and to wait for easy answers instead of puzzling over his life or wondering about it on his own. We may be caught in unwitting bondage and fail to discover the freedom of the Christian person which defines the self in genuine decisions carried through to action.

Evaluation

To make a choice or decision is to exercise judgment about alternatives. It is a mental juggling of the possibilities before us, sorting out the claims into some order of priority. It calls for the strenuous mental activity of arranging our values and goals into a hierarchy. Life, biblically conceived, is a struggle to hear God's will in the midst of the claims and counterclaims upon our time, resources, and energy. To his followers, Jesus says, "No one can serve two masters . . . You cannot serve God and mammon" (Matthew 6:24). The Sermon on the Mount says to those who insist that their first attention must be given to the "necessities" of

---

2. Martin Buber, *Good and Evil* (New York: Charles Scribner's Sons, 1953), pp. 133ff.

life, "Your heavenly Father knows that you need them all. But seek first his kingdom and his righteousness, and all these things will be yours as well" (Matthew 6:32–33). It is a matter of priorities.

We almost never see a temptation confronting us as a choice between good and evil. If it were that clear, we would seldom yield to it. Temptation invariably pulls us between two "good" things. That's what makes the decision so difficult.

Consider the problem of moving one's residence. In many cases, the move is occasioned by a father changing his work. For some families, this is no problem. Their priorities are clear. The sacrifices which are necessary to guarantee father's success in business or profession are accepted. Such advancement is considered valuable for the whole family. They all want what a higher standard of living can bring, and gain prestige from father's new job status. They are all in favor of the move.

But sometimes families must rationalize because they feel forced to "cooperate with the inevitable." Many corporations make it practically impossible for a young executive to *not* move on its suggestion, both because of the benefits they promise to bestow *and* because of the penalty that not moving would bring in stagnation or the loss of a valued job. In some ranks of labor (migrant farm workers, for example) families have no alternative but to go where the seasonal work *is* in order to survive. For other families, there is a greater range of alternatives. They may not be lured only by success or survival but by a host of other goals such as friendship, community responsibility, and so on.

A crucial decision involves both a promise and a cost. Suppose the breadwinner of a family gets an offer of a new job which requires a move of residence. He and his family must evaluate what would be gained and what would be lost by such a move. Their discussion might be outlined something like this:

Promise	*Cost*
1. having interesting work for father	1. giving up our nice house
2. earning a higher salary	2. moving away from our friends

3. living in a part of country we haven't seen
4. having greater educational advantages
5. getting away from unpleasant neighbors
6. being closer to father's aged mother
7. may not have another chance like this

3. taking the children out of a school they are happy in
4. losing school credits by transferring at midyear
5. leaving the church in which father is a strategic officer and feels useful now

To appropriate the promises one must be ready to renounce something "good." This is not a popular idea in affluent America where we like to think we can "have our cake and eat it too." This notion is simply unrealistic from a biblical perspective. We become real persons in real families to the degree to which we think through and act upon a *hierarchy of values*. If we are Christian, the order of those values is clear. Theologian D. T. Niles expresses it this way:

> It is irresponsible . . . to think that Christians can find time and money and strength for everything that everybody else does, and that with spare money in spare time with spare strength they can serve the ends of God's Kingdom. The great pearl is bought only by selling small pearls (Matt. 13:45-46). Where no pearl has been sold, there obedience to the demand of the Kingdom has not begun."[3]

A decision which does not count the cost realistically is an irresponsible decision. I decide to realize some purpose in the future; I resolve to create a reality which is not now an actuality. It may be a college education, or a new home, or a responsible leadership position in my business, or children of whom I can be proud. None of these things will materialize unless they are brought into being by the mobilization of my energy, time, and

---

3. D. T. Niles, *The Preacher's Task and the Stone of Stumbling* (New York: Harper & Row, Publishers, Incorporated, 1958), p. 114.

resources. God wants us to think, ponder, and count the cost. When a young man, caught up in enthusiasm, wanted to follow him, Jesus had to remind him soberly that the animals had their holes or their nests but the Son of Man had no home to call his own. He also spoke of the "shallow soil" in which the seed (the Word of God) immediately sprouted but then withered away under the heat of the sun (the pressures of life and its competing gods). We cannot enter his service thoughtlessly.

As Christian parents, we are to be "reality testers" for our children. We can help them to rehearse the possible consequences, the promise and the cost, of their decisions and of our own. By asking the right questions of each other, we can learn something of our motives and of the possibilities of achievement. When children are very young we must judge for them. The small child cannot evaluate whether or not it is safe to dash across a busy street or touch a hot stove. We can and must. The average adolescent who wants to quit school cannot always see the doors that will be closed to him later if he acts upon his impulse now. Sometimes we must decide *for* our children even at the cost of incurring their anger. Concerning any decision, a Christian should ask himself, "Can I carry it through to a successful conclusion?" One does not start out in childish dependency, certain that a rescue squad will pull him out of the quagmire of his own carelessness.

> Whoever does not *bear his own cross* and come after me, cannot be my disciple. For which of you, desiring to build a tower, does not first *sit down and count the cost*, whether he has enough to complete it? Otherwise, when he has laid a foundation, and is not able to finish, all who see it begin to mock him . . . Or what king, going to encounter another king in war, will not sit down first and take counsel whether he is able with ten thousand to meet him who comes against him with twenty thousand? (Luke 14:27–31; author's italics.)

Unreflective enthusiasm is no match for disciplined planning. The parable suggests that the odds are two-to-one when Christians fight the battle against evil in the world. Christians in families must think through and count the cost of their decisions, for each decision is related to the Christian's ability to carry on a reconciling ministry.

Total Involvement

Responsible decisions involve a struggle of the whole self with the issues at hand. It is so easy to agree to an idea that we sometimes ignore what will be involved if we take this road instead of that. The Bible sadly comments on those who honor him with their lips while their hearts are far from him. A decision must be reflected in the whole life of the person, not merely in his verbal extravagances. How easy it is to *seem* to have made a decision to serve God when we use the proper religious language! Jesus brings wordy enthusiasts up short with his question, "Why do you call me Lord, Lord, and do not do the will of my father in heaven?" One of Jesus' shortest parables illustrates this:

> . . . There was a man with two sons. He went to the first and said, "Go and work in my vineyard today, my son." He said, "All right, sir"—but he never went near it. Then the father approached the second son with the same request. He said, "I won't." But afterward he changed his mind and went. Which of these two did what their father wanted? (Matthew 21:28–32; Phillips translation.)

The first son assented with his words; it was an easy way to "decide." It was a decision without thought, without wrestling with the cost, without even a shred of resentment against the authority of the father. The second responded with a No, a refusal, but this was a gesture of real selfhood; he later chose to obey. And this is the son of whom Jesus approves.

What does this mean for parents in their everyday family living? We can probably force outward conformity upon a child when we discipline him. We can, with punishment and threats, get him to "assent" to our will. But the real object of discipline is to get the controls *inside* of the child so that when we are out of sight he will be able to decide for himself not to act in the unacceptable way. If we insist only upon the immediate Yes and fear-ridden obedience, we will not be of much help to him in the long run. He may say, with the boy who had to sit in the corner for hurting his brother, "I may be sitting down on the outside but I'm standing up on the inside!" Real discipline ought to involve a struggle with oneself and with the reality of his relationships. The child who says Yes too easily may never learn to decide to obey or to figure out why he was asked to do so.

There is another implication for us. People who are active in communities and churches frequently say Yes too easily. They must belong to "three clubs and four movements" or they feel empty and guilty. They are flattered into taking too many major responsibilities. "We know you can do this, Ann; you've got real talents that we need. You wouldn't let us down, would you?" They accept the office, willingly or not so willingly. Later they wonder why they took on so much. Overextended, they find themselves fatigued, irritable, and letting responsibilities slide. Faced with numerous half-finished projects, they feel even more guilty than if they had said No in the first place. Real decisions demand inward struggle. Often our need to be liked makes us "assent" to rather than decide our future course of action. We've neglected the struggle of real choice which takes into account the stubborn factors of time, energy, and our need for reflection on the mind of Christ.

THE FREEDOM AND LIMITATIONS OF COMMITMENT

Decisions both bind and free a person. To many Americans, freedom is the ability to do as one chooses moment by moment. To be bound by commitments seems to them to be fettered and unfree. At the "bachelor party" before any wedding one can hear snide remarks about the "ball and chain" which will soon slow down the new bridegroom. It is true that if you choose this, you cannot have that. A pessimist, for example, would focus upon the sacrifices involved in marriage. He might fail to see that the commitment of a man and wife to each other frees them to be their whole selves to a degree not possible outside of marriage. He does not think of the personal fulfillment that can come from experiencing the warm love of those in one's home, and from the joys of seeing life brought into being and developed. Few men would trade the "freedom" of bachelorhood for the discovery of the deeper reaches which he can find in a faithful lifelong intimate relationship, even with its heavy responsibilities. As one binds oneself in decision, he also finds a new kind of liberty.

If we have not really committed ourselves to being man and wife "as long as we both shall live," we may keep taking our affectional temperature daily to see if it warrants our continued union. How unstable such a marriage would be! Without a binding pledge, this covenant of man, woman, and God, few couples would willingly bear the unpleasantness or the boredom which curse every marriage at times. Few would work hard to find a way to eliminate it. If we have decided, with eyes-open realism, to keep our marriage intact "in plenty and in want, in joy and in sorrow, in sickness and in health," it will be difficult to seriously entertain the thought of leaving without exerting the extra effort and understanding which might redeem the relationship. A responsible commitment to each other frees us to work toward improving the existing relationship, with outside help, if necessary.

Consider the matter of worship. All habit and custom can become sterile, but the habit of attending worship regularly can free one from those changing feelings within us all, which may become our master. "I don't feel like going to church today." "I'll go to church only if Dr. So-and-So is preaching." When we do not feel like worship or prayer we *most* need what such a relationship can bring. To give in to momentary feelings, which may be up today and down tomorrow, is not freedom at all but slavery to our impulses.

Freedom and determinism are involved in each other. As my daughter decides to bind herself to the practice of the piano for an hour a day, month in and month out, she becomes progressively free to play and interpret some of the great music of the ages. She gains a freedom to do what she could not do before. This paradox is expressed in the phrase, "for freedom Christ has set us free . . ." (Galatians 5:1).

Time

Each of our decisions has a *history* and a *destiny*. Just as freedom and commitment are interwoven in our lives, so the decision of this moment is always bound with past and future choices. Contrary to the views of certain existentialist thinkers, there is no absolute freedom for every alternative in each moment. Man is both an historical and a social being. The past actions of myself and others in large measure determine the actions I can decide to take now. For example, one who does not finish high school, cannot now go on to college; that alternative no longer exists; and if we decide to have a child and start the process as God intended, the consequences of that decision will be experienced over a lifetime and will cause a multitude of other decisions to be made. If we look back at that chain of events which finally led to our decision to marry, we may see that, although unrealized at the time, the hand of God was upon the confluence of events and persons which brought about this particular relationship; it may even frighten us to think that we might have taken one of these small steps differently.

Society

Personal decisions are not individualistic. To be sure, we must make decisions within and for ourselves. They are personal decisions *but they always involve others*. The persons in our lives are not only touched by our decisions; they have also contributed to them. We may think we are self-contained or even insignificant, but the reverberations of a major decision by us will affect the lives of many people, They cannot be the same because we have moved in a new direction.

A wife decides, after talking with the family, that she will take a part-time job in a nursery school. This will call for a different division of labor within the home. The children must assume more responsibility for homemaking tasks and her husband must expect less time with her. No significant change can take place in any one member of the family without all being affected by it.

We do not live to ourselves. This is true in everyday events, but perhaps we see it best in cases of extreme change or threatened change in a family. Divorce represents a major sign of disruption and disorganization of the family unit. Something damaging and painful has happened to the members of a once intact family group. No one of them can ever be the same again. And the *effects of divorce go far beyond husband, wife, and children.* Shock waves from the disruption ripple out to the parents, and brothers, and sisters of the divorced couple, to employers, friends, neighbors, co-respondents (the "other women"), and their families. The sum of all the persons affected can conceivably amount to ten times the number of reported divorces!

Consider the problem of suicide. A person contemplating self-murder is a very lonely person. Superficial gregariousness may mask the depth of the alienation existing between such an unhappy person and his family. The would-be suicide is lonely within and wants to reach out to touch other persons, but is afraid to do so. Often an appeal to this person on behalf of others will help him to make a responsible decision. If he has children, he may be asked to consider what those children will have to suffer in pain and embarrassment if he does this irrevocable thing. The vision of his children, hurt and lonely, may be the only way to his sensitive, pained soul. He begins to look at life again and dares to look at his insoluble problem. Our decisions are never merely individual for no man is an island.

THE GUIDANCE OF FAITH

The covenant community of faith is a forum for the decision making efforts of Christians. American individualistic Christianity (a contradiction in terms) has robbed us of one of the greatest promises of the New Testament for our decision making. A body of people can only call themselves Christ's church if they care for one another and minister to each other. We are set in the midst of a people who are called together to "be a Christ to one another," as Martin Luther put it. We covenant together, in Christ, to be helpful members of one another. This family of families, the church, is a community which lives and works and wrestles with decisions together. No person or family need make his basic decisions "in solitary splendor," but whatever help he is given by the community, he is still left with the responsibility of his own decision.

Fellowship

Biblical ethics, the decision making of the Christian life, are born, not in the individual conscience, but in the covenant community. Because the Christian is freed *from* the law, from the bondage of hundreds of minute requirements and clear "rights" and "wrongs" for every occasion, he must find out, in his new freedom, what it means to "bear one another's burdens, and so fulfil the law of Christ" (Galatians 6:2). Neither Paul nor anyone else can spell out precisely how this is to be done in our specific circumstances, but a community of Christians can try to discover what this means concretely.

In that first church, our Lord shared fully the temptations and decisions he was facing with the Twelve. Toward the last of his earthly sojourn with them, he says, "You are those who have continued with me in my trials [temptations] (Luke 22:28). He was probably referring to the uncertainty and weariness and discouragement which he must have experienced in their itinerant life together. Jesus also continued with the disciples in *their* temptations, which were mainly of two kinds: *ambition* (illustrated by James and John's wanting the places of honor in the Kingdom) and *self-pity* (shown in Peter's pointing out how much the disciples had given up). When we see Jesus and the Twelve and their life together as a model of what the church really is, we see a supportive but fallible company bound together in their common life, dealing with issues as down to earth as tomorrow's electric bill, in the presence of their Lord.

Christians see the church as *koinōnia,* the common sharing of the Holy Spirit in the corporate fellowship of the community. Our Lord said "Where two or three are gathered in my name, there am I in the midst of them" (Matthew 18:20). The Spirit dwells in the Body. We know the Spirit through Christ and Christ through the witness of the Spirit.

People of the covenant seek the guidance of the Holy Spirit who dwells within the community of believers. It is the Holy Spirit who guides us to the Scriptures; who affirms to us that Christ is Lord; who works to bind us who are strangers, having no natural affinity with each other, into church fellowship; who makes us members of one another so that we might share in each other's joy and suffering; who equips us to witness in the various arenas of our daily lives.

Today's church recognizes that small groups of people who have learned to trust one another and care for one another can help immensely in decision making. It also recognizes that the small, mobile family unit needs to examine its experience with those who have had similar problems with such things as the discipline of children, relations with in-laws, the pros and cons of a wife working outside the home, living in a neighborhood that is becoming racially integrated, developing strategies of creative conflict in the home, business ethics, community standards, and so on.

Members of small groups are able to share on a deep level their practical concerns about Christian nurture. A discussion group allows parents to explore the motivations for and their utilization of the various standards they hold. For example, one group of church mothers was caught in this familiar dilemma, "Should we insist that the house be neat and orderly or should we let everyone relax?" The answer may not be either/or. A discussion of this topic revealed the various values connected with "things," "order," and so on. Animated discussion was started by a member reading a quotation which suggests that a sign be attached, at least figuratively, to the front and back doors of the house:

> We own this place and it's never going to own us. We have a place to sleep, rest, and eat, so we took over this place and we expect to have a lot of fun here and to be happy here and that's the whole purpose of our home. If Mrs. Grundy doesn't like the way we run things, we give her full permission to go out in our back yard and have a nervous breakdown. Come

in any time you want, but if you want quiet we suggest a tomb, and if you want painful order and neatness we suggest a museum, and if you want strict discipline and unbroken routine we think you might prefer a prison.[4]

It is not a sign of weakness to trust a church group of which we are a part with some of our thinking about decisions confronting us. In such trust there is a recognition that we understand what the body of Christ is.

Prayer

Responsible decision making needs the guidance which God gives through prayer. A Christian family without prayer possesses only a theoretical Christianity. When a man is at the crossroads of a major decision, he will usually pray for guidance. It may be an emergency measure because he is at the end of his rope. Or prayer may be the context for his thinking about decisions and this is a natural step for him to take. Whatever his motives and practices, he is assuming that somehow through prayer he will receive guidance for the choice he must make. But he knows that, with all the information he can get, he must still make his move without absolute certainty. He assumes that God does act responsively to our requests for help.

Christ's own prayers contained definite requests and he counseled his followers to make definite petitions and to persist in their requests even when it seemed that God was ignoring them. In a time of indecision, a family or an individual can be confident that God, the Father, is at the crossroads with them, eager to respond in a way which will help them become his men and women in the world.

Prayer is not a substitute for the hard work of thinking about the alternatives which face us. Some people erroneously contrast prayer and work or prayer and thought, but these are *not* opposites. These people would become *childish* (not childlike) in their attempt to let God take over the responsibility for their lives.

---

4. James Lee Ellenwood, *Just and Durable Parents* (New York: Charles Scribner's Sons, 1948), pp. 46–47.

They would like to sit back, cease all human activity, and assume that the Spirit will do the work. They would become infants again, relating to God as they did to their parents as small children; they have not put away "childish ways" (1 Corinthians 13). We misread the Scriptures if we think that God wants man to become passive before him as in many eastern religions. "Stand upon your feet and I will speak with you," he says to the groveling Ezekiel. The more active a man is in his total person the more active God chooses to be. The admonition to "Work out your own salvation with fear and trembling, for God is at work in you, both to will and to work" (Philippians 2:12–13) gives no comfort to those who would throw away their humanity by refusing to think, decide, and act. "Ask," "seek," "knock"—these are active words. God wants us to be persons, not puppets.

Jesus regarded prayer as the accompaniment of effort and an alternative to despairing acquiescence and inertia. Prayer *is* work. Throughout the New Testament, the opposite of praying about a thing is to do nothing, and the opposite of working for a cause is to stop praying.

In considering some of the contributions which prayer makes to our decision making we must first recognize that it is impossible to separate prayer from corporate worship—from the reading and hearing of the word in Scripture and sermon, and the receiving of the Lord's Supper.

1. Prayer is one way in which the Christian family is helped to clarify what they really want and need. Prayer is not the *only* way God seeks to communicate his will to us. Experiences of love, sorrow, guilt, beauty, disappointment, hurt are all vehicles of God's communication to us if we have ears to hear and eyes to see.

The Christian with anything on his mind or heart should open his soul to God; nothing is too small to consider, no feelings are too mean to express. As John Baillie has said, whatever is big enough to *worry* about, is not too small to *pray* about.[5] Paul said, "Have no anxiety about anything, but in everything by prayer and

---
5. John Baillie, *Christian Devotion* (New York: Charles Scribner's Sons, 1962), p. 47.

supplication with thanksgiving let your requests be made known to God" (Philippians 4:6).

When we express our real feelings, desires, and thoughts to our Father we can begin to discover what we really want. If we think we want to control a wayward adolescent, we may discover in prayer that we really desire a way to help him become a loving, responsible person. If we think that we want revenge on a person who has hurt us, what we may really desire is to have that enemy become a friend. If we think we want to be married (as many teen-agers do), we may really want to get away from home. There are easier ways to get away! If we think we want a new job, we may actually want to get along better with fellow workers and to find some significance in what we do for a living. If we think that what we desire above all else is a new home in the suburbs, we may really be seeking the joy that we had as a young couple working hard for something together.

It is a good thing that many of our expressed wants are not granted. "Hell" has been defined by the Right Reverend James Pike as "getting what we wanted when we wanted the wrong things!"[6] It is the promise of the New Testament that when we pray in the Spirit of Christ, our real desires and his will for us are clarified.

2. Through prayer a family can come to share the same goals for life. This is not to say that prayer can be "used" to bring a reluctant family member over to one's side. It is not a divine weapon. Participation in prayer and worship can enable families to discover their real order of priorities in life, and hopefully to agree on them. There are three basic questions that must be asked in any decision making situation. All of them must be answered before we can work toward a solution: What do we want? What are our *goals*? How shall we get what we want? What *means* can we use to achieve our goals? Who shall do what to get what we want? What *roles* do we take? The most basic of the three is the agreement on goals. A family cannot go far if they cannot settle on this.

---

6. James A. Pike, *Beyond Anxiety* (New York: Charles Scribner's Sons, 1953), p. 93.

3. Through prayer and corporate worship we are assured that any mistakes we make in our decisions are not the last word for our lives. God's grace is such that he can show men how missteps might be redeemed. We have all made mistakes and we will continue to make them. Some of our reactions may have seriously damaged our family and work relationships. We may have decided to act in a way that now seems to threaten our future. Yet God can take even these wrong decisions and say to us, "Behold, I make all things new" (Revelation 21:5). We know we cannot retrace our steps, but it may be that a way will be opened to us to join the highway at another point. Maybe an altogether new route will be found. It is the Good News that we can start from where we are now, even when we think that we are on a dead-end street.

This conviction about the sovereignty of God can free us from the fear of taking risks. All of life is a risk. All decisions involve uncertainty. Sometimes we act as if *everything* depends upon our decision. Thank God it does not. Our God is one whom no happening can surprise, the New Testament reminds us. And thus he is able to lead us into a *future of grace* and out of a past of error, of guilt, and of fear.

Part III
Families in the Church and in the World

10 Christ's Family of Families............................199
11 Arenas of Family Witness: The Community.............218
12 Arenas of Family Witness: The Economic Realm.........233
13 Arenas of Family Witness:
    National and International Affairs......................247

10
Christ's Family of Families

Several years ago our dog had pups, seven squirming little creatures who became the delight of our home. The mother dog made herself available to them in as self-sacrificing a way as she could. They were dependent upon her for nourishment, for warmth, and for the daily job of cleansing. And although those puppies did not know it, they were indebted to another world, another family beyond their canine sphere of life. The mother dog also needed care and warmth and feeding and this was supplied by our human family. We occasionally intervened to see that all went well. When, for example, the runt of the litter was crowded out at meal time or was in danger of suffocating, we reached down to remedy the situation. And the mother dog seemed to know and appreciate our efforts on their behalf. Just so, God's family is the source of care and concern for every particular household within it.

THE FAMILY OF FAITH BIBLICALLY UNDERSTOOD

The Christian family does not stand alone. One of the joys of life together is the discovery that we are not left to our own resources in the arduous task of fashioning a family after God's design. Life in Jesus Christ is not a solitary life; we are part of a larger family. That family, called together by God, is related through his Spirit. "Whoever does the will of God *is* my brother, and sister, and mother" (Mark 3:35; author's italics), Jesus reminds us. Is it possible that here, in this larger family, we can claim the promise of new direction and strength for the daily task of being Christ's men and women in the world and in the home?

Through membership in Christ's family the individual family can define who it is. Each family needs that larger family in order to go beyond their own puny goals. We all need a renewal of love for our family members and inspiration for service beyond the household.

Rightly understood, the church is the body of Christ, all people, past, present, and future, who have been raised from death to life. They are sent into the world as true, restored human beings. The home participates in Christ's body when its members are faithful in helping members of the larger family to understand and exercise discipleship in the world.

Many families both within and on the fringes of local congregational life do not share this view of the church as a body of people whose task it is to exhibit God's reconciling power. Often our own wants and desires and misunderstandings are substituted for the biblical understanding of the covenant community. For example, some parents use the local church to help them achieve other values, goals which are not in line with Christ's purpose. A recent study of adults who came into a Protestant denomination by "confession of faith" revealed that they did not join the church as a result of their own faith but *for the sake of their children.*[1] One mother says, "Since Johnny started Sunday school, I decided that we'd better be in the church too or he would begin to ask why we didn't go." It was important to this mother that her child be involved in the church in order that "he could receive some training in right and wrong which he can't get in his other activities. It will round out his education." This is typical of a growing number of parents who come into the church.

It has been said that "a little child shall lead them," but these fathers and mothers are being led into an institution which is only vaguely understood by them. The church is considered useful for character building, for fighting Communism, or for building desirable neighborhoods. Vagueness and confusion about the Lord of the church is found in abundance among church members. What Will Herberg has called an "objectless faith"[2] is

---

1. Dennison Nash and Peter Berger, "The Child, the Family and the 'Religious Revival' in Suburbia," *Journal for the Scientific Study of Religion,* Vol. II, No. 1, Fall, 1962, pp. 85–93.

2. Will Herberg, *Protestant-Catholic-Jew* (New York: Doubleday & Company, Inc., 1955).

held by a great many faithful church attenders. "If you can have the faith that things will work out all right," says one parent, "I think you can work toward better things." For such a person, Christianity has no historical or theological rootage and embodies few unique qualities that are not duplicated by other worthwhile efforts of society.

Such confusion about Christian faith is bound to spill over into the child's life. A child who had just lost a baby tooth was interviewed on the radio by Art Linkletter who asked, "How do you suppose the new tooth will come in?" "Well," said the boy, "the tooth fairy tells Jesus and he will tell Santa Claus who will bring them for Christmas." To which Mr. Linkletter replied, "Well, that's some chain of command!" This child's notion demonstrates the result of hit-or-miss Christian education.

Many parents in the congregation think of the church primarily as an *institution*. In some parishes the organizational structure is the most obvious aspect of their ministry. They are bundles of busy activity, three-ring circuses with each member of the family in a separate ring. Sunday can be the busiest and most tension-fraught day of the week. Worthwhile activities which were originally planned to nourish Christian people now require people to keep them alive; they have lost their purpose.

For a great many parents the church is only a *building*, judging from their answers to the question, "Where is your church?" In the New Testament the church was a brotherhood of men and women in Christ and it did not matter *where* they met; *why* they met together was the crucial thing. The church began with a group of twelve called by their Lord *"to be with him, and to be sent out"* (Mark 3:14; author's italics). That, in a nutshell, is the purpose of the church. We often forget both elements of the purpose. It is sometimes hard to believe that Christ is in the midst of us in the congregation. And it is easy to forget that we are "to be sent out" to serve the world in his Spirit. Most parents memorized John 3:16 in their Sunday school days. But their life in the church often says the opposite to the outsider: "God so feared the world, that he gave the church that some might be protected from the world."

Often when we think of the life and work of the church, we think primarily of what goes on within the four walls of the church building. This insulates us from the world in which life is lived and compartmentalizes our "religious interest" as something apart from what we do on the job, in the home, in the community, and in the school. But "Christ is either Lord *of all* or He is not Lord *at all*."[3] Hendrik Kraemer, the theologian, once said that a man needs two conversions: a conversion to Christ and a conversion to the world.[4] So often Christ's family of families is turned in upon itself and its own life to the point of excluding their real witness in the world.

Almost every Christian family is asked three questions at some time or other: Do you go to church? Where is your church? What does your church do? A mother's answers might go something like this:

Q. Do you go to church?
A. Yes, usually about twice a month except for the Women's Association meetings which I attend regularly.
Q. Where is your church?
A. Fifth and Main Streets. You've probably seen it on your way to work.
Q. What does your church do?
A. Well, let me show you our church calendar. The activities listed here will best answer your question. Look: the Youth Fellowship, the church school, the Women's Association, the Men's Bible Class, the Day Nursery School, the membership-visiting committee, and so on. As you see, we have two, and sometimes three, activities going on daily at Old First. We are usually buzzing with people. Everyone finds some group that fits him.

If the inquirer seems particularly interested in how his talents might be used for such a church, he may be given a talent

---
3. Attributed to Dr. W. A. Visser't Hooft at the Second Assembly of the World Council of Churches, 1954, Evanston, Illinois.
4. Hendrik Kraemer, *A Theology of the Laity* (Philadelphia: The Westminster Press, 1958).

search sheet on which to check such abilities as singing, typing, flower arranging, working with youth groups, carpentry, church school teaching, and the like. The "talents" listed are almost always those which can be used *within* the institution to carry out the many activities listed on the calendar or in the weekly newspaper. These are important only as *they prepare us as families to minister to the world.*

After a thorough study of the New Testament understanding of the church, Paul M. Van Buren has concluded that we consistently give the wrong answers to these three questions. A Christian with a New Testament view would answer in a quite different way.

Q. Do you go to church?
A. I am part of the Church. But the Church does meet together, if that's what you're asking.

Q. Where is your Church?
A. Well, let's see, about this time of the morning, most of it is at work, except for those on the night shift, or those who are sick. Some are at work in this factory and that, others are working in this office or that store, some are in school, some in their kitchens, the church is infiltrated through the whole town right now.

Q. What does your Church do?
A. I've already told you. It's spread all through the town involved in all sorts of work, doing that work in such a way and talking in such a way as to let others know what is already true: that Jesus Christ is the boss of this city and all that goes on in it. This is the Church's work. And then, *one day a week, we rest from our Church work and gather together to hear again our Lord speaking to us,* that we may go back renewed to the task he has set before us.[5]

---

5. Paul M. Van Buren, "The New Biblical Theology in Parish Life," *Religion in Life*, Vol. XXVIII, No. 4, Autumn 1959, pp. 535–536. Copyright © 1959 by Abingdon Press. Author's italics.

THE FAMILY OF FAITH GATHERED

God's Call and Covenant

Who are these people who make up Christ's family of families? According to the Bible, the church is different from all other communities. It is a *covenanted community* and its difference from a natural community is apparent at three main points.

1. The church is not just a voluntary fellowship of people who want to get together for some reason. Although we may speak of "joining" the church as we would a club, the P.T.A., or an art society, the authentic Christian note is that we have been called into a community of people which acknowledges that it is loyal to the center of its life, Jesus Christ. It is simply because God loves us that he calls us into this fellowship. By calling us to be "a people," a congregation, God enters into an agreement, a covenant, with us. God's part of the agreement, to which he is always faithful, is that his people will be assured of his presence and his love and that he will empower them to become what human beings were meant to be. Our side of the covenant, to which we are frequently unfaithful, is that we will tell the world through word and deed what God has done and is doing in Jesus Christ to restore men to himself and to each other.

2. God calls us into this family of faith which is unlike any other fellowship. In any congregation there will be all sorts of people, some like us and some quite unlike us; some we would choose for friends, and others we would like to avoid. Every age, condition of life, social class, and racial group may be represented in our particular church because these differences are not essential to our basic unity in Christ.

The households of the family of faith are likely to differ widely. They may include the common household of father, mother, and children living in the suburb; a man living alone in a big city; college students occupying a dormitory; and business girls sharing an apartment. In some congregations, the majority of families will be incomplete, composed of "empty nesters" whose children have left home, or single people, or retired adults. Others will boast a population explosion with preschoolers to be seen everywhere. The household within the covenant community may be an army barracks or a convalescent hospital. A particular church will have a unique makeup of households; it will not be a replica of any other congregation. Each household contributes to the others by its differentness. No matter what his marital status, each person finds his place in the family of God.

3. Christ's family of faith is a fallible, human family. His forgiven people are not morally perfect people. On the contrary, we are in the midst of people who are always failing. When we feel tempted to sentimentalize the early church and say, "If only the church today could resemble the saints of the New Testament," we had better look again. For those saints ("saints" in the Bible simply means forgiven sinners who take Christ seriously), as Paul's correspondence with the Corinthian church shows, are not very promising material to do God's work. He admonishes them for boasting and quarreling, for jealousy, incest, homosexuality, adultery, idol worship, and even for getting drunk on the communion wine! Yet, somehow, out of such a group and out of our own congregation God is able to make a people, a community through which his love comes clearly: "For we have this treasure in earthen vessels."

Our Response: Confession and Participation

How do families come into this reconciling fellowship? They are called by God and their calling is made known to all by their participation in the sacraments of the church which are the *enactment of the gospel.* They act out or demonstrate the meaning of Christian faith.

Baptism. Baptism is the sign of identification with the Christian community. It requires one to make an inner confession of his sin and a public profession of his faith. As Paul put it, he had died and risen with Christ and was born to newness of life. Remembering that in his baptism the early Christian was submerged beneath the waters of a river or pool, we can easily grasp the dramatic symbolism of being buried and emerging again from the grave.

An adult can understand what this means. As he is baptized,

he also makes his confession of Christ. The grace of God which is given to him is met with the response of his faith; both the action of God and the action of men are necessary. But what about small children? The infant does not know what is going on when his parents present him to be baptized. Because of the baby's lack of understanding of the meaning of the sacrament, some denominations limit baptism to adults. Others believe that the child is regenerated by the act of a priest, quite without the response of faith. By the very act of baptizing, the child is supposed to be "transformed," made fit for eternal life.

Protestants believe that the sacraments are the outward and visible sign of an inward and spiritual grace. But baptism does not *cause* God's grace to come into the life of the child. Protestants who present their infants and children for baptism do so with the understanding that the child's baptism is a dramatic symbol that God loves him, as he loved us, even *before* he is aware of that love. God's love does not wait upon our faith; God comes to us so that we might later respond in faith to him! Baptism is a sign that God is with the child who is welcomed into the sphere of grace, the community of believers. Baptism is God's enrolling his child in the church. You do *not* have to believe first and then receive assurance of God's love. That is the message.

Faith is a response to God's initiative of which baptism is a dramatic demonstration. The child's response of faith and trust in God who loves him does not have to follow immediately. Baptism aims at that later response, that delayed reaction.

The baptized child is a *member* in the household of faith. His membership is acknowledged by an affirmation to the question, "Do you, in the name of the church, undertake responsibility for the Christian nurture of this child?" The whole aim of the Christian teaching of the child in congregation and home could be summed up in one sentence: to help the child grasp the promise of his baptism so that he can make a decision for God who has acted in his behalf. The meaning of the child's baptism is explained to him again and again until he grasps its import and is able to make a genuine decision regarding Christ. He is to *confirm* the promises made. No one can respond in faith for him.

It is up to the parents, acting as the church in their home, to bring a child to understand the meaning of his baptism. Without the parents' own loyalty and faith, there is little chance that a child can grow to be a Christian. That is why we have given so much attention to life within the family. One day the child may come to deliberately identify himself with the covenant people of God because, in truth, he has been a "child of the covenant." A child is born into a family without willing it, without choosing the parents he is to have. For many years he is cared for, nourished, and loved. But one day he must decide consciously on his own that he will *be* a true member of the family by reflecting what it represents and carrying responsibility for its welfare. In the same way the profession of personal faith, following a long period of study and experience in the covenant community, is a necessary step for full *communicating* membership.

The Lord's Supper. When he has come to a mature decision, the child participates with the adult congregation in the climactic sacrament, the Lord's Supper. The enacted word is given the highest expression when God conveys to the believer his own presence and reality through ordinary objects used in daily family life. Because Jesus was known to the disciples after the resurrection "in the breaking of the bread" (Luke 24:35), Christians do this also for his remembrance. Whether the sacrament is served in an elaborate sanctuary, around the kitchen table in a slum home of London's East End, or on the deck of a cruiser just before battle, it symbolizes the "body of Christ which is broken for you" and the "New Covenant in the blood of Christ" (*The Book of Common Worship*, p. 164). The sacrament enacts the gospel by signifying:

- that by his death Christ has redeemed our lives;
- that by taking the elements into our bodies, we wish Christ to dwell in our hearts by faith;
- that we recognize the place God has for the commonplace elements of our lives used in his service; and
- that, as we bind ourselves to Christ, we are united together in *koinōnía* in a new way.

Like the spokes of a wheel, the closer we come to the Center, the closer we are to each other. We realize we cannot despise, ignore, or offend our brother without offending Christ. And we cannot love Christ without loving him in our brothers. This sacrament is the center of the church's life; in it we find communion with God and with each other.

Our Response: Worship and Study

The church exists primarily to *say* something to the world with its words and through its life. It exists to tell and act out a story, the incredible story of God who was not willing for us to remain subhuman and lost, who came into our concrete life as one of us in Jesus Christ, lived his life with us, fulfilled in himself our deepest needs, and was willing to suffer and die the death of a common criminal for us. When we respond to him in worship, study, brotherly love, and service to the world, we demonstrate our break with the past and become transformed. However it comes alive to us, whether in preaching, or in breaking bread at his table, in group study or family Bible reading, this story is *the* essential ingredient in the life of the church's families. From it proceeds everything which makes that family of families a church.

There are three main avenues by which families come to understand God's word.

The Sermon. When the church is gathered together, the proclamation and interpreting of God's Word to us comes most often in the service of worship. We hear the *written* Word read from the Bible, hear the *spoken* Word delivered through the sermon, and participate in the *enacted* Word in the Lord's Supper or through the Sacrament of Baptism. God's Word is also studied intensively in the schools of the church in classes of all ages, where its meaning and implications for life are explored.

The pastor in a congregation is appointed the chief interpreter of Christian faith by virtue of his long, exacting training. These are validated by his ordination which designates him as one who works to "equip God's people for work in his service"

(Ephesians 4:12).[6] The other ministers of the congregation (all Christians are "ministers") also have a part in proclaiming the story and relevance of Jesus Christ. A well-trained lay teacher in the church may have far more to do with Bible teaching and the interpretation of Christian faith and history to children and adults than the pastor has. And those who do not teach in the schools of the church may enter sermon discussion groups which examine the content of the sermon and its implications for life in the world. This is a new and exciting way to learn. A growing number of families are involved in these groups which meet following the worship service to discuss their understanding of the sermon. If the pastor is present, he can learn about the thinking of the families and can also discover how to communicate more effectively with them. The sermon's application to life is explored in such a group. Enterprising pastors and families are finding this means of participating with each other an important way to break open the meaning of the Bible for today's world.

Group Study. God speaks to us as we seek his living word through a study of the Bible. The Bible does not offer "ideals" toward which we should strive, but projects keen diagnoses of our condition which cut into our rationalizations and pretense of goodness. In their educational efforts, a study group can shuttle back and forth from an understanding of the Bible to an understanding of their own existence in order to make sense of both.

Parents can come to understand that through simple but profound stories, God is speaking to our adult lives today. The life of Adam, for example, is the life of Everyman. The Hebrew name "Adam" means "mankind." When the book of Genesis tells us that Adam hid from God in the garden, we are not to imagine with the mind of a child that God is a large manlike deity, looking under this bush and that when he calls, "Adam, where are you?" Adults who are really listening to the word of God hear and see more than this. We see that *we*, like Adam, are caught in a situation of guilt for not being what we were made to be.

---

6. *The New English Bible* © The Delegates of the Oxford University Press and the Syndics of the Cambridge University Press, 1961.

Consider an experience common to all as husbands and wives or parents: Have we not found ourselves in our family life listening but not hearing, speaking but not communicating, demanding affection and recognition but being unable to give tenderness, inviting closeness but not really wanting intimacy? We often proclaim hope, but act out despair in our lives as we hurry desperately through our paces. Caught in this kind of life we feel guilty and we begin, like Adam, to hide from one another, from God, from ourselves. We are caught in duplicity, saying the opposite of what we feel and wearing masks with one another. And God's voice comes to us, as to Adam, "Where are you, really, after these thirty, forty, or fifty years? How far along are you?" The word of God always addresses us this way. It shows us our need for a Savior—and it reveals that Savior to us.

Without serious study of the Bible *and* of the world to which it speaks, how can we give a good account of ourselves in the battle with the forces of darkness? How can we be expected to be the educators of our children in the meaning of Christ for their lives? How can Christians see the distinctions between Christianity and what is going on in our society if we have not gone beyond the ABC's in our understanding of Christian faith?

The Worship Service. It is very doubtful that families will worship in their homes if they cannot worship with the gathered community of faith. Corporate worship offers the opportunity for the entire family to worship together in the sanctuary.

What is the value of such a service? Will not children disturb the worship of adults? To worship as a family may be Christian education at its best, even when everything that goes on is not understood. Albert Schweitzer is convinced that his own experience of worshiping in the sanctuary with his family was crucial in the growth of his own faith. He asserts that the important thing is not that the child understand every word, but that he realizes that something serious and solemn is taking place, and sees his elders full of devotion, worshiping One who is above them all.[7]

---

7. Albert Schweitzer, *Memoirs of Childhood and Youth* (New York: The Macmillan Company, 1949), p. 45.

To understand the value of family corporate worship for the child, it is necessary to know that not all learning involves intellectual understanding. The first stage of learning for the child is his *identification with the people of God*. As he participates with his parents in the worship service and in their discipleship in the home and in the world, the child senses that he is a part of a special people who do things in a particular way. They pray; they praise God through song; they listen attentively to the Scripture; they give of their substance and energies to the work of God; they attempt to be Christ's men and women in the world. As the child begins to wonder why we do these things he will ask what they mean. As he is ready, parents are able to explain what the Lord's Prayer is, why we confess our sins, why we sing the Doxology, and why our job in the community is to be ministers to others in their need. In short, as children begin to identify themselves with this community of faith, they begin to hear the story which explains *why* this covenant community does what it does and *how* it all began. The time for a *systematic approach to theology* is when the child is older and begins to sense a conflict between the story of Christ and the views of life the world accepts as the deepest truth. At this point we wrestle chiefly on the intellectual level as we evaluate the claims of the various points of view and try to see the relationship of our faith to the ideas of philosophy and science, and to the world's condition. The progression of Christian learning, then, is

>from
>
>identification with God's people through participation
>
>>to
>
>personal encounter with the gospel story
>
>>to
>
>efforts to relate the gospel to the world's knowledge and problems.

Our Response: Ministering to One Another

Christ has called us to be members of one another. Set in the midst of these people as we are, if we study together, pray together, and plan together, we become a working unit of the body of Christ. Families begin to see that they need one another, that none of us is self-sufficient for the ministry Christ has given us. We share a ministry to one another. We need one another's care and concern.

In any congregation there are many with secret troubles, fighting bravely to keep their flags flying; people wearing chains who may need us to loose them. Families who have eyes to see and concern for fellow Christians will be aware of the young couple who have just buried a child, a woman who is struggling with a paralyzing fear, the family down the street in which a beloved mother has just died, a well-known man who ruins his professional life through alcoholism, the middle-aged couple whose home is going on the rocks, the respected leader who has been caught in embezzlement, the young college woman who is plagued by intellectual doubts, the young man who is facing a cancer operation within the month, the young girl who is left with an unwanted pregnancy. These are all crying for redemption. Some of them are deplorable figures to whom it is so easy to feel superior. But at their point of need suddenly the Savior appears hungry, cold, imprisoned with them (Matthew 25). He is not ashamed to be their brother; are we? Unless we are a community of people who care, how can we convince the world that his so-called Kingdom of God is not a pipe dream?

Caring does not mean snooping, or tracking down people to do something for them in order to make ourselves feel important. In describing one such "helpful" person, a friend of mine said you could always tell those she helped by their hunted look! No, to our brothers in Christ we are to be available, alert to need, sensitive to those hurt by life, practical in our concern.

How a person comes through a crisis depends more upon the *kind* of help others give him than upon any "strength of character" or inward courage he may possess. The importance of the community of faith and service is underlined. A person may know that the way to overcome his trouble is to come to grips with it, but in the midst of his difficulty what he knows is often forgotten. People in crisis—the man who has suddenly lost a job, the woman who is recently divorced, the child who is uprooted and moved away from his friends, a mother who loses her baby in the sixth month of pregnancy—all these need help from fellow Christians.

We can help such a person in several ways. *We can help him look at the crisis squarely;* to talk about unspoken fears and dangers, to grieve, and even to cry. So many, living in dread of "what might be," can be encouraged to check with medical or other authorities about the realistic facts of the illness or crisis. Only then can realistic action be substituted for fearful speculation. *We can avoid giving false reassurance.* Dr. Caplan of Harvard University says, "You want to lend him a shoulder as an equal instead of reassuring him like a parent. By doing this you give him the more important kind of reassurance—the reassurance that you have faith in his ability to handle the crisis."[8] He needs to know that God walks with him through the valley and that we are standing by. *We can help him to not blame others.* Blaming, finding a supposed villain, including oneself, to hold responsible for the trouble may relieve one temporarily but prevents him from mobilizing his resources to do what can be done now. Blaming is an unproductive waste of energy. *We can help him to receive help.* It is difficult for some to accept the practical assistance others can give. This may be a denial that help is needed, or may reveal an inordinate need to be self-sufficient. Christians must learn to receive as well as give. The church gathered together becomes in this way "a fellowship of conversation and consolation," as Martin Luther put it.

THE FAMILY OF FAITH SCATTERED

Some people separate religion and life to such an extent that they even use a different vocabulary for their life in the church and their life in the world. A clergyman spent Sunday afternoon at a house in an English village where he had preached. After tea he was sitting in the garden with the hostess when in dashed her little boy, holding a dead rat over his head. "Don't be afraid,

---

8. Dr. Gerald Caplan, in a lecture at the Harvard University School of Public Health.

mother," he cried, "It's quite dead. We beat him and bashed him and thumped him until . . ." Then catching sight of the parson, he added in a lowered voice, ". . . until God called him home." If we read the New Testament aright it is precisely where the beating and bashing and thumping go on in life that God in Jesus Christ has business with us. Life within the four walls of the church building exists for one reason: to provide boot training for Christian battle in the world.

As Christians, we are always involved in the "world." In our jobs, our buying and selling, our family relations, our recreation, we participate in the institutions and organizations which constitute our world. Here is where our service to Christ is meant to be. For the Christian, his various activities are interlocking circles of the influence. Whether he is a Democrat, a Rotarian, a Giants fan, or a father, the Christian is to have an understanding of himself as Christ's man in the world. That means he is concerned with justice, with mercy, with helping human beings find their greatest opportunity to be truly human.

Often, however, there is little carry-over of faith into life. We tend to live a split-level existence, divorcing our religious and church life from the rough-and-tumble experiences which make up our daily lives. We let our separate group affiliations be a world to themselves, not allowing them to interfere with each other. Thus the job, the union, the school, the veteran's organization, the political party, the club may be separate worlds with totally different values by which we live within each of them. This spiritual schizophrenia is illustrated in this story by Leroy Collins, ex-governor of Florida:

> Months back in one of our towns here in Florida we had a woman doctor, one of our public health doctors, who served three towns. She needed to have a conference with the Negro nurse who worked under her supervision. All of her day was filled with appointments and she couldn't find the time for that conference, so, she asked the Negro nurse to meet her in the back of an eating place downtown where they could have a sandwich and discuss their work. And they did meet

and they ate a sandwich together as they discussed professional matters.

The people heard about it and the mob gathered. Citizens went down to the county commissioners of the town and of the other two counties and cried: "Fire her! She has violated the traditions and customs of the Southland. Fire her!"

Where in that situation were our Presbyterians? Where were our Methodists? Our Episcopalians? Where were all of our churchmen? Where were all of our people who are dedicated to this proposition of *All for Christ?* Did they go before these county commissioners and say, "Don't! This is wrong!"? No, they called for the bowl, and they washed their hands, and they said, just as Pontius Pilate said: "The blood of this innocent, righteous person won't be on my hands. See to it yourself." And she was fired, to the everlasting shame of our citizens.[9]

This world attempts to take the teeth out of the gospel by a partial and eviscerating acceptance of it. We are likely to be lulled into thinking that our Lord's will and the status quo are one and the same. It was to this kind of situation that Amos spoke when he castigated those who would separate religious ceremony from a concern for justice. God says through his prophet:

> I hate, I despise your feasts,
>   and I take no delight in your solemn assemblies.
> Even though you offer me your burnt offerings . . .
>   I will not accept them,
> and the peace offerings of your fatted beasts
>   I will not look upon.
> Take away from me the noise of your songs;
>   to the melody of your harps I will not listen.
> But let justice roll down like waters,
>   and righteousness like an ever-flowing stream
> (Amos 5:21–24).

---

9. Leroy Collins, former Governor of Florida, speaking to the Miami Convention of Southern Presbyterian Men; reported in *The Presbyterian Outlook,* October 28, 1957, p. 6. Used by permission.

At times, the first expression of Christian love in the world is to develop a sense of outrage, a burning sense of indignation against the encrusted, well-established evil of the world. Compassion for others cannot be severed from the shock which comes when we see, with the eyes of Christ, human beings trapped by sin and sacrificed to the ruthlessness of other men who are sometimes the best-intentioned people in the world and in the church. When a Christian family loses the conviction that sham and cruelty, misery and callousness are worth striking out against and striking hard, it has ceased to be "an agent of reconciliation." When such a family enters the fray it may be called upon to suffer. Two men, both Presbyterian deacons, did fight for the public health doctor mentioned above. And one of them lost his job as a result.

In a former day, Christians attempted to understand their ethical responsibilities by developing simple rules by which they might tell whether or not an action were "right" or "wrong." Some asked, "What would Jesus do?" only to find that this was not much of an answer in a bureaucratic organization where decision making was often done by someone higher up. Or they said simply, "live by the Sermon on the Mount," only to find that while they could sometimes control their aggressive actions, they could not control their thoughts and feelings (see Matthew, chapters 5 and 6).

The biblical basis for ethical decisions is related to the real situations which face us. The Christian is part of a covenant community which cares about him; he does not stand alone. In this fellowship of the Holy Spirit, families can wrestle together with their difficult choices and inevitable compromises and find strength and support to try them out. In the gathered community, families can *think* and can rehearse what they might do as Christian workers, students, parents, or community participants. It is not enough to study Christian faith or the Bible in abstraction; such study must go on while we wrestle with concrete problems.

One church, for example, takes a vocational census of its people to find out where God has appointed his people to serve and discover what it means to be a Christian in and through the roles they enact in life. The leaders of this congregation found answers to questions such as these: Which of the people in our church have the same kinds of jobs in different offices, plants, or communities? Who are our stenographers, teachers, accountants? Which of our congregation have different jobs in the same company? Which of our independently employed people face the same conflicts in real estate, medicine, or public relations? Which of our women share similar situations in their families? Who are pregnant with their first child? Which homes have been split by divorce, separation, or death? Which husbands and wives are couples again after their last child has left home? These situations all have problems built into them and we need to meet together with Christians who share a particular sphere of life and to help each other witness to Jesus Christ in that sphere.

A Christian style of life is an ethic worked out by a Christian community concerned to deal faithfully with concrete problems of living in the world in the Spirit of Jesus Christ. This is our training for Christian battle, training for which Christian families do not wait to be drafted.

11
Arenas of Family Witness: The Community

"When the Stranger says: 'What is the meaning of this city?
Do you huddle close together because you love each other?'
What will you answer? 'We all dwell together
To make money from each other'? or 'This is a community'?"[1]

Never let your brotherly love fail, nor refuse to extend your hospitality to strangers—sometimes men have entertained angels unaware. Think constantly of those in prison as if you were prisoners at their side. Think too of all who suffer as if you shared their pain (Hebrews 13:1-3; Phillips translation).

Throughout the ages the church has wrestled with the problem of living as "a colony of heaven," having its basic citizenship in the Kingdom of God while living and working in the world. At different times and within different traditions the people of God have come up with different ways of doing this. Some have literally pulled apart from the mainstream of society to live in their own world and build their own institutions, supposedly uncontaminated by the evil of "secular" society. Others have entered a pact with the world and sharply divided it into secular and sacred spheres in which they live, depending upon the day of the week. The descendants of John Calvin do not take either of these routes. They see Christ as the *transformer of culture*.[2] They do not flee from their concrete life in the imperfect institutions of the world, nor do they allow these groups to completely control them. They are convinced that because the

---

1. From "Choruses From 'The Rock'" in *Collected Poems 1909-1962* by T. S. Eliot, copyright, 1936, by Harcourt, Brace & World, Inc.; © 1963, 1964, by T. S. Eliot. Reprinted by permission of the publishers.

2. H. Richard Niebuhr, *Christ and Culture* (New York: Harper & Row, Publishers, Incorporated, 1951), p. 190.

Word became flesh and dwelt among us, God has entered human culture and will reorder it from within, using Christians as his agents.

Unless Christian families can infuse humanity into the impersonal relationships of our modern cities and towns, they may become the graveyard of the human spirit. Christian families can be the starting point for real community in the neighborhood. Such families take their clue from the Apostle Paul who was very much aware of the pressures on the covenant community in his day: "Don't let the world around you squeeze you into its own mold, but let God remold your minds from within, so that you may prove *in practice* that the plan of God for you is good, meets all his demands and moves toward the goal of true maturity" (Romans 12:2; Phillips translation; author's italics).

In these last chapters we will inquire into the nature of the family's Christian witness in the world outside the four walls of the home. We may call the home our castle but, for better or worse, we have neither drawbridge nor moat to keep the world out. The family lives in the midst of a sea of influence. Residing in a town, working at a job, living under a government and in the midst of international tensions, we are subject to the pulls and counterpulls that often jeopardize the witness we may make.

Can we find a way of being thoroughly "in the world but not of the world"? What might a Christian style of life look like in our communities, in our earning and spending life, in our life as citizens of this country? Can we train our children to become a part of a creative Christian minority which can face the constant bombardment of less-than-Christian ideas and practices in our society? How can a church family learn to "filter" the values of society which influence all of its members?

WITNESSING RESPONSIBLY

Through careful reflection we can learn to check our fast and furious pace as families. No problem is more insistently voiced by Christian parents than the pressure of time and the competition of the many community demands which make life a hectic rush. The resulting busy-ness of the average family reduces them to a state of frustration and irritability. They find themselves responding to the rat race either with exhausted indifference and apathy or by carrying out their many responsibilities from a sense of compulsion rather than love and interest. They begin to feel like failures at the many things they take on—because no one person or family could master them all. And their resentment grows because in the face of these many demands on family time and energy, family members find that tensions mount, communication deteriorates, and family freedom is crowded aside because of their seemingly relentless schedule.

When asked who makes the schedule, we are tempted to say our schools, community leaders, and friends, as if *we* had nothing to do with it. When we allow external attractions, invitations, and requests to rule and control us we have ceased to live and only exist. The temptations for parents and children to live in a whirl of activity is so subtle and comes so gradually that we often do not realize what is happening until it is almost too late to arrest the dis-ease. We dislike being left out and are so afraid of offending by turning down an invitation that we often find ourselves spent at the end of the day, sinking into our beds with exhausted bodies and racing minds and no thought at all of him who said, "Be still, and know that I am God" (Psalm 46:10).

In our society few homes have time for persons. The Society of Friends presents queries to its membership each year to guide Quakers in their lives. One such reads, "Are you endeavoring to make your home a place of friendliness, refreshment, and peace, where God becomes more real to all who dwell there and to those who visit it?" We allow ourselves to be pushed around, letting noise and reckless haste rob us of time and quiet for reading, meditation, and for finding that rested spirit which can feed others' needs for companionship. It is easy to fall into the habits of hospitality that seem to be expected by a particular social set, neighborhood, and even by some business concerns. Studied artificiality reigns. Uncomfortably elaborate suppers and a monotonous round of cocktail parties on the one hand and silent television evenings on the other seem to be the order of the day. Can Christian parents find the courage to provide the simple entertainment of good conversation or creative craft work and singing? It is interesting to observe the sophistication of some modern people peeling off as they begin to recover themselves in an atmosphere of genuine warmth and naturalness. What would happen if Christian families began to rely upon their own resources for their entertainment and refused to be fitted into a depersonalized stereotype?

Only as we "sit loose" to all the activity the world offers can we find leisure which is truly re-creative. The Christian family needs wholesome leisure, long stretches of it, to come to know each other, rest their tired minds and bodies, and gain a new perspective on life. Most of our leisure today is mere diversion, "killing time" to fill the emptiness of life. It is appalling to realize that there are fifty-five million TV sets turned on six hours a day. Just how many hours of variety entertainment, sports events, and phony dramas can a person absorb without denying his real life to be lived? The anticipated increase in leisure time will only compound the problem unless we are able to discover those activities which are truly restorative of mind, body, and spirit. Christians who must keep busy forever might ask themselves why. A feeling of guilt or the desire to keep at a distance from people (usually the result of the guilt) is frequently the cause of compulsive activity. Christians need not apologize to anyone for needing rest and renewal. Indeed, the biblical teaching of six days of labor and one day of leisure should enable them to "rejoice and be glad in it" (Psalm 118:24).

In their extra time most people naturally want to be with those with whom they share common interests. But Jesus asked, "If you love those who love you, what reward have you? . . . And if you salute only your brethren, what more are you doing than others?" (Matthew 5:46,47.) The Christian is to be a neighbor to those who are unlike himself; even to the least, the lost, and the dispossessed. Being able to arrange our lives deliberately instead of letting ourselves *be* arranged by outside pressures gives us opportunities for service to those without homes in our community.

There are many lonely people in our communities, people who long for the warmth of a home, even temporarily. Older persons in our churches and our neighborhoods are hungry for some experience to remind them of their life in a family. But many are too proud to say so unless we take the initiative. In every community there are a great many children without adequate homes these days. Here our home might carry on a ministry of reconciliation. College students from other countries constantly express their gratitude for the opportunity to visit in an American Christian home. Christian hospitality may prompt us to bring people of different races, religions, and political ideas together in an atmosphere in which they can be open with one another and know each other as real persons.

One mother reports: "I really can't say whether we or they have profited more from the visits of our overseas guests. They seemed so grateful for the experience of being in an American Christian home. And we no longer think vaguely of Indians or Pakistanis or Filipinos, but of Joel and Chaman and Dolores. The world is truly one for us."

If we hold our homes as stewards of God, we cannot pray as did that Puritan of old: "God bless me, my wife, my son John, his wife, we four, no more. Amen."

Without cluttered lives we might have the time and energy to push the walls of our houses outward by bringing many of the lonely of the world within its atmosphere of genuine warmth and understanding.

"Blessed are those . . . who are glad to have time to spare for God."[3] We cannot be busy with what God is about in his ministry "to the least of these," until we realistically face our limitations. This does not mean that we are to neglect our community responsibilities. It simply means that there are some vital things that will not get done until Christians get involved in doing them.

WITNESSING TO YOUTH

Christian parents can help youth find a more meaningful life in the community. One of the marks of the modern home is that

---

3. Thomas á Kempis, *The Imitation of Christ*, quoted in Douglas V. Steere, *Time to Spare* (New York: Harper & Row, Publishers, Incorporated, 1949), p. 9.

children spend as much time away from it as in it. The junior rat race is no less severe than the adult version. Often parents regard their children as extensions of their own egos, pushing them to "advantages we didn't have." With a nervous urge toward success, they virtually drive their children into a precocious social life which robs them of childhood and of finding out who they are in the sight of God. A dozen clubs, athletic leagues, and other social activities jam their schedules. By eleven, girls are dating and prematurely wearing nylons and high heels. By sixteen many are jaded; they've run the whole course and wearily succumb to an easy marriage and the monotonous cocktail circuit.

Should we spend our time perpetuating these existing competitive social patterns and proliferating groups which do very little except to fill our children's lives as well as our own with hurry and rush? Christian parents must let children be children and help youth to reclaim youth. And we must resist, in the name of our humanity, the forces of the community which rob us of a time of growing, searching, and just *being* what we are.

Young people yearn for something meaningful to do and for an opportunity to perform to the limit of their capacities. They want the comradeship that develops only under rigorous conditions. Yet they are confused about their place in the world because as they look around them they find:

- adult life an empty, meaningless treadmill, an uninspired, mechanical pursuit of "success";
- adults who are apathetic about world problems and even community responsibility;
- adults who have lost their dreams of a better future and have settled for the pleasures of the moment;
- a great chasm separating youth and adults from each other in any significant enterprise;
- a confusion of morality in their communities among the church, teachers, parents, disc jockeys, police, the tastemakers of their schools, and advertisers;
- a lack of opportunity to take a responsible part in the political, economic, or cultural aspects of the community;

- a frightening future of automation, rockets with thirty million horsepower thrust, shifting populations, and Kinsey reports;
- a life in which personal choice seems insignificant in the light of the two gigantic international forces hurtling toward each other at breakneck speed or living in an uneasy truce.

Is it any wonder that many youth have chosen to stay "cool" and detached, uncommitted, unenthusiastic, punctuating boredom with sex, narcotics, drinking parties, and speeding automobiles.

If they have no example in adventurous adult pursuits, they will create their own excitement. Adult society has forced youth to be passive students, consumers, dependents, and bored observers of an adult life which proves its manhood on the greens of a country club. Paul Goodman observes, "It's hard to grow up when there isn't enough man's work."[4]

Unable to test their limits in a constructive way, gang life becomes a substitute. Gang life is terrific fun. In the hunt and the chase, the display of genuine skill, the fierce loyalties and brushes with danger, gang life offers drama, adventure, and thrills. So we find, for example, one hundred girls in a wealthy Eastern suburb engaged for one whole year in systematic shoplifting before they are apprehended.

Children and youth do not need these means to find adventure and meaning if their homes, churches, and communities have offered them something better, a life robust and absorbing enough to compete with the excitement of belonging to a gang. But most churches and church families do not recognize the need for adventure and for a sense of identity and accomplishment in these growing young people. On the one hand, adults insist on treating them like children; the same eighteen-year-olds who are taught to launch ICBM's and fly B–47's are not allowed to pass the offering plate or to give their opinions to adult

---

4. Paul Goodman, *Growing Up Absurd* (New York: Random House, Inc., 1960).

policy makers in some congregations. On the other hand, we want to turn them into old men and women too soon. We expect them to be content with a sedate youth group, gathering quietly on Sunday evenings to listen to "inspiring" talks and sing songs, the words of which they do not understand.

Parents, teachers, law-enforcement officials, and other responsible adults must plan with youth for a more significant part in the real life of the community and the church. It is no accident that the Peace Corps concept has put new life into many youthful dreams. But since nothing is real until it is local, we must come to understand our own community and its possibilities in detail. Promising starts have been made when churchmen, merchants, and community leaders worked hand in hand. Increasing opportunities for part-time employment and part-time schooling have been made available in some deprived areas of our larger cities. Work camps and "workreation" programs in public recreation centers during the summer have increased. Social service opportunities for teen-agers in hospitals, children's institutions, schools and camps for mentally retarded and crippled children are being set up by enterprising community committees. In Boston, through an integrated, church-stimulated program called, "Operation Kindness," over 7000 high school students serve part-time in 106 cooperating agencies.

The value of these imaginative enterprises is not in "keeping youth busy" or "off the streets," but in giving them an opportunity to try out the adult world in a meaningful way and to stretch their abilities to the utmost. As they increase their competence and as adults decrease their fears of our sometimes unpredictable, rebellious adolescents, we can collaborate together in fashioning new goals. Such opportunities can help youth to find their way vocationally as well as challenge their commitment to a Christian style of life. How much more meaningful it is for young people to be able to discuss with adults their work experiences in the light of a Christian understanding of vocation than to "put on" canned programs on the same subject!

A number of churches have created adult "youth ministry"

teams. These teams include those who work with youth in the gathered church as youth advisers and church school teachers as well as adults who have demonstrated competence in their professions and jobs and who have started to think about the Christian meaning of their work as the "scattered church." These families invite to their homes a few young people who might be interested in their particular line of work. As they get acquainted, and as time permits, the youth may visit the man or woman at work to see what it means concretely to be an engineer, teacher, or accountant. Youth and adults may sit down together then and talk about the problems and promises of the occupation and study its meaning in the light of the Christian faith with the pastor.

Another group of particular concern to church families is the youth of the community who are in trouble. We must not assume, however, that it is always the youngster and not the institution or community that needs "adjusting." Bored, anxious, defeated youth and the parents who have abdicated their guidance of them is a lethal combination found with alarming frequency these days. Following the lead of such guides as the excellent pamphlet *Youth in Court*,[5] responsible church women have studied about and visited juvenile courts where they have seen the efforts of their local communities in the rehabilitation of troubled youth. Some churches have set up neighborhood supervised study halls where the youth of crowded homes could be helped to prepare for their future life by adults of the church. Potential school dropouts have been visited, interviewed, and encouraged to return. Psychiatric interviews are provided for the mentally ill child. Church parents "with time to spare for God" have become court assistants and Big Sisters or Big Brothers to teen-agers who lack parental guidance at home.

Dedicated Christian imagination linked with a willing mind and hand can teach us how to be leaven and salt and light relevantly within a community where both youth and adults can find a new pattern of life together.

---

5. *Youth in Court* (Philadelphia: United Presbyterian Board of Christian Education) is the triennium study guide for United Presbyterian Women, 1961–64.

WITNESSING TO LOCAL SITUATIONS

Christian families can work for genuine community in the towns where they live. Christians throughout history have always worked to relieve human suffering—slaves, deprived children, prisoners, the aged, the mentally ill, the physically incapacitated. Occasionally, but not often enough, such concern has been stretched to a desire to change the institutions which gave rise to the distress. So Christians, for example, started hospitals and worked for the reform of prisons and the abolition of slavery.

Housing and Schools

Two persisting community problems claim the attention of Christian families in our times: housing and schools. The health of the public schools is of vital concern to the home. The schools are an extension of family responsibility for the education of children. While we should not expect them to carry on training in family values and religious nurture, they do have the responsibility for educating our children for useful living in our society. As a cross section of our democracy they are a training ground for citizenship in our commonwealth. Christian parents must keep alert to the school's program and needs. They must learn what is being taught in the schools and how much of our children's outlook on life is formed by what they see and do there. We have a responsibility for the public schools. To be responsible means to be able and ready to respond, and Christian parents will respond on various levels: some will serve on school boards; others will keep the public informed about school needs; others will simply vote for bond issues. All will guard against the danger that the growth of private and parochial school systems will jeopardize the educational institution of *all* the people, the public school.

Housing is of vital importance to families. Slum conditions in cities and the shack towns of heavily populated areas impose harsh handicaps on families. One can only imagine what effect seven people sleeping in one poorly heated room has on a growing child. Our efforts at urban renewal often make low-cost housing impossible for just those families that need it. And our pattern of residential segregation of the races severely limits the opportunity of the Negro and other minorities for getting decent housing in line with their economic ability.

The Racial Crisis

The existing racial crisis is, of course, intimately related to a Christian concern for adequate schooling and housing. One cannot underestimate the agony of Christians of all races who are wrestling to find an answer to the problems of racial injustice as members of minority groups, especially Negroes, are clamoring for their rights as citizens to be acknowledged. That full rights to all public facilities, including schools, and the right to own property without regard for the color of one's skin will eventually be granted, no one can doubt. Whether or not these rights can be granted quickly enough to avoid an outburst of indescribable violence, we cannot say. White Christians cannot compromise on the conviction that there must be equal opportunity for all. It must start with the church and extend to integrated neighborhoods which are even more basic in the long run to the school problem. In this time of racial crisis Christian families should remember three things:

1. Christ came precisely that he "might create in himself one new man . . . so making peace" (Ephesians 2:15). "Here there cannot be Greek and Jew, circumcised and uncircumcised, barbarian, Scythian, slave, free man, but Christ is all, and in all" (Colossians 3:11). In Christ, human beings remain male and female, black and white, of course. But it *does* mean that any discrimination on the grounds of race, sex, or class is impossible for a Christian without denying the gospel itself. As Robert Spike has said, "There is only one Lord, one faith, one baptism for Christians. That one baptism makes us all the same color."[6]

2. It ill behooves any Christian to point the finger of scorn at his brother in any other part of the country; all parts of the United States erect their own obstacles to racial justice. Racial segrega-

---

6. Robert W. Spike, *Safe in Bondage* (New York: Friendship Press, 1960), p. 131.

tion and tension is a worldwide phenomenon, not limited to one region of the United States. White people scamper to the suburbs, leaving the cities to become Negro, Puerto Rican, Mexican, and Oriental ghettos. Equal access to schools, jobs, voting, or housing is not a reality in any region of our country.

3. Christians can find ways of changing attitudes towards their neighbors. A single courageous family can do a great deal, but it must be ready to suffer. When one begins to work for reconciliation in an area of life as tense as the racial situation, one discovers why Christ called attention so forthrightly to the suffering his people must undergo. "Blessed are you when men revile you and persecute you and utter all kinds of evil against you falsely on my account. Rejoice and be glad, for your reward is great in heaven, for so men persecuted the prophets who were before you" (Matthew 5:11–12).

One family in Pennsylvania which decided to reject the restricted housing covenant and racial discrimination of their neighborhood was plunged into worry and concern as it decided to create a new pattern. The children were snubbed by some of their friends. Some fellow church members refused to speak to the family, while some of other denominations or of no religious affiliation at all suddenly warmed up to them. "We discovered more venom *and* more goodwill in our neighborhood than we had ever realized existed there."

When we break decisively with surface living and superficial manners, anxiety and strong feelings are not far off. Genuine witness and creativity which breaks with the status quo in any area of life walks hand in hand with suffering. The word "witness" comes from the same New Testament Greek root from which the word "martyr" is derived.

One father represented his church at a denominational conference where a resolution was passed supporting "fair housing" laws. When a Negro schoolteacher in the local high school system wanted to move closer to his work, he and a few others from the congregation located a home for sale and persuaded a group of neighbors to welcome this teacher. "They've turned out to be fine neighbors," one of them reported after a few months.

WITNESSING IN THE NEIGHBORHOOD

Christian families can be a unit of the church in their neighborhoods. In one community a family discovered that no one had more than a casual relationship with his neighbors. They invited a group over for an evening. Each person was invited to tell how his family had come to America and how he had happened to move to that town. This discussion of common human experiences helped to build a bridge between their lives which later led to a consideration of neighborhood problems and common rules for children's behavior on the block. This beginning of cooperative living later became the basis for discussing the issues of faith and life in the homes.

One newer idea coming from overseas is the "house-church." In the New Testament the Apostle Paul wrote to at least two kinds of groups in the church: "Paul . . . to the church of God which is at Corinth" (1 Corinthians 1:1-2), and "Paul . . . [to the] church in your house" (Philemon 1:1-2). He recognizes both the local, particular congregation, and the house-church. If we are so convinced that the church is only "that brick building on the corner" it will be difficult for us to see that the church can genuinely exist in other forms. When Paul writes, "Greet Prisca and Aquila . . . also the church in their house" (Romans 16:3-5) he was *not* talking about churches which were still so small they could not have buildings of their own. He was recognizing a legitimate form of the church in his day and ours.

In many parts of the world the house-church is being reestablished as a means of recovering the vitality of the early Christian fellowship. St. Wilfred's Parish in Halton, Leeds, England, may offer a key to a quality of church life in which the family takes a major part. Here the church, under Canon Ernest W. Southcott, has sought new ways of being the church among the many unchurched people of that fogbound industrial town. An increasing number of homes have become meeting places for discussion, Bible study, prayer and the celebration of the Lord's Supper. The family of the house is usually present and they have added to their number some regular and irregular worshipers from the parish and even some outsiders who have no relationship to the church except that they are baptized. (In Britain perhaps 75 percent of the population is baptized, but only about 15 percent maintain any affiliation with a church body.)

What happens in the house-church? Different patterns have emerged. One is reported by Faith Willcox after she had visited many a house-church in Halton, a suburb of industrial Leeds:

> The morning I had to leave, I joined my last "House Celebration" in the home of a young couple who had just had their second child. It was 7:00 A.M., the mother was nursing the baby in the bedroom, the father was dressed for work—his tram left at 8:00 A.M. He had moved a small table into the center of the living room and laid on it a white cloth and a dish of bread from the kitchen. Two neighbors came in, also ready for work. The vicar arrived and was warmly welcomed by the pajama-clad two-year-old son of the family, who clearly knew who were his friends and who were just grown-ups. We chatted about the fog, the tram schedule, the vicar's stiff neck, and the new baby while we watched the completion of preparations. Silence settled on us very gently. We heard the baby smacking her lips as her mother tucked her back into bed in the next room and quietly joined us. The first words of the Eucharist rose very naturally and seriously out of our "gathered meeting."
>
> The special intercessions this morning were for a member of the congregation who had died the night before, for his family, each one slowly and quietly by name; for all who were known to be ill in the immediate neighborhood; and for each street in the neighborhood. . . . Each man's and each woman's work for the coming day was lifted in prayer; the boy grinned as the children of the house were named. After our communion, the vicar moved to me and, laying his hands on my head, blessed the departing visitor. A moment's silence followed the benediction. Then the father went quietly to the stove and produced a plate of porridge for the boy, who tucked into it without more ado. As we put on our

coats and wished each other well, the father sat down to his breakfast.[7]

Christian families in the United States might see themselves in a new way by making their homes the focal point of a "house-church." Two things might happen: The church might become bigger than its building, and Christians might discover that they do not *go* to church; they *are* the church wherever they live in the community.

---

7. Faith Willcox, "The House Church" (Reprinted by permission from Christian Education *Findings,* October, 1958. Copyright © 1958 by The Seabury Press, Inc.), p. 14.

12

Arenas of Family Witness: The Economic Realm

Most churchmen and churchwomen see little or no relationship between their faith, their families, and their work outside the home. Some are very careful to keep faith and life in separate compartments. To others, it has just never occurred that there *is* a connection. It seldom occurs to them to think or speak of their job and their faith "in the same breath."

To be sure, they may have noticed that there is some relationship between the kind of job they have and the particular church they belong to. Corporation executives, senior and junior, are ten times as likely to list "Episcopal" and six times as likely to list "Presbyterian" as their denominational preferences as are Americans at large. As in other social institutions, we have a strong tendency to seek our own.

A church conference of laymen and ministers held on the West Coast clearly illustrates this point. Asked to introduce themselves by name, occupation, and community activities, the delegates instead introduced themselves in this manner: "I'm Tom Smith, elder in the _____ church." "I'm Ernie Handley, senior high superintendent in _____ church." Almost no one identified himself by his occupational involvement in the world. It was later discovered that one man was a member of his town's board of supervisors, one was a district attorney, and another was a delegate to the Republican National Convention of 1956! To them *the church was basically a weekend, leisure-time concern* and, as such, related primarily to the family and not to the job. They could not imagine of what interest their jobs and community affiliations might be in a church conference. If the average man had to decide in which area of his life—family or work—the church was most relevant, he would choose the family. Yet, these arenas of life are like overlapping circles; each affects the other whether we are aware of it or not.

THE RELATIONSHIP OF HOME AND WORK

Are home and work two separate worlds? "When I get home I'd like to forget about work. That's one reason I moved to the suburb," one man answered. But our work does have a great deal of influence on the home. Not only does the pay that comes from our job efforts make a home possible, but the life work of a man (and woman) has an impact on the home in a deeper sense. The enterprising young man lives his work on a twenty-four-hour basis. A psychiatrist recently stated, "Women love men, but men love work," and there is enough truth in this to start a heated discussion among couples to whom the quotation is introduced.

How persons in the family evaluate themselves is often related to the breadwinner's work. Much of their feeling of status and identity is derived from what the father does. When a wife or children are asked, "What does your husband do?" or "What does your father do?" they know they are being asked a question about his job.

In our society a man's work is the most personal thing about him. Most fathers get their sense of identity from their job. Perhaps Reinhold Niebuhr was thinking of this fact when he said that while motherhood is a vocation, fatherhood is always an avocation.[1] A man defines himself by his "success" in his work. He can be made or broken more easily in this area than in any other. If a man is having a hard time at work, it is almost immediately felt at home; but if he is having trouble at home, his job might relieve him of his sense of frustration.

Our society, which upgrades prestige but often downgrades usefulness, leaves some workers and their families without much self-respect. For example, the man doing a useful job on the assembly line may still find it hard to respect himself because of his low-status work (according to American, but not Christian, standards). Perhaps he resists coming into a congregation of

---

1. From a lecture at a Consultative Conference on Theology and Family, Atlantic City, October 17–20, 1957.

professional and managerial people for this reason. At home, his wife may be reading about actors, statesmen, or professional men, or watching their exploits on television. His children learn about "Dr. Kildare" and "Perry Mason" and even the rescue squads of fire departments. But when do they see their father's work praised? When is the factory worker ever portrayed as a hero? "Why don't you do something important, Daddy?" is a question many of these men face at home. Perhaps that is the reason that he feels like a statistic, a machine handle, and drowns his feeling of insignificance with a beer bottle and TV movies.

There are other ways in which work and home overlap. The father's work and income not only determine at what level they can live, but deeply influence where and in what kind of house they live, where and to what extent their children are educated, how they vote, what they read, who their friends are, when they move, and what their basic loyalties are.

Both fiction and nonfiction have vividly portrayed the ways in which high-pressure, competitive business, especially the corporations, require the absolute loyalty of their executive employees, including their travel, social life, and the location of their homes. Uprooted families find themselves dependent upon the corporation community for health plans, chaplains, recreation and vacation centers, insignias, and even family counseling services—all of which were once provided by the local community. C. Wright Mills is probably right in contending that the economic institution is becoming a more important character influence than the school, the church, or even the home.[2]

The implications for Christians are clear. If we are interested in nurturing "Christian families" we must also pay close attention to the work life of family members. It may be, as Dr. Robert Lynn has suggested, that the reduction of the father's role as teacher and priest is closely related to his increasing concern with his occupational role as the source of his identity.[3] To focus our

---

2. C. Wright Mills, *White Collar* (New York: Oxford University Press, 1951).

3. Robert W. Lynn, "Fifty Church Families and Their Role Expectations," an unpublished paper. Used by permission.

attention only upon the internal life of the family is not really to understand the family today.

THE RELATIONSHIP OF FAITH AND WORK

It is not hard to see why the modern businessman, shop foreman, or dentist would prefer to keep his work life and religious life in different compartments. He may think that it is necessary for his mental health. If he worships with the gathered church on Sunday he may very well be asked to sing these words of the famous Reformation hymn:

> Let goods and kindred go,
> This mortal life also;
> The body they may kill:
> God's truth abideth still;
> His Kingdom is forever.[4]

What he does during the week is designed to secure goods, to keep his family intact and happy, and to assure that his body is in tip-top shape. He knows that business is a fundamentally impersonal organization, however much industry tries to infuse human-ness into worker-boss relationships. Labor and management are there for a purpose: to make profit. This is the way a business must justify its existence. Not to recognize this is to be confused and unrealistic. Even in the "service professions"—medicine, teaching, and professional church work—the churchman is not without a conflict between self-aggrandizement and loving one's neighbor in the Christian sense. Caught in this tension, the sensitive Christian does not know what to do.

There are always some who claim that there is no conflict between business ethics and a Christian profession of faith. They say "I run my business or operate in my union according to the Sermon on the Mount or the Ten Commandments," thinking that is what it means to be Christian. We were told by a former President of the United States that our foreign policy was based on the Sermon on the Mount. All one can say about such statements is: Their authors have never read these sections of the

---

4. "A Mighty Fortress Is Our God," Martin Luther, 1529.

Scripture; or they have not understood the words they read; or they are deceiving themselves in a dangerous way.

How could modern business in the United States exist if it took the words, "You shall not covet" at face value? Modern advertising assumes that there is a basic covetousness in the hearts of men. Can the businessman really abandon all self-interest and give to everyone what he asks, as the Sermon on the Mount indicates is the condition for "blessedness"? It is more honest to face the conflict between the ethics of the Sermon on the Mount and the commitment to business.

> A group of Presbyterian elders who were also realtors in a Pittsburgh community were asked by their pastor to open the way for a cultured Negro family to purchase a home in their neighborhood. After a lengthy discussion in which they consulted Scripture, prayed, and generally agonized over a decision, they summoned their minister and reported: "Our duty is clear. We know that as Christian men we ought to give the word that would make it possible for this man to find a house here, but, God help us, we cannot do it. Most of us have spent a lifetime building up our businesses. The reprisals from the realty board, the banks, and certain other groups would be more than we could take and stay in business. Not only our businesses but our families would suffer all kinds of threats and social ostracism. We just can't do what we know we ought to do as Christians."[5]

Not all Christians resign themselves to the status quo. Some are finding a way to break with the usual "rules" of their business and professions and work for more humane values. But such a departure is almost always accompanied by economic suffering and is accomplished only with the support of the community of faith. The Holy Spirit will teach those who are attentive to him how to be "wise as serpents and innocent as doves" (Matthew 10:16). One realtor, for example, gathered together his church

---
5. From *The Secular Relevance of the Church* by Gayraud S. Wilmore, pp. 49–50. Copyright © 1962, W. L. Jenkins, The Westminster Press. Used by permission.

friends to build a number of houses for middle-income groups of all races in an undeveloped section of town. Other concerned Christians have found ways of changing the personnel policies of large corporations, of fighting unscrupulous landlords, of leading enlightened movements against police graft. And their "work" is motivated by the love of Christ who loves all men and in whom all men must be loved.

Christian men and women are in continual conflict between the demands of the gospel and the demands of the world. Their identity as Christians does not depend on the particular decision they make, but on their loyalty to Jesus Christ. Often we do not know what is demanded of us as Christians. At times we know what we should do but are unable to do it. This was exactly the situation Paul was in when he agonized, "I do not understand my own actions. For I do not the good I want, but the evil I do not want is what I do. . . . Who will deliver me from this body of death? Thanks be to God through Jesus Christ our Lord!" (Romans 7:19, 24–25.) Christians do live in two spheres. The man who lives in the world must *expect* to find himself in conflict with his commitments. He tries to reconcile his commitments and bring his work more into line with God's will for him in this place. But he relies in his anxiety and conflict upon the forgiveness of God, knowing that if he is faithful the Father will help him to work toward a more perfect obedience than he is now capable of. Christians are justified, not by their actions, but by God's grace which is appropriated through faith! It was this discovery, and the recognition that all of us do live with uneasy compromises, that led Martin Luther to say that Christians must "sin bravely, but believe more bravely still." Does this realization cut the nerve of our effort, our desire to change the pattern? Not at all. The congregations of Christians should help every family man to bear this inevitable conflict while seeking God's will about what he *can* do within his daily life. His ultimate confidence is in God to whom he is finally responsible. He will not deceive himself, however, that his actions in business are always good. Nor will he fool himself by thinking that what is good for his pocketbook is good for God.

The Dangers of Modern Business and Industry

Modern work is meaningless for countless men and women today. It is a boring, monotonous grind to be finished as soon as possible. When the factory whistle blows, one does not want to be in the way of the feverish attempt of thousands to get away from work—and fast. A few decades ago the usefulness of a man's job was apparent to all. What he did with his hands or mind fitted into the pattern of society. As a cobbler, he knew those who were to wear the shoes he made and exactly what he was putting into the product. The carpenter lived in the community with the neighbors whose houses he had built. They could see the results both in the product and in the lives of people who used the product.

Today our complex industrial and commercial life, in which the worker is often a small cog in a big machine, robs the worker of a feeling of accomplishment and usefulness. This is not true only of factory workers. Few men in any area of work create anything by themselves anymore. The whole range of occupations has, in large measure, lost a sense of purpose and meaning. This generation finds it hard to take seriously Paul's words: "Whatever your task, work heartily, as serving the Lord and not men, knowing . . . you are serving the Lord Christ" (Colossians 3:23-24). Sociologists frequently speak of the depersonalization of modern work. Man has become a function only: a statistic, a seller of products, a consumer of goods, a recorder of accounts. He sees himself as a thing. Studies of job satisfaction among the middle- and upper-income groups show that many men are dissatisfied and unhappy in their work by the time they are in their middle forties, when they should be making their greatest achievements and their best contribution to the world. They have lost a sense of purpose in their jobs. Many an executive living in a plush suburb, caught in the "organization," dreams secretly of one day doing something creative but his mounting indebtedness caused by his station in life frequently eliminates this as a realistic possibility.

Perhaps the most common response to the general frustration

and monotony of work life in the modern day is "living for payday." There is nothing wrong with being glad to receive the income that puts food on the table, a roof over our heads, a child through college, but if "Thank God it's Friday" means "Another useless five days are over and I can finally be myself for two days," we may be in difficulty. If leisure becomes an escape from the nonsense of what we do five days a week, it is doubtful that it can, by itself, provide an antidote to low morale. One has to face the fact that some jobs (and some features of *every* job) seem meaningless. In this case a man can do one of several things, depending upon circumstances and willingness to sacrifice, for each decision has a cost as well as a promise: he can leave his job for another if he has talent and opportunity; he can grit his teeth, put in his time at work, collect his paycheck, and fulfill his real calling outside the "job"; he can work for rewards on the job not connected with the work itself, such as developing his social relationships or occupying a position of responsibility in a union, or another work-oriented association.

Some men and women have directed their efforts toward "security" instead of productivity and toward "status" instead of creativity as compensation for the loss of meaningfulness on the job. Such benefits exert a subtle pressure upon those who receive them. With material and psychological comfort, one is not likely to strike out on one's own or to take another job more in line with one's talents and ethical convictions. Gradually one learns to "play it safe," to fuzz over personal responsibility in the name of team effort or "groupthink." But too much security can deaden the Christian's nerve endings to human hurt, to inefficiency, and to the uselessness and destructiveness of certain products.

The Biblical Understanding of Vocation

In understanding what the Christian faith has to say about work, the Christian man or woman will also begin to understand how his work can be an arena of witness. The Christian man is a "new being." He has been called by God to put away his anxiety about his life, past, present, and future, because it is in the hands of God. No longer is he worried about his standing with his

Creator; Jesus Christ has given him a new status through God's initiative. In joyful response then, to God's unspeakable gift, the Christian takes his responsible place within the community of forgiven sinners, the church, and seeks to express his gratitude by his service to God in the world as a citizen and as a worker.

We must first understand the Christian meaning of "vocation" or calling. God calls men first of all to be Christians, to carry on his ministry of love in the world. Their fundamental vocation is to be agents of reconciliation. Becoming a prophet, pastor, evangelist, teacher, bricklayer, engineer, or lathe turner is a secondary choice of the Christian. His witness is the total expression of his being in the context of his life. His work represents the particular circumstance in the world in which his "vocation," his ministry, can be discharged. What he does is almost incidental as long as he has an opportunity to convey the meaning of reconciliation and love in obedience to God.

What are the insights by which a Christian might look at his job? The Christian on the job should ask whether or not his work is *useful* in the world. Does the work we do contribute to the meeting of the plain and practical necessities of life for people as well as meeting their needs of purpose and meaning? Or is it destructive of life or does it contribute to the wasting of lives? All sorts of rationalizations can take place in an affluent society which continues to glut the market with such nonessentials as a battery-driven cocktail stirrer. We are told that our economy could not survive without thousands of such nonessentials each year. We build obsolescence into products which would otherwise have a longer life. The Christian must decide what is essential and what is luxury.

A young man commented to an older, successful man he greatly admired, "Just think, you've accomplished every major thing you've set out to do." To which the older man sadly replied, "There's just one thing more important and that is to feel that the work you've done has been worth doing." To the Protestant Reformers, the true test of a job was its *social utility*, not its glamour and professional status. To the magistrate, artisan, soldier, servant girl, and housewife, Martin Luther insists that if they do their work as appointed by God, they have a status higher than that of a bishop! Such labor ministers to the common good and is, therefore, as "spiritual" as that of the clergyman, physician, or teacher. We turn our backs upon the Bible and our Protestant heritage if we regard some useful work as more holy than others. We fall into this trap when we talk about "full time Christian service," meaning professional missionary or church work. This whole idea is a mistake and the phrase should be stricken from our vocabulary. Some people erroneously feel that if they were "really dedicated" or "spiritual" they would choose to enter the ministry or a related occupation. They may also conclude that in such work they would be free of the frustrations, competition, and monotony that they find in their present jobs.

Status-conscious Americans often have the idea that one who works with his mind is more significant than one who works with his hands. At no point does the Bible ever make this comparison. *Whether one works primarily with mind or hand, in a machine shop or a pulpit, in a hospital or a kitchen, depends not on our degree of spirituality but upon the abilities and responsibilities God has given to each of us personally.*

The first question, then, that should be answered by Christians as they seek to discover their lifework, is: "Does this work meet human need wherever it exists throughout the world?" If one cannot answer "yes" to this question, by any stretch of the Christian imagination there may be no alternative but to get out of it as quickly as possible, especially if he cannot make a redemptive contribution. To those who cannot get out, the way is still open to make their leisure hours their real job and attempt through the church and the community to bring wholeness and reconciliation to men in everyday life.

Responsible Use of Abilities. For the Christian, his job should put his *abilities* and talents to the best possible use. Each person has unique capacities and God intends their development for use in the world. If a man decides to enter a church occupation the decision should be based primarily upon his proven abilities, not merely upon the search for significance or a religious experience, or the need to relieve a feeling of guilt. Some Christians ought to make such a decision and will, with the proper encouragement. By the same token, others now in training or in service should ask themselves if their talents do not lie in another area of work. The man most like Christ is the man who is faithful to God in using his own abilities as Christ was faithful in using his.

This criterion calls for the Christian to be a good workman at whatever he does. If he is a plumber, he should be a good plumber. If he is a teacher, he needs to develop all of his skill and exercise it. If one is not a competent workman and a reasonably friendly person, no amount of talking about his faith will impress those with whom he works. The impact of his words depends heavily upon his faithfulness to God's gifts.

A part of our faithfulness to our abilities is expressed in an honest product and service rendered without misrepresentation. This is a tall order in a day when the interdependence of our industrial life deprives us of control over production, advertising, and sales, and "bearing false witness" has become the cardinal commercial sin.

Responsible Work Relations. We have an opportunity to minister to people in existing work relationships. Everyone works with people. When students, considering their occupational choice, say that they "want to work with people," they often mean that they are more interested in people than in ideas or things, or they may be saying that they need to be needed in personal relationships. But the fact is that we *all* work with people. Manual work and intellectual work do not separate one from people. In fact our most fruitful contact with them is usually while working jointly on the product of head or hand.

In this day of specialization in which many people and many institutions work on a single product and countless people unknown to each other may be a part of a single team, there is all the more reason for the Christian to emphasize the personal elements of his relationships with others.

How often do we see our secretary or the milkman as a useful function instead of a unique human being with a personal life? We can get by in life by simply treating them in terms of the work they are to do, but to discover the richness of their nonwork life can give a feeling of significance that the depersonalization of modern life erases. When we regard a fellow workman as a means to an end, we not only lower his work efficiency, we denigrate him to the status of a "thing." Modern industry has increasingly called upon psychologists to help management and supervisory workers develop sensitivity in human relations. Through courses, workshops, and conferences, the boss is helped to become a human being to his employees, learning to view them sympathetically. If this is done for the sake of good business, how much more should Christians be humane and interested for the sake of the whole person? The Christian's motive is the desire to stand by a fellow human being who needs the experience of being loved and worthwhile.

Relationships are complicated in the modern work world. We are caught in a web of loyalties which include obligations not only to the work itself but to our employer (if we have one), to members of our union or professional association, and to the consumer public. To be concerned about Christian love at work is to delicately balance the claims of all of these.

As Christians we may have to challenge the work and its conditions from the side of management or the side of labor. Labor unions grew as a result of exploitation of laborers in a day when Christian conscience was confined to the peccadilloes of individual morality. Now unions, too, must come under judgment as the potential enslavers of men's loyalties. It may be necessary at times to choose the side of one against the claims of another in our struggle for right relationships on the job. A community indwelt by sin must work toward *justice* which may be the chief expression of love under these conditions. Christian men, whatever their position, must share responsibility for bettering the conditions under which men work. This is part of our Christian vocation.

Responsible Spending. A further insight about the Christian and work recognizes that every worker is also a consumer. The management of his spending is often more within his power to determine than the conditions of his work life. If he can serve God by doing needful work, by using his abilities faithfully in that work, and by working toward better human relationships on the job, it is also possible for him to serve God in his dispersement of his earnings. In an era of "conspicuous consumption" this is especially important. There was a day not too long ago when the church said nothing at all about how a man earned his money. He could gouge, cheat, ruin his competition, exploit his workers. His "philanthropy" would wash away all of his sins: "Tainted money will do just as much good as money earned honestly," it was averred. But the most direct answer to that expression of social irresponsibility is found in men like Isaiah, Amos, Hosea, Micah, Jeremiah, and our Lord himself in whom the love of man and the love of God came together.

Modern economists tell us that we live in a consumer-centered economy, and anyone barraged by TV advertisements is well aware of the pressures to buy every sort of product whether we need it or not. We are caught between the advice which urges us to save money and the counsel which encourages us to borrow money painlessly. We have haunting memories of our parents' frugality and yet are told that the health of our economy depends upon our spending to the hilt. Department stores often earn more from the interest on charge accounts than they do from the sale of products. These are some of the conflicts of an affluent society.

A noted psychiatrist described one of the dominant neuroses of our time as "the wish to have everything." That wish is being stimulated on all sides. The advertisers' ability to contact millions simultaneously through newspapers and TV gives them the power to mold our thinking on a scale never before possible. The Christian family should read Vance Packard's *The Hidden Persuaders* in order to discover what massive attempts are being made to make us buy impulsively and nonrationally.

There is an insidious attempt to wear down the sales resistance of children and youth to certain products so that in later years a market is ready-made. Teen-agers now control fantastic sums of money and the advertisers know it. Almost half a million dollars a day has been spent by the tobacco industry to show teen-agers the glamour and enjoyment of smoking cigarettes, but nothing is said about the proven link between cigarettes and lung cancer. Yet, if we declare the immorality of advertising designed to recruit young smokers, we must also be prepared to sacrifice television shows which are sponsored by advertising money.

How, in the face of this onslaught, can Christian families decide how to spend the money over which God has made them stewards? Christian parents who make their decisions as before God must find ways of evaluating the appeals to luxury, comfort, and prestige. They must decide to what use their money, energies, and abilities can be put to further God's purposes. By losing our life, we will find it in abundance again. By the proper control of expenditures we might even continue Christ's ministry in a desperately needy world:

> . . . to proclaim release to the captives
> and recovering of sight to the blind,
> to set at liberty those who are oppressed,
> to proclaim the acceptable year of the Lord (Luke 4:18–19).

Our true vocation—whatever our specific work—is to serve him and live in the kingdom of right relationships. In *this* calling we are never out of a job.

13
Arenas of Family Witness: National and International Affairs

"Why do we even discuss these huge questions? We are wasting our time on something we can't do a blessed thing about," a mother blurted out at a church meeting. National and world problems are of such great magnitude that it is not difficult to understand the apathy and sense of pessimism about the chances of affecting or altering the great social forces set loose in this generation. The international situation is so complex that it is easier to devote our time and energy to something we feel we *can* do.

But a Christian response is more positive. It cannot omit God from the picture and is therefore willing to do even a little with more confidence than the non-Christian can claim. One seventeenth-century writer is reported to have said, "I had rather see coming toward me a whole regiment with drawn swords than one lone Calvinist convinced that he is doing the will of God." An overstatement in our day, perhaps, but the point is clear. We are not alone.

WORLD CRISIS AND TENSION

No family, however happy internally, can escape the social unease and worldwide fears of our day. The shadow of nuclear holocaust falls across every plan we have, every effort we make to nurture Christian families. "Why should I bring up more children to live in this crazy, unpredictable world?" asks one mother. "Why study eight years toward a profession when it may be all over in our lifetime?" is the reaction of a thoughtful college boy.

We know that we are living on the edge of a crisis, not unlike the crisis which faced the first-century Christians and pervaded most of the books of the New Testament. The average American does not move to a remote part of the globe to escape the possibility of extinction, nor does he consciously carry the emotional burden of world crisis into his daily life. Nevertheless, he reacts to life as if he knows deep inside that crisis is there. Youth has become fatalistic, timid, and unadventurous. With a few exceptions, college students have retreated into "privatism," concern for a rich, full personal life and apathy about wider social issues. Their parents bury their anxiety in job, or garden, or power tools, or children. Many Americans seek peace in various forms of Oriental mysticism, such as Zen.

We are unaccustomed to living with prolonged crisis in America. Most feel immobilized by a feeling of helplessness in the face of a continuing crisis. Other Americans panic in the midst of continual danger. Those who panic quickly look for someone to blame for the crisis, a scapegoat upon whom all anxieties may be laid. Thus we have extremists on the left and the right who attack, who are suspicious of all, and who, because they cannot tolerate the strain, would do away with the very democratic processes we are trying to preserve.

The problem, then, is to know *how* to look at crisis. Too much fear could cause panic and unwise actions; too little could lead to a sleepwalk into oblivion. This is true of both the international situation and the racial tension in our own land.

CHRISTIAN RESPONSE

A Christian's belief in God and his providence is his balance wheel in these times. God is the Lord of history; he is One whom no happening can surprise. This is not to say that everything that happens is according to his ideal will; far from it. The gift of freedom is a terrible gift that involves making a choice and also taking the consequences of the choice. The Christian knows that our scientific advances are good, but they may also lead to unthinkable evil in the wrong hands. What could be more deadly than the union of high intelligence with destructive purpose?

A Christian may not have more wisdom about our national

and international crisis than other men. He may not sense God's purpose in this time of tension any better than they. But he *does* have resources which give him staying power and which enable him to do what is useful without discouragement.

In International Affairs

The Christian is continually conscious that he is a part of God's larger family. What implications does this have for relevant action? It means that his biblical awareness that all men are God's children keeps him from being an isolationist in a world which grows smaller by the day. He would bring his family to accept their citizenship in the world instead of retreating to an island of happiness in a world of tumultuous change. He is sensitive to the plight of that world and will help his children to visualize the need.

If the population of the world (about 3,000,000,000 persons) were compressed into a single community of just one thousand persons, we would see some striking contrasts: Sixty persons would represent the U.S. population; the rest of the world would be represented by the remaining 940 persons. But the 60 Americans would receive *half* of the total income of the entire community; the other half would be divided among the other 940. Out of the 1000 people in this community, 330 would be classified as Christians (100 of these would be Protestants), and 670 would be non-Christian. Classified according to skin color, 303 people would be white, and 697 would be nonwhite.

The 60 Americans would have a life expectancy of 70 years. The other 940 would average less than 70 years. Our 60 compatriots would have 15 times as many possessions as all the rest of the people. Although Americans would raise 16 percent of this community's food supply, they would consume all but a paltry 1.5 percent of what they raise themselves, storing that surplus in expensive bins. The other 940 people would be constantly hungry and would wonder why Americans eat 70 percent above their actual food requirements. "Of the 60 Americans, the lowest income groups would be better off than the average in much of the rest of the town." With shame we would also notice that the average Christian American family spends, chiefly through taxes, 850 dollars each year for military preparations but less than four dollars a year to share their Christian faith with the rest of the world.[1]

David Head has his "natural man" pray:

> We miserable owners of increasingly luxurious cars, and ever-expanding television screens, do most humbly pray for that two-thirds of the world's population which is undernourished: *You can do all things, O God.*[2]

And praying thusly, we continue our pursuit of the contented, happy life, rallying around the barbecue and the dry martini.

Living in awareness of this larger family, the Christian family knows it cannot live to itself. It attempts to meet human need through such available channels as the ecumenical mission, Church World Service, CARE, CROP, UNICEF, and other agencies. It dedicates a portion of its income to minister to "the least of these," with whom Christ identifies himself. Insofar as possible, this family builds a personal bridge with persons of other lands through correspondence, gifts, and other means. The Christian family remembers above all that statistics are people.

Families need to realize that they do not have to travel far to express their influence for peace and goodwill. Here in the United States tens of thousands of students, homeless refugees, and migrant workers from other countries are within the range of the ministry of the Christian home.

Myron and Helen Wicke tell about their "adopted family" which now lives in every corner of the globe. Their family lived near or on college campuses for many years. Foreign students were frequent guests in their home, much to the delight of their twin sons who got acquainted with strange costumes, unusual foods, and unfamiliar languages. In the midst of differentness they also discovered a common humanity as they pushed their

---

1. Henry Smith Leiper, "Our World in Miniature," *Presbyterian Life*, October 15, 1959, p. 12.
2. David Head, *He Sent Leanness* (New York: The Macmillan Company, 1959), p. 23. Used by permission of The Macmillan Company.

world horizons outward. These friends, now returned to their homelands, are symbolized by flags on top of the television set—India, Pakistan, China, Japan, Korea, the Philippines, Uruguay, Brazil, Argentina, and Mexico. These strangers from other lands brought much into this home, and now, back in their homelands where they serve in responsible positions, they will remember the Christian witness of friendship to them.[3]

Christian families need to be aware of the worldwide repercussions that occur when nationals of other countries are snubbed or hurt while visiting here. Many a responsible person from India or one of the newer countries of Africa have been deeply hurt by the refusal of service in some restaurants. It does little good for the cause of peace to have our reputation for bigotry and prejudice broadcast throughout the world. That may wipe out any gains so laboriously made on the diplomatic front.

When the morning headlines in the California newspapers read: "Teen-Ager's Sport—Beating Up Farm Migrants," our relationships with Mexico, the country from which these seasonal laborers came, suffered enormous damage. Parents were asked to talk with their families about the attacks and damage of property. In case after case, the young people of these church families exclaimed, "But they are only foreigners!" Had they missed the point that migrants were also people with feelings and needs like ourselves? As a result of this episode, parents learned that their own messages to their children about people unlike themselves were yielding bitter fruit. World friendship begins with the ordinary, everyday lessons of tolerance and understanding.

Church families will support efforts to realize a larger family of nations and churches. This is not a day to go it alone. The isolationist in world politics is as outmoded as the individualist on the religious front. The church is not a happy island of retreat in the midst of a sea of tumultuous change. Accepting the uniqueness of our own group, we need to cooperate with agencies which demonstrate that working together holds the promise of peace.

The United Nations, fallible though it is, is a family of

---
3. Myron and Helen Wicke, "Our Adopted Relatives," *The World from Our House* (New York: Friendship Press, 1956), pp. 16–22.

nations. It is a forum in which the differentness of each people can be expressed. We should keep in mind that the United Nations is not designed to be a world government. It has no way of compelling great powers to do its will; its only decisions are the collective votes of the member nations who vote according to their self-interest. This is the nature of the *family* of nations who have contracted together to "rid the world of the scourge of war."

Likewise, the National Council of Churches and the World Council of Churches are *families* of churches, churches which differ deeply in their traditions, practices, and government. Yet they find one thing against which all differences pale into insignificance: their commitment to Jesus Christ and their desire to see his gospel spread throughout the world.

Few places are better able by example and precept to teach the basic humanity of man across all artificial barriers than the homes of Christian families. Our homes need not be isolated chambers; we can bring the world into them. Through such means as mealtime discussions of Berlin, Hiroshima, or Southeast Asia, we can develop in our children a sense of unity with, and sympathy for, their fellowman wherever their homes may be. And broadening experiences outside the home may include church-sponsored seminars on international affairs, a year of college abroad, a study tour of mission installations, a visit to the United Nations, personal friendships with people of other lands, or even a stint in the Peace Corps. To have instilled in our children the desire to devote themselves to the cause of strengthening the bonds between the world's peoples through Christian love and understanding is one of the deep joys of Christian parenthood.

In Politics

No thoughtful analysis of the church family can overlook the potent effect of government upon that family. The Christian family cannot escape involvement in political life. No home is immune from decisions made in Washington, D.C., or by city and state governments. A bill is signed in the Oval Room of the White House, and our grocery bill may reflect the change. Hurried conferences are called in the Cabinet Room. The Cold War chills and Wall Street flurries, and what we have to spend may be increased or decreased. The President's wife holds an open house, and new fashion trends are stirring the hearts of America's women. Old-age insurance and health plans; fire, police, and military protection; the proliferation of schools and child-care centers all remind us how our elected representatives in government, national or local, influence our lives.

This is why Christian families must become politically minded. Some Christians try to separate *morality* (which usually means "self-perfection") from *politics* (which usually suggests "dirty business"). They will take action when they think a moral issue is at stake, such as the mobilization of votes for prohibition, but will not raise a voice in the political or economic order.

"Freedom" in our day is such a moral issue. Political freedom is the setting wherein we may learn to live for truth, to care for other people, to develop personal potential. We want to produce and extend this freedom to others. Political freedom is not to be equated with the *liberty* Christ brings. All men are bound by the tyranny of their own selfish interests and desires in spite of political freedom. They are the slaves of sin and lesser loves until freed by him. The Christian knows that we need both in order to be truly free to recover our essential humanity. The earliest Christian creed, "Jesus is Lord" carried with it the implication, "Caesar cannot be Lord."

Many Christians want the church to stay free of the affairs of society and the real issues that confront us on the political, economic, and international fronts of life. Perhaps they fear for their own undeclared allegiances. Perhaps they are saying that God has no relationship to what happens to men apart from Sunday and outside the four walls of the church building. It is a private religion of satisfied but fearful Americans instead of the biblical concept of the church. That the church should be interested in politics does *not* mean, as in some European countries, that the church should form a political party to vote church members into office. But it does mean that, both individually through its members and corporately by its pronouncements and actions, the church must declare itself against issues that deprive people of their freedom and of their status as children of God, equal before the Father of us all. All Christians are not expected to come to the same decisions and have the same political opinions, nor will they necessarily all be lined up against non-Christians. It is simply a matter of Christians together working out their decisions on the basis of a Christian understanding of life rather than some other point of view.

In his book on the East Harlem Protestant Parish in New York City, George Webber tells of one member of their ministering team who was standing on a corner in Harlem one afternoon when a coal truck raced through a red light, knocking an old man down in the gutter. His instinctive response was to pick up the man and rush him to the hospital, but the law requires that an ambulance be called. (One can be a good Samaritan only by calling for help and making the victim comfortable until the government sends a means by which the injured can be conveyed to proper medical care.) He did this and sat for an hour and thirty-seven minutes waiting for the city ambulance! This church, as the body of Christ concerned about its world, found the only way to be a good Samaritan in this kind of situation was to get better ambulance service for East Harlem. And the only way to do that was to put pressure upon the local political boss. And you cannot exert this pressure, they discovered, unless you have been actively engaged in the political enterprise.[4] Christians may have to change their attitude toward getting involved in politics (which is simply the power structure of a society) if they are to give a relevant response to their faith in our complex society.

In the reference to the final judgment (Matthew 25), it is the meeting or failing to meet the needs of others which determines whether or not a person is accepted into God's Kingdom. In our day of corporate life this parable includes being concerned for food surplus and shortage, water supplies, housing, hospitals, and prisons. If we think that in our day of great *inter*dependence and corporate life, our concern for our neighbor stops at the level of personal kindness or evangelism without drawing us into politics,

---

4. George Webber, *God's Colony in Man's World* (Nashville: Abingdon Press, 1960), pp. 93-94.

we are simply being escapists. Our involvement as Christians in the common life of men is our reaffirmation of the Incarnation, wherein we recognize that God was not afraid to get mixed up with this poor, sad world of ours *in person.*

In the church, Christ's family of families, we find a community in which we may rehearse our attempts at reconciling the world; we find the mutual service of brothers; and we find him who is with us to the end of the age.

We do not begin by making decisions on a worldwide scale; we cannot choose between peace and war. We begin with the choices that are open to us day by day within our homes and at our jobs. We stand with others as we make crucial decisions, knowing that in Christ's name bold action must be taken.

Is our family a bridge to the larger family of God in the world? Christian parents may decide that they can no longer insulate their havens of security from the hell of national and international insecurity. Unless the Christian home we so often call our castle lowers its drawbridge and claims all men as part of God's family, the home, with all of its togetherness, will become an enemy of Jesus Christ and we will discover that our castle is built upon the sand. To those who would lose their little preoccupations to become a part of the larger family of God, he promises a life more abundant than we can imagine.

O God, our Heavenly Father, who hast set the solitary in families: look in favor, we beseech Thee, upon the homes of Thy people. Defend them against all evil, and supply all their needs according to the riches of Thy grace. Make them sanctuaries of purity and peace, love and joy. Bless those dear to us wheresoever they are, and grant that they and we may so follow Thee, that, though our paths may lead us far from one another, we may yet abide within the safe shelter of Thy love; through Jesus Christ our Lord. AMEN.[5]

---

5. Reprinted from *The Book of Common Order,* p. 300, by permission of The Church of Scotland Committee on Public Worship and Aids to Devotion.

A Problem Index

This is an index of 115 questions about issues facing thoughtful Christians in families. Numbers refer to the pages on which the issues are discussed.

American Family Life

How can we define the American family? **11-13**
What basic family types are found in the United States of America today? **27-29**
In what direction are the goals of Americans changing? **35-46**
What conflicting ideals are pressing upon the American family? **14; 25; 35-46; 96-97**
What do Americans look for in marriage? **37-44**
What are the prevailing models of the "good wife" in the U.S.A.? **32-35**
Who is the "head" of the American home? **29-32**

Bible

What kind of help does the Bible give in understanding family problems? **15-23; 48-50; 160-174**
Why does the Bible not speak of the "Christian family"? **50-51**
What is the Bible's view of sex within and outside of marriage? **54-59**
How does the Bible state the purposes of marriage? **54-66**
What are the functions of Christian parenthood? **97-121**
Why can't we take biblical families as models for ourselves? **17-18**
What is the place of family love in the Kingdom of God? **69-70**

Children

What does it mean to bring up children "in the nurture and admonition of the Lord"? **106-117; 120-121**
What do children contribute to their parents? **99-100**
In what ways are children likely to be different from one another? **107-109; 130-131**
What makes for effective discipline? **110-115**
Why do our children quarrel with one another? **161-165**

How are Christian values learned? 86–92; 110–117
How are children related to the church? 105–106; 205–211

Christian Education
Can persons be educated into Christian faith? 48–50; 101–106
Why is the Christian education of adults important? 101–106; 199–203; 209–210
Is family worship Christian education? 118–120
When is family conversation Christian education? 136–144
How can family members be trained for life in a world of conflict? 161–165; 205–215; 247–248

Church as Covenant Community
What marks the church as different from other institutions? 199–205
When is the church in the home? 50–51; 230–232
How does a church minister to its members and to the world? 211–217
What are the consequences of seeing the church as a family of families? 199–205

Christ
How does faith in Christ bear upon life in the family? 104–105
Are Jesus' views of the family too idealistic? 21–23
What is meant by a Christocentric view of family life? 17–21
What is Jesus' view of divorce? 60; 66–68
How did Jesus speak of his family? 71–72; 199

Communication
What is the problem of family communication as seen from a biblical perspective? 128–136
Can we really understand each other? 125–127; 130–131
What stands in the way of good communication among family members? 128–136
In what ways can people communicate without words? 115; 117; 127–128; 158
In what ways will our faith change our way of communicating? 136–144; 219–222

A PROBLEM INDEX 259

Conflict

How is the family of Christians in conflict with secular society? **218–222; 227–232**

What, if anything, can Christians do about world conflict? **219–222; 248–255**

Why is conflict inevitable within the family? **61; 159–161**

What strategies for disagreeing creatively may be found in the Bible? **161–174**

What effect does faith in Christ have on family conflict and reconciliation? **60–62; 64–66; 102; 160**

Decision Making

In what ways does the Holy Spirit heighten the individuality of life? **179–185**

How do families differ in making up their minds? **177–179**

How does God guide us in our decisions? **189–195**

Divorce

What various points of view toward divorce are found in the U.S.A.? **45–46; 66–68**

Are divorce and remarriage ever justified? **66–69**

What various points of view toward divorce are found among Christian people? **66–69**

Economics and Family Living

What conflicts are likely to arise for a Christian engaged in business? **236–240**

Under what conditions do money problems disrupt a family? **170**

What principles (guidelines) to consumership may be offered the Christian living in America today? **244–246**

Faith

What distinction does the Bible make between faith and religion? **19–21; 118–120**

What is the relationship between Christian faith and faithfulness in marriage? **59–62; 64–66**

Why do parents have difficulty giving faith to their children? **48–49; 101–104**

How can you reconcile the apparent conflict between the life of faith and daily work? **236–246**

Freedom

What are the dangers of sexual freedom? 78–85
What differences exist in the idea of freedom of American society and that held by Christian faith? 136–144; 186–187
What does the gift of freedom mean in the Christian family? 136–144

Holy Spirit

In what ways does the Holy Spirit heighten the individuality of family members? 130–131; 142; 149; 153–154; 242–243
Is the "sacred" or the "secular" the arena of the Holy Spirit in life? 19–21; 56–58; 213–217
How does the Holy Spirit act in the Covenant Community? 189–195; 204–217

Love

What is the prevailing American idea of love? 40–42; 79; 145–147
What is different about Christian love? 69–72; 80–81; 150–151
How is forgiveness most often misunderstood? 131–132; 171–174
How does God's love transform ours? 69–72; 136–144
Why is "falling in love" not enough for stable marriage? 40–42

Man

In what ways is modern man depersonalized? 128–130; 219–222
What are the basic differences between male and female? 62–63
In what way is the Christian doctrine of sin relevant to an understanding of family life today? 99–101; 104–105; 131–136; 177–181

Marriage

What effect does the husband-wife relation have upon children? 55–56; 155–158
What do Americans expect of marriage? 38–40
What needs does marriage satisfy universally? 53–54
How is Christian marriage different? 54–66
When is a marriage idolatrous? 40; 69–72
What standards of mate selection do American youth hold? 40–45

Morality
What is the nature of our families' moral confusion? **90–92; 96**
Is a new morality evolving in the U.S.A.? **85; 90–92**
What is the difference between a moralistic view and a Christian view of sex and marriage? **56–59; 75–78; 87–90**
Where does the Christian family find its bases for ethics? **86–92; 190–192; 213–217**

Parenthood
When does parenthood become a crisis? **69; 97–99; 174–176**
What are the major problems of the modern parent? **14; 35–37; 56; 96–97; 107**
What is the teaching task of Christian parents? **101–104; 110–117; 144**
What constitutes parental teamwork in a family? **155–158**

Psychology
When does psychology help and when does it hinder our parenting efforts? **56; 96–97; 145–150; 174–176**
When do families need professional help? **174–176**

Research
What is the relationship of scientific findings to biblical insights about the family? **15–17**
What can scientific advances in contraception mean to responsible parenthood? **93–95**
What confidence can we place in scientific studies of sexual behavior? **85**

Self
What is the place of self-love in the Christian's life? **78–95**
How can we discover the courage to be real? **142–144**
What, in family relations, promotes a sense of self-esteem and well-being and what diminishes it? **125–126; 137–144; 147–148; 173**
What sharpens a child's sense of identity? **107–109; 161–165**

Sex
What are the prevailing philosophies of sexual expression in the U.S.A.? **78–84**

What would you say are the characteristics of the sexual revolution in America? 73–85

What difference does it make that sex is a part of God's creation? 56–59; 73; 80

What guidance for sex education can Christian parents find? 56–59; 73; 80–92

Society

How does social change contribute to family problems? 14; 29; 32; 73–76

What family patterns exist in other cultures? 51–54

What are the evidences that there is a distinct teen-age society (culture)? 35–37; 223; 245

In what ways do Christians participate in political life? 252–255

Work

What can be done to prevent modern work from becoming meaningless? 239–244

What constitutes a Christian witness in daily work? 240–246

How does one's work affect one's home life? 233–236

Can one live at work by the Sermon on the Mount? 236–237

World

Church or world: Does the Christian have to choose? 213–217

What do we mean by saying adult education is "boot training for Christian battle"? 216–217

How can parents bring the world into the family? 221–222

How can a Christian family influence international relations? 221–222; 247–255

Youth

How can youth still be helped to find a Christian view of sex? 56–59; 73; 80–92

In what ways do adults add to youth's confusion? 222–226

In what ways do young people search for meaning in life? 42; 224

What does youth really look for in marriage? 37–42

THE RESOURCES FOR HOME AND FAMILY NURTURE
THE COVENANT LIFE CURRICULUM

The resources for the Home and Family Nurture aspect of the Covenant Life Curriculum are designed to confront families with the gospel and to help them fulfill the responsibilities laid upon them by the gospel. Specific materials are offered to help accomplish this purpose. The intended use for these materials and their working titles are:

To help leaders develop a program of Home and Family Nurture through which the local congregation may minister to its families:
> *Principles for the Development of Christian Family Education: A Leader's Guide*—Malcolm C. McIver[1]
> *Home and Family Nurture* manual—Richard F. Perkins[1]

To help families come to grips with the whole gospel and interpret the nature and mission of the family in the light of the gospel:
> *Families Within the Family*—Elaine E. Lubbers[1]
> *The Image of a Christian Family*—Richard F. Perkins[2]
> *Christians in Families: An Inquiry into the Nature and Mission of the Christian Home*—Roy W. Fairchild[2]
> *Christian Parenthood: A Lifetime Guide*—Helen H. Sherrill[2]
> *The Nature of Christian Worship*—John F. Jansen[4]

To help parents in their unique task of nurture so that they may establish and maintain in their homes a personal commitment to Jesus Christ as Lord and Savior:
> *The Educational Ministry of the Family*—Richard E. Lentz[3]
> *Use of the Catechism*—Marshall C. Dendy[4]
> *Theology for Families*—Winfield Burggraaff[3]
> *Youth Entering into Covenant: For Parents*—William A. Benfield, Jr.[3]
> *Story Book of the Bible*[5]
> *Stories from Church History*—Iris V. Cully[3]
> *Story Book on the Christian Life*[5]

To lead youth and adults to a Christian understanding of the meaning of personal maturity, sexual development and relationships, marriage:
> *Anticipating Adult Maturity*—Gladys Guy Brown[3]
> *The Blue Light: Christian Dimensions in Marriage*—James M. Godard[2]
> *Personal Christian Maturity*—William B. Oglesby, Jr.[4]
> *Teen-Age Problems*[5]

To help the family to be a witness to and instrument of the claims of Christ in all of life:
> *The Social Ministry of the Family*—Roger H. Crook[3]
> *The Economic Ministry of the Family*—Roger H. Crook[3]
> *Ministering to Others*[5]
> *The Church Utilizes Community Resources*[5]

1—available 1963, 2—available 1964, 3—available 1965, 4—available 1966, 5—available when possible.

ABOUT THE AUTHOR

Dr. Roy W. Fairchild is an ordained minister in the United Presbyterian Church, U.S.A. Since 1959 he has served as Professor of Christian Education at the San Francisco Theological Seminary in San Anselmo, California.

Dr. Fairchild received his A.B. degree in Psychology and Social Sciences from the University of California. His B.D. degree was earned at San Francisco Theological Seminary, his M.A. degree in Counseling and Religious Education at the University of Chicago, and his Ph.D. degree in the Psychology of Religion at the University of Southern California.

The native Californian has a wide background, including practical experience, in the fields of theology, psychology, sociology, counseling, and research. He has made numerous literary contributions to these fields in the form of books, articles, and book reviews. He cites one of his books, *Families in the Church: A Protestant Survey*, in this text.

Dr. Fairchild is married and has three daughters.

M. MILTON HULL, the illustrator of CHRISTIANS IN FAMILIES, operates an art service in his native city of Richmond, Virginia. Mr. Hull and his wife, Helen Schuyler Hull, both attended the Pennsylvania Academy of Fine Arts. Mrs. Hull is now primarily a portrait painter. They have three children, aged 20, 18, and 16, and the oldest works with Mr. Hull in his office.

8612–ACJ